ASPEN PUBLISHERS

⚖ TeachingLaw.com Companion

LEGAL RESEARCH AND WRITING

Diana R. Donahoe

 Wolters Kluwer

Law & Business

AUSTIN   BOSTON   CHICAGO   NEW YORK   THE NETHERLANDS

To contact Customer Care, e-mail customer.care@aspenpublishers.com,
call 1-800-234-1660, fax 1-800-901-9075, or mail correspondence to:

Aspen Publishers
Attn: Order Department
PO Box 990
Frederick, MD 21705

Printed in the United States of America.

1 2 3 4 5 6 7 8 9 0

ISBN 978-0-7355-7907-1

ABOUT WOLTERS KLUWER LAW & BUSINESS

Wolters Kluwer Law & Business is a leading provider of research information and workflow solutions in key specialty areas. The strengths of the individual brands of Aspen Publishers, CCH, Kluwer Law International and Loislaw are aligned within Wolters Kluwer Law & Business to provide comprehensive, in-depth solutions and expert-authored content for the legal, professional and education markets.

CCH was founded in 1913 and has served more than four generations of business professionals and their clients. The CCH products in the Wolters Kluwer Law & Business group are highly regarded electronic and print resources for legal, securities, antitrust and trade regulation, government contracting, banking, pension, payroll, employment and labor, and healthcare reimbursement and compliance professionals.

Aspen Publishers is a leading information provider for attorneys, business professionals and law students. Written by preeminent authorities, Aspen products offer analytical and practical information in a range of specialty practice areas from securities law and intellectual property to mergers and acquisitions and pension/benefits. Aspen's trusted legal education resources provide professors and students with high-quality, up-to-date and effective resources for successful instruction and study in all areas of the law.

Kluwer Law International supplies the global business community with comprehensive English-language international legal information. Legal practitioners, corporate counsel and business executives around the world rely on the Kluwer Law International journals, loose-leafs, books and electronic products for authoritative information in many areas of international legal practice.

Loislaw is a premier provider of digitized legal content to small law firm practitioners of various specializations. Loislaw provides attorneys with the ability to quickly and efficiently find the necessary legal information they need, when and where they need it, by facilitating access to primary law as well as state-specific law, records, forms and treatises.

Wolters Kluwer Law & Business, a unit of Wolters Kluwer, is headquartered in New York and Riverwoods, Illinois. Wolters Kluwer is a leading multinational publisher and information services company.

Contents

How to Use TeachingLaw.com Companion: Legal Research and Writing

This TeachingLaw.com Companion is intended for use in conjunction with the TeachingLaw.com ebook as a supplement, an alternative to reading the longer sections online, and a convenient way to study offline.

Icons in the text [➥] indicate where the ebook provides linked material that will greatly enhance your learning and help you to better understand the concepts and skills being taught. In addition, the ebook includes quizzes, self-assessments, exercises, checklists, annotations, and multimedia material (all indicated here by their ebook icons); turn to the "More Ebook Interactivity" section at the end of each Companion chapter for a listing of these materials.

For a complete learning experience, make the ebook your primary resource.

Research Sources

Research Sources — Introduction to Legal Research — The Importance of Effective Legal Research

All lawyers must know how to research the law. Good lawyers know how to research efficiently and thoroughly. TeachingLaw.com provides you with research knowledge as well as research strategies and interactive practice to help you become an efficient and a thorough legal researcher. To use this online book effectively, read the text, click on sample pages, and perform the interactive exercises to make sure that you understand the material before you go to class. The interactive features of the ebook help to explain the material, provide immediate feedback, and allow you to link directly to certain research sources instead of simply reading about them in a textbook.

You will need strong legal research skills no matter what type of legal profession you choose. If you become a practicing attorney, clients will ask you for advice. They might ask whether they can perform some action such as purchase another company or build on a particular piece of land. In these situations, you will need to find the law to answer their questions and provide advice. Clients will also come to you with preexisting legal problems. They might want to sue someone, for instance, or they might be defendants in a lawsuit themselves. Here, you will need to research the applicable law to argue the case on behalf of your clients. Other clients will ask you to draft documents such as contracts or wills. For these clients, you will need to know the applicable law in order to bind the parties to the contract or to distribute your client's estate according to his or her wishes. If you choose a legal profession in which you do not practice the law directly (for instance, teaching), you will need to research the law to prepare for your classes or to publish scholarly articles in your field.

Regardless of the type of profession you choose in the law, remember that the legal audience is a doubting audience. A judge will not believe your argument unless you cite to precedent. The opposing side will look for sources to prove the opposing point. A lawyer will argue that your contract provisions are not legal. Another scholar will argue that your theories are irreconcilable with other legal positions. Therefore, to be effective, you will need to prove every argument you make. To do so, you will need to ground your arguments in the law by citing to legal sources. Of course, you need to know how to find those sources first and to make sure that you have found all the applicable law on point.

Research Sources — Introduction to Legal Research — Overview of Types of Legal Authority — Primary Law

Legal researchers find the law they need in a variety of places. The research process will become more manageable if you first understand the various legal sources and how they function together. The broadest categories of legal authority are (1) primary law and (2) secondary sources.

PRIMARY LAW

Primary law refers to those legal sources that are the law itself. Primary law is created by different branches of the government, both federal and state. The three main categories of primary law are (1) constitutions and statutes, (2) cases, and (3) administrative law.

1

Constitutions and Statutes

Constitutions are created on federal and state levels; they establish the form of government and define individual rights. The United States Constitution provides the framework for our laws, and no other law created can violate the United States Constitution. States create their own constitutions, which can grant further protections for individuals but cannot lessen the rights granted by the federal constitution. Legislative bodies create constitutions.

Statutes are also created on federal and state levels. They are written by the legislative branch (and approved by the executive) and published as statutory codes. Statutes cover a broad range of topics, from criminal to civil, and apply to all citizens, whether individual or corporate. They are usually written in general terms to cover a wide range of circumstances. Often they contain definition sections, purpose clauses, specific penalties, and other provisions. The intent of the legislature in creating statutes becomes important when courts are asked to interpret the statutory language on a case-by-case basis.

🔍 ➥ **Federal Constitutions and Statutes**

🔍 ➥ **State Constitutions and Statutes**

Cases

Federal and state judges interpret the law when they hear cases between specific parties. The case opinions judges write to resolve these disputes not only bind the particular litigants, but also provide precedent for future cases. In writing cases, judges can decide that a particular law is unconstitutional. Otherwise, judges apply the laws to the particular facts of the case according to the legislative intent of the statute. If there is no statute on point, judges use legal principles to create rules to apply to the factual situation; this body of law from case opinions is called common law.

🔍 ➥ **Federal Cases**

🔍 ➥ **State Cases**

Administrative Law

Regulations are created by the executive branch. The executive branch has the power to create agencies, such as the Federal Trade Commission (FTC) or the Federal Communication Commission (FCC). These agencies create regulations and decisions for that particular industry. There are both federal and state regulations and decisions.

🔍 ➥ **Federal Administrative Law**

🔍 ➥ **State Administrative Law**

BINDING VS. PERSUASIVE AUTHORITY

It is important to understand that primary law itself falls into two separate categories: (1) law that is binding or mandatory, and (2) law that is merely persuasive.

Mandatory or binding law is law that is binding in that jurisdiction; it must be followed under the principle of stare decisis. For example, a trial court in Maryland must follow Maryland state codes and decisions from higher Maryland courts because they are binding authorities.

Persuasive law is law from a lower court or a different jurisdiction that that gives guidance but does not have to be followed. For example, a New York court does not have to follow a California court's decision. Likewise, a justice who sits on the Supreme Court of California, that state's highest court, is not required to follow a California trial judge's opinion.

The distinction between mandatory and persuasive law is important when deciding the best cases to rely on when writing a legal document. Usually, you want to show the judge that she is bound by certain law. However, at times, you will need to rely on persuasive authority. For example, although an opinion from the same level court is not binding on that court (one trial court judge is not bound by his colleague's opinion) because it is technically only persuasive authority, an opinion from the same level court would be extremely relevant to the judge making the decision. In addition, when no binding authority exists on an issue, you will need to use persuasive authority to make your argument.

8? → **Mandatory vs. Persuasive Quiz**

Research Sources — Introduction to Legal Research — Overview of Types of Legal Authority — Secondary Sources

SECONDARY SOURCES

Secondary sources are materials that discuss and comment on primary law. They are written by scholars, judges, and others to provide commentary and background materials on the law. Although they are not the law itself, secondary sources can help a legal researcher understand a particular body of law as well as find primary law on a subject. They are especially helpful for first-year students, who tend to know very little about most legal subjects, as well as for experts in a particular field, who refer to these sources when developing law in their areas. Secondary sources come in a variety of forms. As a legal researcher, you will need to decide if you want to use a secondary source or whether it makes more sense to start researching the primary law first.

DECIDING WHETHER TO USE A SECONDARY SOURCE

Secondary sources are handy in certain situations and can help you research primary law efficiently. However, a secondary source is not always the best starting place in your research strategy. Consider using a secondary source in the following circumstances:

If you are asked to research a subject area that you do not understand
Often, you will be asked to research an area of law that you have never studied. In these circumstances, referencing a secondary source, such as a legal encyclopedia, will help you understand the general law in its basic form.

If you are asked to compare the law in different jurisdictions
You might be asked to write a comparative piece in which you contrast a particular law in different jurisdictions. Instead of tediously researching each state's law on point, consider using a secondary source, such as American Law Reports, which compiles trends on the law in different states, explains those trends, and provides citations to the law in each jurisdiction. If you find a secondary source on point, you might save days of research on your issue.

If you are asked to criticize the law or develop a new theory
There might be times when you are asked to criticize existing law or create a new theory. Chances are that scholars have already written about the subject area. Referencing law reviews will help

you find legal theories and criticisms about the area as well as references and citations to other legal sources on point.

If your initial research of primary law yields poor results

There may be times when you start your research in primary law but find too little or too much law on point. In these circumstances, consider using a restatement or treatise to help you learn more about the general subject area, to help formulate search terms, and to find primary law to act as a starting point.

DECIDING NOT TO USE A SECONDARY SOURCE

Oftentimes, it will not be useful to use a secondary source at all in your legal research. For example, if you are asked to research a statute in a certain jurisdiction, it makes the most sense to look in that state's code directly instead of finding information about the code first in a secondary source. In addition, if you are very familiar with an area of law, you probably do not need to learn more about it in a secondary source. You want to find the most streamlined research strategy to help you locate primary law. Therefore, secondary sources are not always the best starting point.

Remember that secondary sources are not binding on courts, so you should cite to them only sparingly in court documents. (On the other hand, scholarly articles are replete with secondary source citations.) In addition, if you use a secondary source to find primary law, you should always find that primary law as well to make sure that it is accurate and up to date.

SECONDARY SOURCES IN GENERAL

Secondary sources are considered persuasive authority. However, at times, a secondary source, such as a restatement, might be adopted by a specific jurisdiction — at which time it becomes binding law on that jurisdiction.

Q → **Binding vs. persuasive law information and quiz**

Secondary sources come in a variety of forms. Regardless of the secondary source you choose, finding information within it usually entails referencing a table of contents or index, finding the material itself within the main volumes, and updating that information by locating the primary law or making sure you have the most recent secondary source on point. For specific information and exercises on each secondary source, click on the links below.

Q → **Legal Encyclopedias**
Q → **American Law Reports**
Q → **Treatises and Hornbooks**
Q → **Law Reviews**
Q → **Restatements**

Research Sources — Introduction to Legal Research — Overview of Process and Strategy

THE IMPORTANCE OF A COHESIVE RESEARCH STRATEGY

Many students fail to recognize the importance of a cohesive research strategy. Instead, when they are given an assignment, they often log onto Westlaw and Lexis and begin searching. As a result, the students waste time and become frustrated or they find too many "hits" and have a hard time wading through the sea of authority. To avoid this pitfall, you should begin to think like a lawyer by following some basic research strategies.

THINK FIRST

Before launching into your research, think about a plan of action. You should ask yourself or the supervisor important questions, brainstorm ideas for search terms, write an issue statement and a cohesive plan, and take notes. In addition, questions about cost and time might not seem relevant as a student, but they are very important when you begin billing clients.

🔍 ➝ Asking the Right Questions

IDENTIFY APPROPRIATE LEGAL SOURCES

Once you have brainstormed ideas and focused on your issue, you should consider which authorities will be most relevant. Your thought process should include the following factors.

1. **Jurisdiction**

   First, you should be sure what jurisdiction's law applies. Usually, the supervisor giving you the assignment will tell you the jurisdiction, such as New York State law or federal law in the Second Circuit. However, sometimes you will need to figure out the appropriate jurisdiction. If so, you might need to research civil procedure rules or conflict of laws materials. Once you know your jurisdiction, focus your initial research within the law of that jurisdiction.

2. **Primary Law vs. Secondary Sources**

   While your ultimate goal will usually be to find primary law, sometimes you will find it more easily by looking first in secondary sources, especially if you know nothing about the issue. A secondary source will provide you with background information, context about the issue, and oftentimes citations to get you started. However, if you know something about your issue or have an idea about what category of law applies (contracts, torts, property), it makes more sense to begin with primary law — statutes, cases, and regulations.

3. **Statutes, Cases, and Regulations**

   It is often helpful to figure out which sources are most likely to address your issue. Statutes are often a good starting point because much of today's law is codified. However, there are still pockets of legal issues that are addressed only by common law, such as privacy torts. Therefore, if you are unable to find a statute on point in your jurisdiction, consider searching for cases. If your topic is covered by an administrative agency, such as food and drug law, consider beginning your research in regulations.

   Official vs. Unofficial Codes: Although you will need to cite to official codes in legal documents, many official codes do not contain annotations (U.S.C.). These annotations contain helpful references to other material such as cases and secondary sources. Therefore, when researching, choose annotated codes whenever possible (U.S.C.A. or U.S.C.S.).

4. **Binding vs. Persuasive Law**

   In general, you want to rely on binding law. However, you may also find (and rely on) persuasive law that will be quite helpful. Therefore, do not limit your research to binding law. Consider starting with binding law but branching out to persuasive authority as well. At times, when you find no binding law, you will need to rely on persuasive authority alone.

5. Dates

The dates of applicable statutes, regulations, and cases are important. For example, if you find a relevant statute, be sure to check the date of enactment; cases that were decided before the statute may no longer be applicable. In addition, older cases, even if they are still good law, may not seem very persuasive to your audience, especially when there are more recent cases on point.

CONSIDER PRINT VS. ELECTRONIC SOURCES

In General

As a legal researcher, you will need to make choices. You can search for many (but not all) legal sources in both print and online sources. Although your natural tendency may be to look online for materials, you might discover that using the books in certain circumstances can save you time and lead to finding more relevant primary law on point.

Print Sources

Print sources are usually organized alphabetically by jurisdiction and then by type of authority. For example, the primary law in your school's library might start with Alabama and end with Wyoming. Within each state, you will find that state's code, its digests, and its reporters. The federal law is usually located separately. Each book will provide citations to other sources, and you will need to use multiple books before you locate all your sources. Once you find those sources, you might want to copy them so that you have them for your files. In addition, you will want to update the law by looking in separate "pocket parts" and supplements stored either at the back of a volume or at the end of a volume set.

Although the process of using multiple sources and making copies might seem tedious, often the research process in print sources takes less time because you can quickly page through, skim irrelevant material, and grasp the context of a subject area due to its relative location within the law. In addition, the index and table of contents are good tools to learn the context and organization of particular bodies of law. Most researchers prefer finding statutes in the print sources because their indexes and categorical organization of the codes make them easier to use than online sources.

🔍 ↪ **Strategies for Book Research**

Electronic Sources

Online searching is often more convenient, and the law is updated more frequently than print sources; however, it is usually not free. The main legal services—Lexis, Westlaw, and Loislaw—are usually provided free for law students, but they cost lawyers quite a bit of money. Legal researchers should consider free databases—such as those linked throughout this book—before researching on a pay-for-use site.

Accessing electronic sources can be accomplished by a variety of methods. Often, a lawyer can choose between researching online by jurisdiction, subject matter, or word searches. Some online services provide a list of authorities but require you to actually find those authorities in print. Most services provide direct links to authority, which you can then download or print. While most services have indexes and table of contents, often researchers focus on word searches either via Boolean searching or natural language searches. As a result, the search terms chosen are extremely important.

🔍 ↪ **Strategies for Online Research**

CREATE EFFECTIVE SEARCH TERMS

Many Internet-savvy students think that legal research is similar to using a search engine. However, legal research is more complicated. Instead of typing a word or two as if performing a general search, the legal researcher should think in terms of the following.

1. **Courses as Categories**

    Oftentimes, a problem can be categorized into one of the typical first-year courses in law school: torts, contracts, property, criminal procedure, and civil procedure. As you move on in law school, you will be exposed to other broad topics such as corporations, tax, evidence, and family law. While there is quite a bit of overlap (consider contracts and torts alone), you can often think of legal problems in terms of typical legal courses. If you are able to break down the issue into these easily manageable categories, you can generate search terms using the language you learned in each class (offer and acceptance, intentional torts, etc.).

2. **Who, What, Where, When, Why**

    Many legal editors break down the categories of legal research into who, what, where, when, and why. If you can do the same thing, you will more easily find search terms that will lead to applicable law:

    Who: Think in terms of parties such as employer or employee.
    What: Think of the legal action (joint custody) or tangible objects (a defective product).
    Where: Think beyond jurisdiction to a more specific location (at a school, in a workplace).
    When: Think about the timing. It will matter in terms of applicable law.
    Why: Think about possible motives (intent) and defenses (self-defense).

3. **Expanding or Narrowing Search Terms**

    If your initial search term does not yield enough results, consider adding a synonym (use "house or home") or making your term searchable by the root instead of the whole word (using "employ!" will find *employment*, *employer*, *employee*, *employed*, etc.). If your search terms yield too many results, consider restricting the terms by limiting the search within a sentence, a paragraph, or a number of words. Also, consider adding more search terms to narrow a topic.

USE HELPFUL FINDING TOOLS

Indexes, tables of contents, and other research tools (such as popular names tables) are very helpful when performing legal research. Both online and print sources now usually have both, and they will help you locate terms either categorically (table of contents) or alphabetically (indexes). By skimming these sources, you will glean a sense of legal terms of art, context, and organization of the law. In addition, it will be easier to find your terms of art when conducting word searches if you have first availed yourself of these tools. As you read through the ➥**strategies for specific sources**, take note of the specific finding tools within each source.

UPDATING THE LAW

Once you have found a statute, case, or regulation on point, you will need to ensure that it is still good law. Statutes and regulations may be repealed or revoked, and cases may be reversed. Be certain to ➥**update the law** for your particular source to verify its status.

USE SOURCES TO FIND OTHER SOURCES AND KNOW WHEN TO STOP RESEARCHING

The sources you find will cite to other authorities. You should read those authorities; they might also lead to other sources. As you can imagine, the loop can become endless. So when do you stop researching? The best time to stop researching is when authorities start to repeat themselves. However, there will be times when stopping will be determined by pure economics (you have already spent too much money on the client's issue) or timing (you have to go to court or meet with your client in ten minutes).

🔍 ➥ **Deciding When to Stop**

For more help with creating a research strategy, use the following links.

🔍 ➥ **Research Strategies**
🔍 ➥ **Updating the Law**
🔍 ➥ **Research Strategy Testimonials**

Research Sources — Introduction to Legal Research — Overview of Process and Strategy — Citing to Sources

CITING TO SOURCES

Because the legal audience is a doubting audience, you will need to prove all your legal assertions by grounding them in the law. To do so, you will first need to find the law, and then you will need to cite to it in your documents. These citations are important to the legal reader because they reference your supporting law and allow the reader to find that law.

Citations are governed by strict formatting rules so that lawyers have a uniform system for finding authority. If you fail to follow those rules, your reader might not be able to find your legal authority and you might lose credibility with the reader. (If you cannot cite correctly, how does the reader know that your research is accurate or thorough?)

There are two main manuals that currently provide the formatting rules for legal citation:

1. The Bluebook: A Uniform System of Citation (known simply as the Bluebook) is now also published online at http://www.legalbluebook.com.
2. ALWD Citation Manual: A Professional System of Citation (ALWD is pronounced "allwood").

🔍 ➥ **Editing and Citation**

Research Sources — Introduction to Legal Research — A Research Plan Example: From Start to Finish

It is helpful to illustrate a research strategy on a client's issue from start to finish. In this section, you will read about a client's particular problem and follow some basic research strategies. While this example is not exhaustive, it will provide you with a starting point for developing your own research strategy.

THE EXAMPLE

Keep in mind that clients do not have fact patterns; they have very real problems. While you might receive your information from a professor in written form like the example provided below, most real-world clients walk through the door and are interviewed—either by you or a supervising attorney. You might also receive information from a case file; however, the file will rarely be a neatly arranged, chronological story such as a fact pattern. Usually, you will need to fit the multiple pieces together to develop a clear and concise story. More often than not, you will find holes in the story and will need to investigate more facts—by meeting with the client or witnesses, going to the scene, or pouring through documents. Below is a neatly arranged, abbreviated fact pattern for convenience in discussing a basic research strategy.

Sally Meets Harry:

On the first day of class, Sally was unable to log onto TeachingLaw.com. In a panic, Sally asked Harry, a student sitting next to her in class, for permission to use his email and password in order to access the first assignment in the ebook. Harry agreed and gave Sally this information. As a result, Sally was able to log onto the ebook and download the assignment.

The next day, Sally told Harry she was now able to log in using her own email and password and asked Harry if he wanted to work on the assignment together. This time, Harry declined and said he preferred to work independently so he could learn all the material himself. Sally felt somewhat slighted and disappointed. Sally worked on the assignment herself and uploaded it that night using her own password. As she was uploading her own assignment, she decided to play a trick on Harry. She logged out of the ebook and logged back in, but this time using Harry's password. When she entered Case Files, she noticed that Harry already had a green check mark on his first assignment (indicating he had uploaded successfully). Sally crafted answers for the assignment that did not make any sense and included sensitive and intimate language regarding Harry's personal life. Sally then uploaded this document into Harry's Case Files. (As long as the new upload occurs before the time period has ended, the new document replaces the old upload.)

After the professor downloaded and read Harry's document, she called Harry to her office and showed him the document. Harry was extremely upset and wound up having a nervous breakdown. He had to withdraw from law school.

Harry has hired you to pursue a claim against Sally.

STEP 1: FIND THE FACTS

Your first job is to make sure you have all the facts. In a real situation, you would ask the client specific questions, take a look at the document in question so you could examine the language that Sally used, and talk to Harry's doctors. You would also want to investigate the damages by copying all medical bills, accessing any lost wages, and discovering any other expenses Harry might have incurred. Keep in mind that being able to prove liability is not, by itself, a reason to accept this case. If Harry cannot collect any real damages, accepting the case makes no economic sense for either the client or for you. In the real world, finding the facts and deciding whether to take a case are often very difficult.

STEP 2: SPOT THE ISSUES

As in any law school exam, you want to determine what potential claims (and possible defenses) are available to the client (and to the other side). You can break the claims into categories such as criminal charges and civil causes of action. Can you come up with a civil claim or a criminal charge to bring against Sally? (Click on each link below for possible claims.)

Potential Civil Claim 1 ➥**Intentional Infliction of Emotional Distress**
Potential Civil Claim 2 ➥**Identity Theft**
Potential Civil Claim 3 ➥**Slander and Libel**
Potential Criminal Charge ➥**Identity Theft**

STEP 3: CHOOSE A STARTING POINT

First, begin taking notes. Consider writing down all possible claims and starting a separate file (either a hard copy or on your computer) for each claim. Then, attack each claim separately so that you do not become overwhelmed with sources and strategies. You will want to keep notes on each claim as you progress throughout your strategy.

🔍 ➥**Research Strategies – Taking Notes**

Let's start with the potential civil claim of intentional infliction of emotional distress.

STEP 4: THINK FIRST

Before logging on to Lexis or Westlaw or running off to the library, begin by thinking about your issue. This might take you five minutes or an hour, but it will save you time in the long run. First, write an issue statement so that you remain focused throughout your research. (Your issue statement need not be perfect.)

▣ ➥**Sample Issue Statement**

Next, brainstorm ideas for search terms. Use the issue statement as a starting point. Keep notes so that you don't repeat a failed search. Ask your supervisor questions.

🔍 ➥**Asking the Right Questions**

STEP 5: IDENTIFY APPROPRIATE LEGAL SOURCES

To streamline your research, consider what jurisdiction applies, whether you will need to research beyond primary authority, and what possible sources will be most useful.

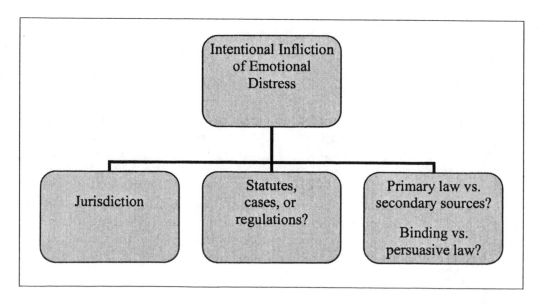

Jurisdiction: Where do Sally and Harry attend law school? If they are in Chicago, then the law of Illinois applies because the action that led to this possible claim took place in Illinois. (This is very simplified; other rules might apply that would make your claim a federal one or one of another state jurisdiction.)

Statutes, Cases, or Regulations: Start by looking in the Illinois state code. If there is nothing in the code on intentional infliction, consider moving onto cases. (You might remember from torts that many intentional torts are governed by common law.)

Primary Law vs. Secondary Sources: If you cannot remember anything about intentional infliction of emotional distress, you might pick up your first-year torts book, research the issue in a legal encyclopedia, or look at the Restatement on Torts to get some background information on the law. However, if you already have some general knowledge of intentional torts, this step might not be necessary.

Binding vs. Persuasive Law: Most (if not all) jurisdictions will have law on intentional infliction of emotional distress. However, if you find yourself in a new area of law or one in which your jurisdiction has little law on point, you might decide to expand into the law of other jurisdictions. Perhaps your jurisdiction has not yet addressed the issue of using the Internet to intentionally inflict emotional distress. Consider expanding your research to other jurisdictions to see if another court has addressed this issue.

STEP 6: CREATE EFFECTIVE SEARCH TERMS

1. **Courses as Categories:** You have probably already identified torts as the overall category for intentional infliction of emotional distress. From here, you want to identify some of the issues and subcategories you discussed in torts, such as emotional distress, mental suffering, or damages. So now you have a few potential categorical search terms from your torts class.

2. **Who, What, Where, When, Why:** Here, you can try to come up with other terms that might help you narrow your search.

   Who: student; peer
   What: caused emotional or mental injury; uploaded document
   Where: Chicago, Illinois; at school; online
   When: when given permission at first; on September 1, 2008
   Why: to offend; intentionally, to harm, to trick

3. **Expanding or Narrowing Your Search Terms:** Choose some of the broadest search terms first and consider making them expandable:

   Intentionally → Intent!

   Emotional → Emotion!

   If your search terms are too narrow, consider creating a broader, more categorical term:

   Torts → Civil liability

   Consider using a combination of both categorical terms and specific search terms:

   Torts or Civil liability and intent! or emotion!

   Narrow the number of hits you might get by making sure that the main terms are only within a few words of each other:

   intent! w/3 emotion! w/3 distress

To quickly find elements of intentional infliction of emotional distress, try:

elements /s intent! w/3 emotion! w/3 distress

4. **Print vs. Electronic Research:** Do not assume that researching on your computer is always the most efficient strategy. Many researchers prefer finding statutes in print. It might make the most sense to head to the library first and find the Illinois code section on intentional infliction of emotional distress. You might also skim through the table of contents or index of the Illinois code for intentional torts. If there is nothing in the code (or even if there is), you could begin to research cases using the digests, which are located in the same section of the library.

However, if you are not near the library or are comfortable with the word search you have created, log on to your computer. Ask yourself first whether a free source is available. For this problem, for example, you might go to the ↪**state map** and click on Illinois. Try clicking on state statutes to search the state code. You can try a word search or search through the table of contents. Instead of finding intentional infliction, you might notice there is a statute on slander and libel (in civil liabilities). Take note of this provision; it might be another claim you could file against Sally.

If there is not a statute on point, this map will not be very helpful in finding cases online since most jurisdictions do not yet link directly to their published cases. Therefore, you would log on to Lexis or Westlaw. Here, you will want to decide your best strategy. Because you know your jurisdiction, it makes sense to start in an Illinois database. If you have already determined that there is no statute on point, you would want to go to the database in Illinois for cases. Here, you would try the word search you have already created and work on expanding or narrowing the search depending on your number of hits.

🔍 ↪**Strategies for Book Research**
🔍 ↪**Strategies for Online Research**

If you find only a few sources, consider printing them to read. However, if you find a lot of law, you might want to read on screen first to cull out irrelevant materials before printing. Annotations will give you synopses of the cases or articles, which will assist your decision-making process.

STEP 7: USE HELPFUL FINDING TOOLS

For this problem, there are many useful tools that would help expedite your research:

Indexes: The index to the state code might be a useful starting point (if there is a statute on point). The digests will also have indexes for searching cases.

Table of Contents: Each state code will have a table of contents. You could use either the table of contents in the print books or the table of contents provided by Lexis and Westlaw to search categorically. Online, these expand as you get deeper into a subject area. You will find as you search the Illinois code that there is no statute on intentional infliction of emotional distress. However, you might note that there is a slander and libel act under the general civil liabilities section. You would want to look in this section to see if Sally's actions fit within this statute.

Key Number System: This system is particular to West (Westlaw online and West published books) and categorizes issues into a uniform numbered system. These also expand online as you click deeper within each subject. Here, you would find the Damages key number 50.10 section helpful for intentional infliction of emotional distress.

🔍 ↪**Key Number System**

STEP 8: USE SOURCES TO FIND OTHER SOURCES

The sources you find will help you find other sources. For example, if there is a statute on intentional infliction of emotional distress, the annotations in the statute will lead you to cases and secondary sources regarding your issue. Cases you read will cite to other cases (or statutes or secondary sources) that are relevant to intentional infliction as well. When you ➥**update** these cases, you will also find citations to cases that have referenced that case.

STEP 9: KNOW WHEN TO STOP

The worst feeling when you walk into court is wondering whether you found all the relevant law for your argument. Therefore, you want to be thorough in your research. A good time to stop your research is when you keep finding the same law. For example, you might update a case and find references to three cases you have already read. You might find annotations in a statute and then cases in a digest that are almost all identical. You might read a secondary source that covers all the issues you have covered in your research.

If you find no statute on point (such as in this intentional infliction example), then the cases you find should not reference a relevant statute. If they do, make sure to read that statute to determine if it applies.

To be thorough, however, consider using a variety of sources — print and electronic, Lexis and Westlaw, indexes and tables of contents — to ensure you are not missing a major piece of law on point. Keep in mind that research is not a linear process; just because you have followed one research strategy from start to finish does not mean you are done with your research. Oftentimes, you will find holes in your argument as you are writing a document; at that point, do more research so you can be thorough when citing to authority.

Once you have finished researching for one claim, repeat the process for each potential claim. In fact, you might have found more potential claims from your research on the first one. You also need to ask Harry how much money he wants to spend on his case. The amount of time you research this issue might be limited in terms of economics.

   🔍 ➥**Deciding When to Stop**

For more help with creating a research strategy, use the following links.

🔍 ➥**Research Strategies**
🔍 ➥**Strategies for Particular Sources**
🔍 ➥**Updating the Law**
🔍 ➥**Research Strategy Testimonials**

Research Sources — Federal Law

There are three branches of the federal government that create federal law:

1. **The legislature:** The federal Congress enacts codes.
2. **The judiciary:** The federal courts interpret and create laws through case opinions.
3. **The executive branch:** Administrative agencies regulate specific areas of the law such as food and drugs.

Research Sources — Federal Congress

The United States Congress is divided into two chambers: the House of Representatives and the Senate. To become law, a bill must pass each chamber. For legislative information on the Web, click ➙Thomas. Click on the following for more information on the ➙House, the ➙Senate, or ➙How a Bill Becomes a Law.

Research Sources — Federal Constitutions and Statutes

Constitutions

What: Constitutions are the highest primary authority. The ➙United States Constitution creates the broad governmental framework, describes governmental powers and restraints, defines political relationships, and enumerates individual rights and liberties.

Where: The United States Constitution is found in print version in the first volume of the federal code (U.S.C., U.S.C.A., U.S.C.S.).

Why: You are more likely to reach for the U.S.C.A. or U.S.C.S. to research constitutional issues because these sources are published more frequently than the U.S.C. and are annotated, meaning they provide references to cases, statutes, regulations, and secondary sources that discuss each constitutional provision.

How: ➙Finding Constitutions and Statutes

⊨ ➙Tutorial on Constitutions and Statutes

Federal Statutes

What: Federal statutes are laws passed by the United States Congress. They are codified in the United States Code, which is organized into fifty titles or subject areas. The titles are then subdivided into chapters, and the chapters are subdivided into sections.

🔍 ➙Statutory Language and Reading Statutes

Where: Federal statutes can be found in chronological and subject-matter sources:

1. The **chronological** form is a ▣ ➙Session Law, which is published in a volume that contains all the laws passed by a legislative body during each year or session. Session laws are published

(very slowly) in the Statutes at Large (Stat.). For a citation to 109 Stat. 2213, you would look in the 109th volume of the Statutes at Large on page 2213.

2. The **subject-matter** form of publication is in either the **official** or **annotated codes.** They are the preferred citations and most often used by lawyers because they are easy to access by way of topical or popular name index. The volumes contain collections of all statutes in that particular jurisdiction and are arranged in broad topics called "titles." The official code is the ➥**United States Code (U.S.C.).** The annotated codes are the United States Code Annotated (U.S.C.A.) and the United States Code Service (U.S.C.S.). Each has its own index, usually located at the end of the set of volumes. You can find these annotated versions in book form and on Lexis or Westlaw. These annotated codes also have **popular names tables** and **conversion tables.** The popular names tables allow you to search for a statute if you don't know its citation but know its name, such as The Americans with Disabilities Act. The conversion tables allow you to search if you know the public law number of your statute. The annotated versions also contain many helpful resources, including **Notes of Decisions,** which provide references to cases applying that statute.

    ▯ ➥**U.S.C.**
    ▯ ➥**U.S.C.A.**
    ▯ ➥**U.S.C.S.**

Why: The Statutes at Large are rarely used for research because the chronological arrangement makes them difficult to access. The U.S.C., U.S.C.A., and U.S.C.S., however, are arranged by subject matter and are heavily indexed so that the legal researcher can easily find a particular code provision. The U.S.C.A. and U.S.C.S., both published by commercial publishers, are updated more frequently than the official U.S.C., which is published by the government. Code provisions, once written by the Congress, are often litigated by lawyers, interpreted by the courts, and criticized by scholars. The annotated codes are therefore the most helpful tools for lawyers to find statutes because they also provide annotations to the various interpretations of each code provision.

How: ➥**Finding Constitutions and Statutes**

↔ ➥**Tutorial on Constitutions and Statutes**

CITATION:

    🔍 ➥**Citing Federal Constitutions Using the Bluebook**
    🔍 ➥**Citing Federal Statutes Using ALWD**

Research Sources — Federal Courts

The federal court system is hierarchical:

> At the lowest level, trials are held in the **United States district courts.**
> The first level of appeal is in the **courts of appeals** or **circuit courts.**
> The highest appeal is held in the **United States Supreme Court.**

The district courts and the courts of appeals are broken down geographically into **circuits.** There are 11 numbered circuits as well as the D.C. Circuit and the Federal Circuit. Each circuit has its own district court and appellate court judges.

⇥**Supreme Court**   ⇥**Courts of Appeals**   ⇥**District Courts**

🔍 ⇥**Function and Organization of the Courts**

Research Sources — United States Supreme Court

Supreme Court cases are cited in the United States Reports (U.S.), which is the Court's official reporter, as well as in the Supreme Court Reporter (S. Ct.) and the United States Supreme Court Reports, Lawyers' Edition (L. Ed., L. Ed. 2d). The Supreme Court sits as the final appellate court for each circuit, but the Supreme Court hears only the cases it decides warrant further appellate review by "granting certiorari." To learn more about the Supreme Court and to search the Supreme Court for docket information, recent cases, briefs, and oral arguments, visit the Supreme Court's website by clicking below.

⇥**The Supreme Court**
🔍 ⇥**Listen to Supreme Court Oral Arguments**
🔍 ⇥**Listen to Supreme Court Justices Discuss Legal Writing**

Research Sources — Federal Courts of Appeals

The courts of appeals are divided into 13 circuits: Circuits 1-11, the D.C. Circuit, and the Federal Circuit. Courts of appeals are cited in the Federal Reporter (F., F.2d, F.3d). Click on each circuit number to link to that circuit's home page for docket or court information or to search for recent court decisions. For all published circuit cases, search on ⇥**Lexis** or ⇥**Westlaw**.

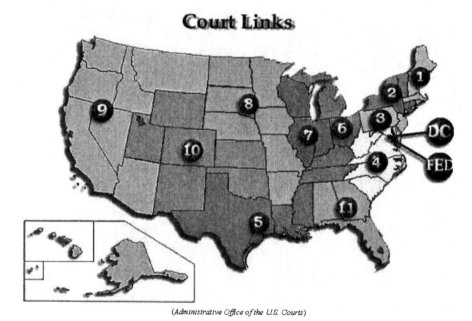

Court Links

(Administrative Office of the U.S. Courts)

Research Sources — Federal District Courts

The district courts serve as the trial courts within each circuit. Some circuits have many district courts, which are divided according to their regions. District court cases are most often cited in the Federal Supplement (F. Supp., F. Supp. 2d). To search for particular district court dockets, information, and recent cases, click on the circuit number below. For all published district court cases, search on ➥**Lexis** or ➥**Westlaw.**

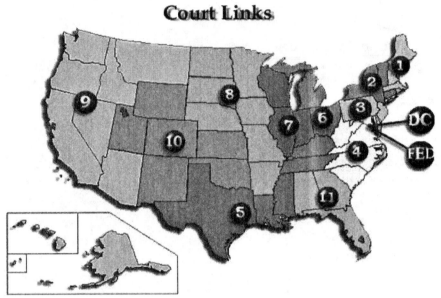

Court Links

(Administrative Office of the U.S. Courts)

Research Sources — Federal Cases

What: Federal cases are written by federal judges. These judges interpret the United States Constitution and federal statutes and create federal common law by deciding on specific cases and writing opinions. Only the written opinion of the court is considered case precedent. However, when published, editors include other helpful information such as:

> **Citation and Heading.** The citation includes the case name, reporter (sometimes there is an official and an unofficial reporter provided in a parallel citation), and the year of the decision. The heading contains a bit more detail by providing the name of the court as well as the actual date of the decision.
>
> **Case synopsis.** The editors usually provide a summary of the opinion. They are identified as the syllabus in a Supreme Court opinion. Remember that they are not part of the official opinion.
>
> **Headnotes.** These are short paragraphs that summarize key points of the opinion. Usually, editors will provide corresponding numbers to the text of the opinion or they will be directly hyperlink to the text of the opinion. West also provided ➥**Key Numbers** to these headnotes.
>
> **Names.** Here, the editor will provide the names of the attorneys as well as the names of the judge who wrote the opinion. *Per curiam* means that no one particular judge is taking credit for the opinion; it is an anonymous opinion. *En banc* means that the full appellate court has heard the argument and rendered a decision (as opposed to a three-judge panel).
>
> **Written Opinion.** The actual opinion appears next in the text and is the only part of the published decision you should cite.

These published opinions become binding precedent. However, only the cases chosen by the courts for publication are considered "published." As a result, only the published opinions will ultimately be placed in the reporters. Although many unpublished decisions are available through services such as

Westlaw and Lexis, most jurisdictions do not rely on unpublished decisions as binding precedent so lawyers are wary of citing them in court documents.

⬚ ↪Anatomy of a Case

Where: Federal cases are published in chronological and subject-matter form.
1. The chronological publication is through a variety of books called federal reporters, which are found in the following volumes:
    1. ↪**Supreme Court**
        1. The United States Reports ⬚ ↪**(U.S.)**, the official reporter for the Supreme Court, published by the federal government
        2. The Supreme Court Reporter (S. Ct.), published by West Group
        3. The United States Supreme Court Reports (L. Ed., L. Ed. 2d), published by Lawyers Cooperative
    2. ↪**Courts of Appeals**
        1. The Federal Reporter ⬚ ↪**(F., F.2d, F.3d)**, published by West Group
    3. ↪**District Court Cases**
        1. The Federal Supplement ⬚ ↪**(F. Supp., F. Supp. 2d)**, published by West Group
        2. The Federal Rules Decisions (F.R.D.)
        3. The Federal Reporter (F., F.2d), for cases decided between 1880 and 1932
2. The subject-matter form of publication is in ⬚ ↪**federal digests.** However, the cases in the digests are not printed in full; instead, they are summaries of cases grouped by subject matter and function as an index to the reporters. Each reporter has its own digest.

Why: Your ultimate goal is to find a case within the chronological reporter. However, you would start with the chronological reporter only if you had a citation or the plaintiff's or defendant's name (to check the names tables). Most of the time, you will be searching for cases based on subject matter. Therefore, the best place to begin your common law research is through the digests. Each digest contains an index and then volumes arranged alphabetically by subject matter. These subjects have been created and maintained by publishers who act as the researchers' first set of eyes to cull and sort case law. Once you find your subject matter, the digest will provide citations to the reporters as well as a short annotation summarizing the case. You should never cite directly to the digest.

How: ↪**Finding Cases in Research Strategies**

    ⬚ ↪**Tutorial on Cases**

CITATION:

    🔍 ↪**Citing Cases using the Bluebook**
    🔍 ↪**Citing Cases using ALWD**

Research Sources — Federal Agencies

Federal agencies fall under the executive branch. They are created through congressional legislation that defines the specialized topic and mission of the agency. Once established, an agency may issue rules and regulations pertaining to its mission and hear and settle disputes arising from them. Law produced by agencies is called administrative law.

Well-known executive agencies include the following:

- ↪**Environmental Protection Agency**
- ↪**Federal Communications Commission**
- ↪**Federal Trade Commission**

To find a particular agency, you can click on the following:

- ↪**Agency Index** (Washburn University School of Law)
- ↪**Federal Web Locator** (Center for Information Law and Policy at Chicago-Kent College of Law)
- ↪**FirstGov** (A-Z Index of U.S. Government Departments and Agencies)

Research Sources — Federal Administrative Law

What: Each executive agency creates administrative law, which includes rules and regulations, decisions, and a variety of other documents particular to that agency.

> **Administrative Rules and Regulations:** Agencies create rules and regulations, which implement statutes that have already been passed by Congress. These statutes give the agencies the power to enforce the statute by promulgating specific regulations and rules that must be followed. Regulations (sometimes called rules) look very similar to statutes. When an agency promulgates a rule or regulation, it must notify the public by publishing the proposed regulation in the Federal Register, solicit comments regarding the regulation, and publish the regulation before it becomes effective.
>
> **Administrative Agency Decisions:** Agency decisions are similar in form to judicial decisions. Administrative agencies exercise a quasi-judicial power in that they make decisions involving issues arising under their regulations. Under the Administrative Procedure Act, agency hearings are conducted by an administrative judge, who acts as a trial judge making decisions of the agency. A party can appeal the agency decision to the federal district court.
>
> **History of Administrative Law Publications:** Before 1936, there was no official publication of rules and regulations. As a result, there was no way to determine whether an act was prohibited by a particular agency. Franklin D. Roosevelt's New Deal created a growth of agencies, which produced thousands of regulations, but there was no method to publish them. In <u>Panama Refining Co. v. Ryan</u>, 293 U.S. 388 (1935), a corporation was prosecuted for violations of a regulation that had been revoked before the lawsuit was filed. Therefore, in 1935, Congress passed the Federal Register Act, which required any administrative rule or regulation to be published in the Federal Register. Since 1936, the Federal Register has published, in chronological order, every regulation having "general applicability and legal effect."
>
> In 1937, Congress provided for a method of subject codification of the regulations into the **Code of Federal Regulations (C.F.R.)**, which was first published in 1939. Since 1968, the C.F.R. has been published yearly, in quarterly installments.
>
> In 1946, Congress passed the Administrative Procedure Act, which required the agencies to publish proposed rules and allowed the public to comment on those proposed rules in the Federal Register. Subsequent legislation requires agencies to publish descriptions of the agencies, rules of procedure, policy statements, and notices of most meetings (the latter from the Sunshine Act of 1976).

Where: Similarly to statutes, administrative regulations are published chronologically and by subject matter:

CHRONOLOGICALLY: THE FEDERAL REGISTER

The Federal Register is published daily (based on workdays), and all issues within a year constitute a single volume. A table of contents page lists all executive agencies and documents produced by each agency. A daily issue publishes material in the following order:

- Presidential documents
- Rules and regulations
- Proposed rules
- Notices
- Notices of Sunshine Act meetings

The Federal Register also contains helpful finding aides, such as:

- List of C.F.R. parts affected in that issue
- Telephone numbers
- A parallel table of Federal Register pages for the month
- A cumulative table of C.F.R. Parts affected during the month
- A list of Public Laws

SUBJECT MATTER: THE CODE OF FEDERAL REGULATIONS (C.F.R.)

The C.F.R. arranges administrative rules and regulations chronologically. It is arranged in a format similar to the United States Code. The regulations are arranged in 50 titles, some of which match the titles of the U.S.C. The titles are then divided into chapters, which regulate a particular agency.

> Administrative Agency decisions are similar in form to judicial decisions. However, there is no comprehensive system for publishing these cases. To find administrative decisions you can try the following sources:
>
> 1. Agency Reporters and Web Sites. Many agencies publish their opinions in their own reporters, such as the Federal Trade Commission Reports or Agriculture Decisions. To find a particular agency, click on USA.gov.
> 2. Lexis. Click on Area of Law by Topic; then within each topic, look for Administrative Materials.
> 3. Westlaw. Click on Directory; Topic Practice Areas; a specific topic; Federal Administrative Materials.

Why: If you work in a particular area of law, such as food and drug law, you will need to become very familiar with the applicable regulations and agency.

How: The best place to find regulation is through the C.F.R., which is a set of soft-cover volumes. To find regulations in the C.F.R., you can search by subject or by citation to the regulation or to the statute. There are a number of sources to find regulations:

1. **Online.** The C.F.R. is available online through a number of sources:

    a. Government Printing Office. There are two versions on GPO Access:

        1) the pdf version, which is the "official" version and is as up-to-date as the print version; and

        2) the e-C.F.R., which is more current but not "official."

    In addition, GPO Access has a Parallel Table of Authorities and Rules so that you can find a regulation from a statute citation.

    b. Agency Web Sites. Agencies will post their specific regulations.

    c. Westlaw. When you have a citation to the C.F.R., use "Find." Otherwise go to "Administrative Code." You can use the C.F.R. index or do a search.

    d. Lexis. When you have a citation to the C.F.R., use "Find a Document." Otherwise, go to "Code of Federal Regulations." Lexis does not have a C.F.R. index.

    e. Registration.gov. This is a government web site where you can find proposed regulations.

2. **Book Research.** To find regulations in the print C.F.R:

    a. The index to the C.F.R. There are three print indexes: the Index and Finding Aids volume of the C.F.R., a special volume of U.S.C.S.; and one published by West.

    b. Annotated Codes. U.S.C.A. and U.S.C.S. frequently cross-reference regulations from the specific statutes.

Updating Regulations: Once you find the applicable regulation, you will need to make sure it is up to date. The C.F.R. is updated quarterly each year:

- Titles 1-16 contain regulations in force as of January 1 of that year.
- Titles 17-27 contain regulations in force as of April 1 of that year.
- Titles 28-41 contain regulations in force as of July 1 of that year.
- Titles 42-50 contain regulations in force as of October 1 of that year.

Each year's volumes are a particular color. Thus, in June, half the set will be one color and the other half will be a different color. By the end of the year, the whole set is the same color. The cover of each volume states the dates of coverage. Because the C.F.R. is updated so frequently, there are no pocket parts. However, because a regulation can be changed after the particular title has been published, you will need to update your regulations carefully using the List of Sections Affected or online resources.

The List of Sections Affected (LSA)

The LSA is published monthly and contains the finalized and proposed changes made since the latest publication of the C.F.R. The LSA arranges final regulations by C.F.R. title and section and provides page references to the Federal Register. The LSA arranges proposed changes by title and part and references pages in the Federal Register. To update a regulation you need to find the most recent issue of the LSA. Look on the inside cover to determine the time period covered. Next, look up your regulation by title number and then specifically by part or section. If your number is not listed, the regulation has not been updated. If it has been listed, you will find a reference to the Federal Register where the information on the regulation will be posted. Next, you will need to update further to make sure that no further action has been taken on that regulation since the publication of the most recent LSA. To do so, use the table on the back cover of the most current issue of the Federal Register (C.F.R. parts Affected).

UPDATING ONLINE

To update online, you can use these sources:

1. GPO Access; The e-cfr provides updating through the Federal Registrar;
2. Weslaw. Use Keycite flags;
3. Lexis: Shepardizing a regulation will only provide you with cases or law review articles citing the regulation. It will not tell you about any changes in a regulation;
4. Regulations.gov. Here, you can find proposed regulations.

🔍 ↪**Research Strategies: Finding Administrative Law**

↤↦ ↪**Tutorial on Finding Administrative Law**

CITATION:

    🔍 ↪**Citing to Administrative Material Using the Bluebook**
    🔍 ↪**Citing to Administrative Materials Using ALWD**

RESEARCH SOURCES - STATE LAW

    Select a state by clicking it on the map or choosing it from the drop-down menu. You will be able to view its home page, constitution, code, courts, and regulations. You may also read information about state law by clicking in the ↪**State Law box.**

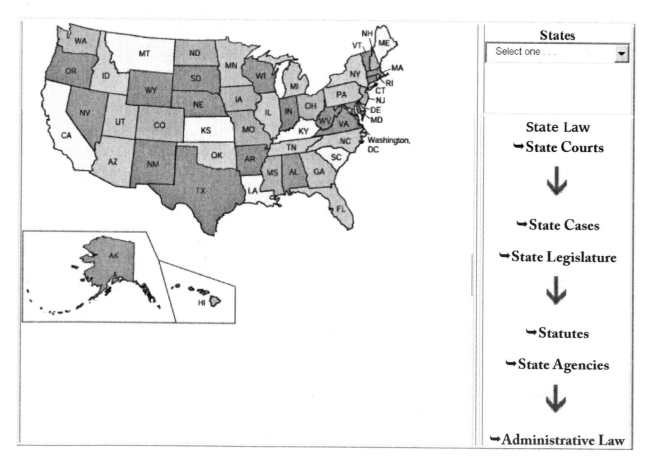

RESEARCH SOURCES - STATE LEGISLATURES

Each state has its own legislature. Like the federal Congress, most state legislatures are broken into two separate houses. Similar to federal bills, state bills must pass each house (and receive the governor's signature) before they become laws.

➥**How a Federal Bill Becomes a Law**
➥**Example of How a State Bill Becomes a Law**

Research Sources — State Constitutions and Statutes

State Constitutions

What: Most states have their own constitutions, which are subordinate to the U.S. Constitution and may enumerate more rights for their citizens. Jurisdictions are not required to have their own constitutions. (The District of Columbia, for example, relies solely on the federal Constitution.)

Where: A state's constitution usually is found in the first volume of the state's code and can be accessed through the index accompanying the state statutes or on the Web, usually via the state's home page.

Why: If you are simply looking for the full state constitution, finding it on the Web is easy. However, if you want to find a particular provision or read law interpreting a particular provision, you should use the state code because it provides indexes and annotations.

How: ➥**Finding Constitutions and Statutes**

▸◂ ➥**Tutorial on Constitutions and Statutes**

CITATION:

      🔍 ➥**Citing to Constitutions Using the Bluebook**
      🔍 ➥**Citing to Constitutions Using ALWD**

State Statutes

What: State statutes (or codes) are laws passed by a state's legislature. States organize their codes differently; some use numbers similar to the titles of the U.S. Code, while others organize by subject matter.

🔍 ➥**Statutory Language and Reading Statutes**

Where: State codes are found in chronological or subject-matter sources:
     1. The chronological form is a session law, which is published in a volume that contains all the laws passed by a legislative body during each year or session.
     2. The subject-matter form of publication is in either the official or annotated codes or statutes. They are the preferred citations and most often used by lawyers because they are easy to access by way of a topical or **popular name index.** The volumes contain collections of all statutes in that particular jurisdiction and are arranged in broad topics called titles. State codes vary in quality and quantity. Some states use commercial publishers to print their official codes; other states publish their own codes, usually more slowly than commercial publishers do. Bluebook Table 1 (T.1) and ALWD Appendix 1 list each state's official code. You can also access each state's code on

the Web or through Lexis or Westlaw. The annotated versions contain many helpful resources, including **Notes of Decisions,** which provide references to cases applying that statute.

Why: The session laws are rarely used for research because the chronological arrangement makes them difficult to access. The annotated state codes are much more useful because of their subject-matter arrangement, indexing, and annotations. In addition, they are often published by commercial publishers and are therefore more current than the government-published session laws.

How: ➥Finding Constitutions and Statutes

↤ ➥Tutorial on Constitutions and Statutes

To access state constitutions and statutes, click ➥HERE for your particular state.

CITATION:

    🔍 ➥Citing to Statutes Using the Bluebook
    🔍 ➥Citing to Statutes Using ALWD

Research Sources — State Courts

Each state has its own court system. Although state court systems differ from each other, in every jurisdiction a case starts in a trial court and has an opportunity for at least one appeal.

Trial courts: Some jurisdictions have multiple trial courts, such as one for criminal cases and one for civil cases.

Appellate courts: Many states have an intermediate appellate court so that a litigant has two opportunities for appeal: one to the intermediate appellate court and one to the highest state court. In these types of jurisdictions, there may be more than one intermediate appellate division.

To understand your particular state's court structure, consult Bluebook Table 1 (T.1) or ALWD Appendix 1. A diagram of the hierarchy of a typical state's court system follows:

Supreme Court

↑

Court of Appeals

↑

Trial Court

Click on the ➥map to access a particular state's court system.

Research Sources — State Cases

What: State cases are written by state judges. These judges decide on specific cases and thereby create common law and interpret state statutes and constitutions. Only the written opinion of the court is considered case precedent. However, when published, editors include other helpful information such as:

    Citation and Heading. The citation includes the case name, reporter (sometimes there is an official and an unofficial reporter provided in a parallel citation), and the year of the decision.

The heading contains a bit more detail by providing the name of the court as well as the actual date of the decision.

Case synopsis. The editors usually provide a summary of the opinion.

Headnotes. These are short paragraphs that summarize key points of the opinion. Usually, editors will provide corresponding numbers to the text of the opinion or they will be directly hyperlinked to the text of the opinion. West also provides ➥**Key Numbers** to these headnotes.

Names. Here, the editor will provide the names of the attorneys as well as the names of the judge who wrote the opinion. *Per curiam* means that no one particular judge is taking credit for the opinion. *En banc* means that the full appellate court has heard the argument and rendered a decision (as opposed to a three-judge panel).

Written Opinion. The actual opinion appears next in the text and is the only part of the published decision you should cite.

These published opinions become binding precedent. However, only the cases chosen by the courts for publication are considered "published." As a result, only the published opinions will ultimately be placed in the reporters. Although many unpublished decisions are available through services such as Westlaw and Lexis, most jurisdictions do not rely on unpublished decisions as binding precedent so lawyers are wary of citing them in court documents.

➥**Anatomy of a Case**

Where: State cases are published in chronological and subject-matter forms:

1. The **chronological** form of publication is through ➥**state or regional reporters**. Regional reporters and their corresponding states include the following:

    1. **Atlantic Reporter** (A., A.2d): Connecticut, Delaware, District of Columbia, Maine, Maryland, New Hampshire, New Jersey, Pennsylvania, Rhode Island, Vermont
    2. **North Eastern Reporter** (N.E., N.E.2d): Illinois, Indiana, Massachusetts, New York, Ohio
    3. **North Western Reporter** (N.W., N.W.2d): Iowa, Michigan, Minnesota, Nebraska, North Dakota, South Dakota, Wisconsin
    4. **Pacific Reporter** (P., P.3d): Alaska, Arizona, California, Colorado, Hawaii, Idaho, Kansas, Montana, Nevada, New Mexico, Oklahoma, Oregon, Utah, Washington, Wyoming
    5. **South Eastern Reporter** (S.E., S.E.2d): Georgia, North Carolina, South Carolina, Virginia, West Virginia
    6. **South Western Reporter** (S.W., S.W.3d): Arkansas, Kentucky, Missouri, Tennessee, Texas
    7. **Southern Reporter** (So., So. 2d): Alabama, Florida, Louisiana, Mississippi

2. The **subject-matter** form of publication is in ➥**state or regional digests**. However, the cases in the digests are not printed in full; instead, they are summaries of cases grouped by subject matter and function as an index to the reporters. Each reporter has its own digest and an index to the digest. The digests are a form of access into the chronological reporters.

Why: Your ultimate goal is to find a case within the chronological reporter. However, you would start with the chronological reporter only if you had a citation or the plaintiff's or defendant's name (to check the names tables). Most of the time, you will be searching for cases based on subject matter. Therefore, the best place to begin your common law research is through the digests. Each digest contains an index and then volumes, arranged alphabetically by subject matter. These subjects have been created and maintained by publishers who act as the researchers' first set of eyes to cull and sort case law. Once you find your subject matter, the digest will provide citations to the reporters as well as a short annotation summarizing the case. You should never cite directly to the digest.

How: ⇥**Finding Cases in Research Strategies**

⬌ ⇥**Tutorial on Cases**

CITATION:

     🔍 ⇥**Citing Cases Using the Bluebook**
     🔍 ⇥**Citing Cases Using ALWD**

Research Sources — State Agencies

State agencies fall under the state's executive branch. Agencies on the state level create and enforce regulations on a variety of matters such as housing, utilities, and public health. Each state has its own agencies, which can be found by returning to the ⇥**state law map** and clicking on a specific state.

🔍 ⇥**Federal Agencies**

Research Sources — State Administrative Law

What: Each state agency creates administrative laws, which include rules and regulations, decisions, and a variety of other documents particular to that agency. These documents mirror the form and function of ⇥**federal administrative law.**

Where: States publish their administrative laws in a wide variety of formats. Some states' publications are similar to federal administrative law in that they have subject sets similar to the subject-matter codification of the Code of Federal Regulations (C.F.R.) that are sometimes supplemented by chronological sets similar to the Federal Register. In other states, regulations are published only by the agency itself. Some states have sold the rights to publish their state administrative codes to private publishers.

Why: You might be asked to find regulations promulgated by a particular state.

How: To find the administrative law resources for a particular state, you can click on the ⇥**state map** and then click on the administrative law link in that state or consult the following sources:

BNA's Directory of State Administrative Codes and Registers

The Book of the States (Council of State Governments)

⇥**Westlaw** and ⇥**Lexis** publish selected states' administrative laws.

🔍 ⇥**State Agencies and Administrative Law Published Online by Each State**
🔍 ⇥**Research Strategies for State Administrative Law**

CITATION:

     🔍 ⇥**Citing to Administrative Law Using the Bluebook**
     🔍 ⇥**Citing to Administrative Law Using ALWD**

Research Sources — Legal Encyclopedias

What: Legal encyclopedias look and function like general encyclopedias in that they are alphabetically arranged into volumes that contain specific topics. Each encyclopedia contains an index, usually located at the end of the volumes, as well as an index to each volume and a table of contents to each topic.

Why: Legal encyclopedias provide very basic introductions to a specific legal topic, but they do not analyze the law or explain its application. You would use an encyclopedia if you need an elementary context for a particular law or if you need a more detailed definition than found in Black's Law Dictionary. A state encyclopedia may be helpful if you are trying to find whether a state has a particular law (i.e., whether Maryland has the death penalty). While legal encyclopedias contain footnotes to legal citations, these citations are only a small sample.

Where and How: Three sets of encyclopedias are most often used by lawyers:

1. **Corpus Juris Secundum (C.J.S.)**
   This West publication is a set of dark blue volumes that uses the ➦**key number system**. The set contains pocket parts, which are located at the back of each volume and reference recent citations. C.J.S. contains lengthy footnotes since it has its origins in West's exhaustive publication philosophy. To access from ➦**Westlaw** : Type "CJS" in the Search These Databases box.

   ➦**Sample Pages: C.J.S.**

2. **American Jurisprudence 2d (Am. Jur. 2d)**
   This encyclopedia set was originally published by Lawyers Cooperative Publishing, but is now a part of West Group. It contains pocket parts, which are located at the back of each volume and reference recent citations. Unlike C.J.S., Am. Jur. 2d has a New Topics binder, located at the end of the set, that introduces new topics. It also contains a "Deskbook," which serves as a handy reference tool that lists items such as the following:

   - Addresses and phone numbers of federal government departments
   - Historical documents
   - Financial and annuity tables
   - Arbitration rules
     - To access from ➦**Lexis**: Go to "Source - Legal - Secondary Sources - American Jurisprudence 2d".
     - To access from ➦**Westlaw**: Type "AMJUR" in the Search These Databases box.

   ➦**Sample Pages: Am. Jur. 2d**

3. **State Encyclopedias**
   Many states publish their own encyclopedias, which function similarly to the national sets referenced above. They have names such as Encyclopedia, Jurisprudence, or Practice. State encyclopedias can be very helpful because they might contain a history of the law in that state as well as citations to statutes and useful cases on point. Remember to look for pocket parts and be wary of citing to these encyclopedias in legal documents.

   - To access from ➦**Westlaw**: View "Westlaw Directory - U.S. State Materials - Forms, Treatises, CLEs and Other Practice Materials".
   - To access from ➦**Lexis**: Go to "Source - Legal - Secondary Legal - Jurisprudence & A.L.R."

⌨ ↪**Sample Pages: State Encyclopedias**

↔ ↪**Tutorial on Legal Encyclopedias**

Citation: It is rare that you would cite to a Legal Encyclopedia in a court document.

Research Sources — American Law Reports (A.L.R.)

What: American Law Reports (A.L.R.) combines features of an encyclopedia with those of a case reporter. It is like an encyclopedia in that it contains annotations and footnotes to particular legal topics. However, a topic covered in A.L.R. is much more detailed than one covered in an encyclopedia, and it also discusses and analyzes national trends. The distinctive feature of A.L.R. that resembles a case reporter is that it contains the full text of selected cases to act as a reference point for the analytical discussion of the particular legal topic. Cases are selected for discussion if they contain novel or important issues. A.L.R. was originally published by Lawyers Cooperative, which published selective opinions. Therefore, one limitation of the series is that coverage is not comprehensive.

Why: A.L.R. is a fantastic source if you are looking to learn all you can about a particular topic in a very short time. If your topic or case is the subject of an A.L.R. annotation, you will have found a gold mine. First, A.L.R. will print, in full, a representative case on that topic. Next, it will print a lengthy (sometimes 40-page) annotative section discussing that topic, including context, particular issue, a survey of states including distinctions among jurisdictions, and citations to other sources within each jurisdiction. As a result, A.L.R. annotations can be quite helpful in discussing, comparing, and citing law from various jurisdictions. If you find your case has been addressed or your particular point of law has been analyzed, then the annotation will be extremely helpful and well worth using. However, because the series is not comprehensive and is often confusing with its many series, it is not always efficient.

Where and How: A.L.R. (now published by West Group) contains seven series: A.L.R., A.L.R.2d, A.L.R.3d, A.L.R.4th, A.L.R.5th, A.L.R.6th, and A.L.R. Federal (A.L.R. Fed., A.L.R. Fed. 2d). A researcher can use the index and digest to find relevant annotations. If an annotation has been superseded, the researcher need only read the later annotation. However, if it has been supplemented, the researcher should consult both annotations. The "Annotated History Table," located in the index, shows if an annotation has been supplemented or superseded. In addition, the researcher should consult pocket parts within each volume for updates.

A.L.R. annotations usually contain the following:

- A scope note, which describes coverage in the annotation
- A summary of the case
- An outline of the annotation
- Extensive research references
- An in-depth index
- A table of cases
- An annotation text
  - To access online:
    - ↪**Westlaw:** Type "ALR" in the Search These Databases box.

🖳 ➙**Sample Pages: American Law Reports**

↤ ➙**Tutorial on Secondary Sources**

Citation: It is rare that you would cite to an A.L.R. in a court document.

Research Sources — Treatises and Hornbooks

Hornbooks

What: Hornbooks are legal aids created for a **student** audience, namely the audience using the legal casebook method developed by Langdell. These textbooks, usually written by one or more law professors, contain excerpts from cases in a particular field of law, such as contracts. The cases are often explained, questioned, and placed in a context within the book.

Why: Hornbooks are used by students in class and in studying for exams.

Where and How: Consult your law library or bookstore to find an appropriate hornbook. Usually, they are arranged by subject matter or assigned by your professor.

Treatises

What: Treatises are legal aids that also cover one particular area of law, but they are more extensive than hornbooks (they are often published in multivolumes). They are often written for the **practitioner**. They contain lengthy footnotes, critical analyses, and sometimes historical or social debates on issues particular to that topic. They are written by scholars, and different treatises are relied on more heavily than others. For example, Weinstein on Evidence or Prosser on Torts is often used by practitioners.

Why: Many practitioners rely heavily on treatises in their particular legal areas. Because they are written by real experts who have spent their careers focusing on the law and explaining and discussing it, treatises play an integral role in the law firm. Consulting a treatise is like asking for help from the smartest student in the class.

Where and How: To find relevant treatises, you should consult your law library's catalog or a book titled Law Books in Print. If you specialize in an area of practice, your office library will usually contain a relevant treatise. Most treatises are available only in print form. If you are working in a law firm, you will often find a treatise in the office of a partner who specializes in that particular subject.

🖳 ➙**Sample Pages Treatise/Hornbook**

↤ ➙**Tutorial on Treatises and Hornbooks**
↤ ➙**Tutorial on Secondary Sources**

CITATION:

    🔍 ➙**Citing to Hornbooks and Treatises Using the Bluebook**
    🔍 ➙**Citing to Hornbooks and Treatises Using ALWD**

Research Sources — Law Reviews

What: Law reviews are student-run organizations that publish heavily footnoted articles, usually written by professors, and notes, written by students. Law reviews, such as the Georgetown Law Journal, publish on any topic chosen and are edited by its students. Other law reviews, such as the American Criminal Law Review, publish in the area of one particular topic.

Why: Law review articles are scholarly documents designed to stimulate thought, argue for a position, or criticize a case. Therefore, you would not use them to find objective explanations of the law. Instead, the value of a law review article is the work done by the author; in writing the critical piece, the author performs thorough research into that particular area of the law and provides prolific footnotes detailing that research. While the commentary often gives useful insight into a subject and its historical or political underpinnings, the footnotes almost always provide helpful references to cases, statutes, and other authorities on the subject matter. These footnotes provide a gold mine in terms of legal sources.

Where and How: To find law review articles on a particular area of law, you can use a number of sources:

1. **Index to Legal Periodicals and Books (ILP)** contains law review articles dating back to 1908 and focuses on academic reviews. Users search the index by using author names, law review titles, or specific cases or statutes. The index is available in a print version, a CD version (Wilson-Disc), or online via Lexis and Westlaw, where it is called Legal Periodicals and Books. (The online version does not contain the older reviews.) You can also subscribe to the Web version; visit ➥**Index to Legal Periodicals Full Text**.

2. **Current Law Index (CLI)** dates back only to 1980, so its coverage is not as comprehensive. However, it covers a wider range of periodicals and newspapers than does the Index to Legal Periodicals and Books; it also includes practitioners' publications. It is published 12 times a year in single editions and is then republished in a cumulative volume. Its online version, **LegalTrac**, is available on Lexis and Westlaw. You can subscribe to LegalTrac directly online as well. Here, you can search by keyword and by author. Once you have a citation, you can search in other sources (such as Lexis, Westlaw, Hein-on-Line, and E-Journal Finder) to find the article.

    ➥**Lexis** - Go to "Look for a Source - Legal - Secondary Legal - Annotations and Indexes."
    ➥**Westlaw** - Type "LRI" or "ILP" in the Search These Databases box.

3. **HeinOnline** is a retrieval source for dozens of academic journals. It houses back journals in pdf format for easy access. Most law libraries subscribe to HeinOnline. You can search HeinOnline by citation, title, author, or by word searches or using a table of contents for individual publications.

4. **Westlaw and Lexis** both publish full-text articles from many law reviews, and they are easy to access. Searching here differs from using the journal indexes because you can search full text, not just the title and subject headings. In addition, you can search each section as well as footnotes for content that does not appear in the indexes. Lexis and Westlaw usually update their sites more frequently than the journal indexes. However, you are likely to find a great deal of "hits" in searching on Lexis and Westlaw since their databases are very large. In addition, coverage for the journals is very mixed, with some starting in the 1990s. On Westlaw, some law reviews publish only selected articles before 1994. To search these databases, do the following:

    1. ➥**Lexis** - Go to "Look for a Source - Secondary Legal - Law Reviews and Journals."
    2. ➥**Westlaw** - Type "JLR" in the Search These Databases box.

5. **E-Journal Finder.** You can find journals that only publish electronically.

      ➡ **Online Law Review Article**
      ➡ **Book Law Review Article**
      ➡ **Tutorial on Secondary Sources**
      ➡ **Tutorial on Law Review**

CITATION:

      ➡ **Citing to Law Review Articles Using the Bluebook**
      ➡ **Citing to Law Review Articles Using ALWD**

Research Sources — Restatements

What: Restatements are similar to treatises in that they cover one particular area of the law. They are written by committees of scholars, judges, and lawyers and published by the ➡**American Law Institute**, which is a nonprofit organization for lawyers' continuing education. However, unlike treatises, Restatements do not contain a great amount of detail or practitioner's hints.

There are 13 Restatements, each addressing a particular area of law, such as the most widely used, Restatement on Torts and Restatement on Contracts. Although they are not the law, they are so authoritative that courts often specifically adopt a particular Restatement as the law in that jurisdiction. The 13 Restatements:

Agency
Conflict of Laws
Contracts
Foreign Relations
Judgments
Law Governing Lawyers
Property
Restitution
Security
Suretyship & Guaranty
Torts
Trusts
Unfair Competition

Why: You would use a Restatement if you need a neutral, concise, black-letter statement of the law. A Restatement is also a useful tool for studying for law school exams. Beware, however: The Restatement might not be the law of your particular jurisdiction, and it does not provide you with analyses of, details or hints about, or answers to a specific legal question.

Where and How: Each Restatement has its own index and is organized by subsection to that topic. The Restatements "state" the law as well as provide commentary, examples, and analysis about the law and its development. The Restatements 2ds also provide cross-references to the key number system and to American Law Reports (A.L.R.). Each Restatement is updated by an appendix, which may contain several volumes.

To access online:

↪**Lexis:** Go to "Source - Legal - Secondary Legal - Restatements".

↪**Westlaw:** View "Westlaw Directory - Forms, Treatises, CLEs and Other Practice Material - Restatements of the Law & Uniform Laws".

⊟ ↪**Sample Pages Restatement**

↔ ↪**Tutorial on Restatements**

↔ ↪**Tutorial on Secondary Sources**

CITATION:

🔍 ↪**Citing to Restatements Using the Bluebook**

🔍 ↪**Citing to Restatements Using ALWD**

↪**Research Strategies: Using Looseleafs**

↪**Research Strategies: Finding Legislative History**

Research Sources — Quick Reference — Statutes

UNITED STATES CONSTITUTION

The U.S. Constitution creates the broad governmental framework, describes governmental powers and restraints, defines political relationships, and enumerates individual rights and liberties. It is found in print version in the first volume of the federal code (U.S.C., U.S.C.A., U.S.C.S.).

The U.S.C.A. and U.S.C.S. are often more helpful than the U.S.C. because they are published more frequently and are annotated.

FEDERAL STATUTES

Federal statutes are laws passed by the U.S. Congress. They are found in chronological order in the session law, which is published in a volume that contains all the laws passed by a legislative body during each year or session. Session laws are published (very slowly) in the Statutes at Large (Stat.). Federal statutes are found in subject order in either the official or annotated codes. These are the preferred codes to cite to and are easier to use. They can be accessed by way of topical or popular name indexes, and the volumes contain collections of all statutes in that particular jurisdiction and are arranged in broad topics called titles.

The official code is the United States Code (U.S.C.), and the annotated codes are the United States Code Annotated (U.S.C.A.) and the United States Code Service (U.S.C.S.). The annotated codes have indexes, usually located at the end of the set of volumes, and can be accessed either with the books or on Lexis or Westlaw.

The commercial annotated codes (U.S.C.A. and U.S.C.S.) are usually the easiest source to use for a researcher. They are updated more frequently than the official code, and the subject-matter organization is easier to use than the Statutes at Large. The annotations are helpful tools for finding additional sources that interpret the code provision.

STATE CONSTITUTIONS

Each state may have its own constitution, which is subordinate to the U.S. Constitution but which can provide additional rights to the citizens of that state. They are usually found in the first volume of the state code and are found in the index. State constitutions are also usually found on the state's website. If you are looking for a particular provision, however, or want to find other sources interpreting a provision, you may want to use the print source rather than the Web source because it provides an index and annotations.

STATE STATUTES

State statutes or codes are laws passed by a state's legislature. They are found in chronological order in the session law, which is published in a volume that contains all the laws passed by a legislative body during each year or session. State statutes are also found in subject-matter order in either the official or annotated codes or statutes. They are the preferred citation and most often used by lawyers because they are easy to access by way of topical or popular name index.

The annotated codes are usually easier to use because of their subject-matter arrangement, indexing, and annotations. They are also frequently more current than the government-published official code or session laws.

Research Sources — Quick Reference — Cases

FEDERAL COURTS

The federal court system is hierarchical. At the lowest level, trials are held in the U.S. district courts. The first level of appeal is in the courts of appeals, or circuit courts. The district courts and the courts of appeal are broken down geographically into circuits. There are 11 numbered circuits as well as the D.C. Circuit and the Federal Circuit. Each circuit has its own district court and appellate court judges. The highest appeal is held in the U.S. Supreme Court.

FEDERAL CASES

Federal cases are the written opinions of federal judges in particular cases; they make up the common law and interpret federal statutes and the constitution. They are published chronologically in the federal reporters. Supreme Court decisions are found in the United States Reports (U.S.), the official reporter, and in two commercial reporters, the Supreme Court Reporter (S. Ct.) and the United States Supreme Court Reports, Lawyers' Edition (L. Ed., L. Ed. 2d). The commercial reporters both contain annotations. Courts of appeals decisions are found in the Federal Reporter (F., F.2d, F.3d), which is published commercially and contains annotations. District court decisions are found in the Federal Supplement (F. Supp., F. Supp. 2d), which contains annotations. The Federal Rules Decisions (F.R.D.) also contains district court decisions, and the Federal Reporter (F.) contains cases decided between 1880 and 1932.

Federal cases are found in subject-matter order in the federal digests. These digests provide summaries of cases grouped by subject matter, and they function as an index to the reporters. Each reporter has its own corresponding digest.

Ultimately, you must find the case in and cite to the reporters, but you can find a case in a reporter only if you have the citation or the name of one of the parties to check the names table. Therefore, the best place to begin your common law research is through the digests. Once you find your subject matter, the digest will provide citations to the reporters as well as a short annotation summarizing the case. You should never cite directly to the digest.

STATE COURTS

Every state has its own court system, and many differ in their structures. However, in all states, cases begin at the trial level and have the opportunity for at least one appeal. Many states have intermediate appellate courts, providing two opportunities for appeal along with the state supreme court. Table 1 in the Bluebook can help you understand the court system of a particular state.

STATE CASES

State cases are the opinions of state judges. They decide specific cases, creating common law and interpreting statutes and constitutions. Cases are published chronologically in state or regional reporters. Regional reporters include the Atlantic Reporter (A., A.2d), North Eastern Reporter (N.E., N.E.2d), North Western Reporter (N.W., N.W.2d), Pacific Reporter (P. P.2d), South Eastern Reporter (S.E., S.E.2d), South Western Reporter (S.W., S.W.2d), and Southern Reporter (So., So. 2d).

Cases are found in subject-matter order in the state or regional digests. These provide summaries of cases grouped by subject matter and function as an index to the reporters. Each reporter has its own digest and an index to the digest. The digests are a form of access into the chronological reporters.

Ultimately, you must find the case in and cite to the reporters, but you can find a case in a reporter only if you have the citation or the name of one of the parties to check the names table. Therefore, the best place to begin your common law research is through the digests. Once you find your subject matter, the digest will provide citations to the reporters as well as a short annotation summarizing the case. You should never cite directly to the digest.

Research Sources — Quick Reference — Administrative Law

FEDERAL AGENCIES

Federal agencies fall under the executive branch. They are created through congressional legislation that defines the specialized topic and mission of the agency. Once established, an agency may issue rules and regulations pertaining to its mission and hear and settle disputes arising from them. Law produced by agencies is called administrative law.

FEDERAL ADMINISTRATIVE LAW

Administrative rules and regulations are published in the Federal Register and the Code of Federal Regulations (C.F.R.). The Federal Register is published daily (based on work days), and all issues within a year constitute a single volume. A table of contents page lists all executive agencies and documents produced by each agency.

The C.F.R. arranges administrative rules and regulations chronologically. It is arranged in a format similar, almost parallel, to the U.S. Code. The regulations are arranged in 50 titles, some of which match the titles of the U.S.C. The titles are then divided into chapters, which regulate a particular agency. The C.F.R. is updated quarterly, and each year's volumes are a different color.

The List of Sections Affected (L.S.A.) is published monthly and contains the finalized and proposed changes made since the latest publication of the C.F.R. The L.S.A. arranges final regulations by C.F.R. title and section and provides page references to the Federal Register. The L.S.A. arranges proposed changes by title and part and references pages in the Federal Register.

FEDERAL ADMINISTRATIVE AGENCY DECISIONS

Administrative agencies exercise a quasi-judicial power in that they make decisions involving issues arising under their regulations. Many agencies publish these opinions in their own reporters, such as the Federal Trade Commission Reports or Agriculture Decisions. In addition, these decisions may be found on an agency's website or sometimes on Lexis or Westlaw.

STATE AGENCIES AND ADMINISTRATIVE LAW

State agencies fall under a state's executive branch. Agencies on the state level create and enforce regulations on a variety of matters such as housing, utilities, and public health.

Each state agency creates administrative law, which includes rules and regulations, decisions, and a variety of other documents particular to that agency. These documents mirror the form and function of federal administrative law.

States differ in the manner in which they publish administrative law. To determine the administrative law resources for a particular state, you can consult the following sources: BNA's Directory of State Administrative Codes and Registers and The Book of the States (Council of State Governments). Westlaw and Lexis also publish selected states' administrative laws.

Research Sources — Quick Reference — Secondary Sources

Source	What is it?	Why would you reach for it?	Where can you find it?	How do you use it?
Legal Encyclopedias	An encyclopedia covering legal topics, organized alphabetically by topic.	To provide a basic, elementary background on a legal issue or to determine if a certain state has a particular law.	C.J.S. is found in the books or on Westlaw. Am. Jur. is found in the books and on Lexis and Westlaw. Many state encyclopedias are found in the books or on Lexis or Westlaw.	C.J.S., published by West, uses the key number system. Generally, these encyclopedias are indexed, with the index found at the end of volumes on the shelf, or can be searched online in Lexis and Westlaw.
American Law Reports (A.L.R.)	A more detailed encyclopedia, with extensive annotations on legal issues. A.L.R. also includes the full text of relevant or important cases and annotations, and discusses and analyzes national trends.	To learn a lot about a particular topic in a short amount of time or to get a national overview of a particular topic and get citations to continue your research in more detail.	A.L.R. contains seven series: A.L.R., A.L.R.2d, A.L.R.3d, A.L.R.4th, A.L.R.5th, A.L.R.6th, and A.L.R. Federal (A.L.R. Fed., A.L.R. Fed. 2d). It is found both in book form and on Lexis and Westlaw.	Use the index and digest to locate relevant topics. If an annotation has been superceded, read only the later one. If it has been supplemented, read both. Annotations usually contain a scope note, summary of the case, outline of the annotation, research references, in-depth index, table of cases, and annotation text.
Treatises and Hornbooks	Hornbooks are legal aids for the student audience on a particular area of law. Treatises are similar legal aids for the practitioner, but often with greater detail and analysis.	To study for a law school exam (hornbooks) or to get an explanation of an issue in your practice area from one of the leading scholars in the field (treatises).	These sources are typically found in book form and are located using either a library catalog or the book Law Books in Print. At firms, treatises are often found in the offices of partners who specialize in that practice area.	Treatises are updated annually and contain indexes and tables for easy reference.

Law Reviews	Scholarly periodicals, published by student-run organizations at law schools, containing scholar-written articles and student-written notes. Articles are typically written from the author's individual perspective to stimulate thought, argue a position, or criticize a case.	To mine the footnotes for helpful sources, such as cases, statutes, and other authorities. Law review articles often provide insight into the issue, but should not be taken to be an objective explanation of the law.	Law reviews are published in print and online. Hein Online houses back issues of legal periodicals in pdf format, and articles can be searched and retrieved in full text on Lexis and Westlaw, although coverage for many journals is mixed. Older articles may be available only in the bound print editions of the journal.	The Index to Legal Periodicals and Books can be used, in print form, using a CD-ROM, or on Lexis and Westlaw (called Legal Periodicals and Books) to access articles via author, title, or specific case/ statute (dating back to 1908). The Current Law Index (CLI) is more comprehensive, but dates back to 1980 and is found in the books or on Lexis and Westlaw. Lexis and Westlaw also provide extensive search and retrieval options for law reviews.
Restatements	A restatement of the law in a particular area (e.g., torts) written by a committee of scholars, judges, and lawyers, and published by the American Law Institute. Although these are not the law, they are very authoritative and are adopted as the law in many jurisdictions.	To get a neutral, concise, black-letter statement of the law. The Restatement may not be the law in your particular jurisdiction, however, and it will not provide you with hints or explanation regarding how the law is to be applied.	The Restatement can be found in book form, on Lexis, or on Westlaw. There are a total of 13 Restatements.	Each Restatement is indexed and organized by subsection within the overall topic. The Restatements state the law and provide commentary, examples, and analysis of the law and its development. The Restatement 2ds also provide cross-references to the key number system and A.L.R. Each Restatement is updated by an appendix.

Research Sources — Quick Reference — Legislative History

Why: Legislative history provides an understanding of the context in which Congress or a state legislature wrote a particular bill. It is often used (to a greater or lesser degree) in the interpretation of a law, although it is only persuasive authority.

What: Legislative history encompasses several types of sources:

- Amendments and prior versions of bills, to compare what was added or removed during the legislative process;
- Subcommittee hearings, providing views of various groups who took an interest in the bill;
- Committee reports, including the purposes and recommendations of a committee;
- Congressional floor debates, indicating the intent of individual congresspersons.

Of these, committee reports are generally the most important and useful source.

Where: Legislative history is available in print and online sources.

- In print:
  - USSCAN
    - Full text of selected committee reports
    - Bill information and list of reports for all federal laws passed
  - Congressional Information Service (CIS)
    - Provides comprehensive records, but only as abstracts (not full text)
  - Congressional Record
    - Includes floor debates from both houses, published daily
- Online:
  - Thomas, via the Library of Congress
  - Lexis databases (current session)
    - Bills – Legis; Bills
    - Hearings – Legis; Hearing
    - Committee reports – Legis; CMTRPT
    - Floor debates – Legis; Record
  - Westlaw databases (current session)
    - Bills – Cong-BillTXT
    - Hearings – USTestimony
    - Committee reports and floor debates – LH

Prior congressional sessions are available in the print and online sources as well.

More Ebook Interactivity

 Research Sources — Quick References & Citations

QUICK REFERENCES

- Statutes
- Cases
- Administrative Law
- Secondary Sources
- Legislative History

CHECKLISTS

- What Source Do I Look In?

 Research Sources — Class Exercises & Tutorials

TUTORIALS

- Tutorial: Statutory Research
- Tutorial: Secondary Sources
- Tutorial: Cases and Digests
- Tutorial: International Legal Research
- Tutorial: Administrative Law Research
- Tutorial: Legislative History
- Tutorial: Internet Research
- Tutorial: Lexis
- Tutorial: Westlaw

EXERCISES

- Federal Statutes
- Federal Cases
- State Statutes
- State Cases

 Research Sources — Quizzes

- Research Sources Quiz
- Congress and Federal Statutes
- State Legislatures and Statutes

- ⚙? Federal Courts and Cases
- ⚙? State Courts and Cases
- ⚙? Secondary Sources
- ⚙? Federal Administrative Law
- ⚙? Legislative History
- ⚙? Looseleaf Services

Research Strategies

This section informs you of your many options as a legal researcher and helps you choose efficient and effective strategies. Here, you will learn how the American legal system guides your research, how to choose between book research and online research, how to determine your research strategies for particular sources, and how to update the law to ensure that it is timely and accurate.

Research Strategies — Briefing Cases

You will brief a case for two different purposes. First, as a student, you will brief cases for your classes to prepare for questions posed by your professors. Second, as a legal researcher, you will brief cases to prepare to write a legal document and analyze a particular legal issue. Although both are often called case briefs, they are very different in product, process, and purpose.

Research Strategies — Briefing Cases as a Student for Class

As a student, you will probably brief assigned cases for class. The purpose of this case brief is to prepare to answer the professor's questions and to begin to digest the law for the course. In essence, a case brief is a summary of the judge's opinion. Therefore, a good case brief will summarize each step of the judge's reasoning by diagramming the various parts of the case and analyzing the legal reasoning. You will need to find the method of case briefing that works best for your learning style. Some students write lengthy briefs while others simply take notes within the case books. Below, you will find the various parts of a case that are often worth diagramming and analyzing in a case brief.

1. <u>Case Name</u>: ↪**Smith v. Jones, 310 U.S. 200 (2000)**. It is a good idea to include the full citation, including the date of the opinion, for future reference.
2. <u>Facts</u>: Usually a judge will have paragraphs of the opinion dedicated to a description of the facts. You need not include all the facts in your case brief; however, try to include facts that are most relevant to the court's reasoning. Important facts usually include the cause of action or claim and possible defenses.
3. <u>Procedural History</u>: Most cases you will read for class are appellate opinions where an appellate judge reviews a trial judge's opinion. Therefore, the appellate judge will explain what happened to the case below in the trial court. These facts are helpful to understand the posture of the case when it came before this particular court.
4. <u>Issue</u>: The issue is the particular question the court had to decide in this case. It usually includes specific facts as well as a legal question.
5. <u>Holding</u>: The holding is the way in which the court decided the issue.
6. <u>Reasoning</u>: The judge should explain the holding using legal reasoning. Here the judge should cite to other cases as well as any particular statute, constitutional provision, or regulation that supports the holding. In briefing the case for class, you usually need not cite to these authorities. However, you should be able to summarize the legal reasoning of the court. Oftentimes a professor will ask questions relating to the basis of this legal reasoning and try to poke holes in the judge's logic. In addition, professors will often ask you how far you think this legal reasoning

should be applied by asking hypothetical problems and asking you to employ the same reasoning.

7. <u>Dissent</u>: The dissent is an opinion written by another judge sitting on the same panel as the writing judge. Although this opinion is not considered law, the professor might ask questions about this judge's legal reasoning or use some of the dissenting judge's arguments to discuss the issue.

🔗 → **Garratt v. Dailey**
🖳 → **Students' case briefs for Garratt v. Dailey**

Research Strategies — Briefing Cases as a Lawyer for Research

As a lawyer or law student, you will need to research cases to provide support and analysis in your legal documents. Therefore, when researching the law for a particular document, you will need to brief cases for research. Essentially, this means you will take notes on each relevant case that you find. A good case brief for researching includes a summary of the facts, holding, and reasoning of the court as well as a list of other relevant sources for future research.

1. <u>Case Name</u>: →**Smith v. Jones, 310 U.S. 200 (2000).** It is a good idea to include the full citation, including the date of the opinion, for future reference and citation. Be sure to include pinpoint cites (cites to a particular page) so you can cite specifically in your legal document.

2. <u>Facts</u>: An outline of the facts is often helpful. However, concentrate on the facts that are used by the judge in his legal reasoning. These facts are called legally significant facts.

3. <u>Procedural History</u>: As a legal researcher, the legal history is important only to understand what "reversed" or "affirmed" means for your particular case.

4. <u>Issue</u>: The issue is the particular question the court had to decide in this case. It usually includes specific facts as well as a legal question. Oftentimes, you will not need to note the issue in your brief as long as it is clear from your notes on the holding.

5. <u>Holding</u>: The holding is the way in which the court decided the issue. It is especially important in case briefing for research as it lays out the answer to the issue as well as the most legally significant facts that led the court to that answer.

6. <u>Reasoning</u>: The judge should explain the holding using legal reasoning. Here the judge should cite to other cases as well as any particular statute, constitutional provision, or regulation that supports the holding. In briefing a case for research, you should note these other authorities as potential supplemental sources. If you are reading the case online, consider clicking on the other authorities to see if they are relevant for your issue. If you are reading the case in print, write down these authorities and their full citations so that you can research them later.

7. <u>Dissent</u>: The dissent is an opinion written by another judge sitting on the same panel as the writing judge. Although this opinion is not considered law, you might garner some information about the legal reasoning and jurisprudence on your particular legal issue. At times, though not often, you might cite to a dissent in your legal document.

🔗 → **Garratt v. Dailey**
🖳 → **Lawyer's case brief for Garratt v. Dailey**

Research Strategies — The American Legal System

Civics Lessons

While most countries rely solely on their civil codes as laws, the United States, considered a "common law country," has three bodies of government that create laws:

1. Congress or the legislature creates ➥**constitutions and statutes**:

   1. Found in state or federal codes
   2. First published in slip laws and session laws

2. Courts ➥**create cases or court opinions**:

   1. Found in state, regional, or federal reporters
   2. First published in slip opinions

3. The executive branch, through its agencies, creates ➥**regulations**:

   1. Found in the Code of Federal Regulations or the state's equivalent
   2. First found in the Federal Register or the state's equivalent

Federalism

Federal and State Government: To complicate matters, states and the federal government have their own legislatures, courts, and agencies. These are parallel systems and the type of issue dictates which body of law and which branch of government applies. This seemingly confusing system arose as a result of the states trying to retain their rights when the federal Constitution was ratified.

🔍 ➥**U.S. History and the Great Compromise**

Federal and State Court Systems: The federal and state court systems have parallel structures and similar functions.

🔍 ➥**Function and Organization of the Courts**

Usually, federal courts will hear matters that relate to federal law. They therefore apply the relevant federal law. State courts will usually hear matters that relate to state law; they therefore apply the relevant state law. However, in some instances, federal law applies within a state court, while state law might apply in federal court. For example:

A federal court might hear a case based on "diversity of citizenship" a concept you will learn about in Civil Procedure. In this situation, the federal court will apply the particular state law, and it will be bound by the decisions of the state court applying state law.

A state court is bound by the U.S. Constitution. The state must uphold the same rights as those granted in the U.S. Constitution, although it may grant additional rights. Therefore, a state judge is bound by both the state and federal constitutions.

The U.S. Supreme Court is binding, in most situations, on all courts — both state and federal.

At times, the appropriate law is ambiguous and litigated. The balance of power between state law and federal law, federalism, is constantly shifting.

Research Strategies — Legal Interaction

The starting point in legal analysis is usually statutes. Courts often define, apply, and analyze the terms of those statutes. Courts also determine whether a statute is constitutional. The courts, through their decisions, create legal precedent, which should be followed by other courts within that jurisdiction under the concept of stare decisis. When a court determines that a statute is unconstitutional, that statute is no longer good law. When a legislature determines that a court has misinterpreted a legal term of art within a statute, the legislature can rewrite the statute.

When no statute is "on the books," often there is common law, or case law, that applies. In these instances, a judge's opinion or a series of court opinions create a body of law. At times, the legislature will codify a body of case law.

Congress has also empowered agencies to create their own law through regulations. These laws are specific to a particular area such as environment, food and drug, and housing. Courts can interpret regulations to ensure that they are constitutional and being applied correctly by agencies.

Research Strategies — Primary Law vs. Secondary Sources

➥ **Primary law** is the actual law on the books such as statutes, rules, cases, and regulations.

➥ **Secondary sources** are materials that discuss and comment on primary law such as law review articles, legal encyclopedias, and hornbooks. Secondary sources are persuasive law.

Research Strategies — Stare Decisis

Stare decisis is a core concept of the American legal system. It means that current cases are treated consistently with past precedent. Stare decisis has a number of benefits to litigants. First, it permits them to predict the outcome of a legal issue or dispute. Oftentimes, clients ask lawyers for advice as to whether they are permitted to perform a certain action; lawyers look to past cases to determine whether the requested action is permitted under the law. Clients can then rely on the prior cases, through the doctrine of stare decisis, to determine whether to perform the particular action. Second, lawyers look to prior decisions to determine whether to bring lawsuits and to determine how best to defend lawsuits. Third, stare decisis provides parties with fair treatment under the law. Each party is treated similarly, based on case precedent.

Stare decisis, while a core concept of the American legal system, operates with some flexibility. Because no one case is exactly like a prior case, courts can still follow precedent but massage the law to fit the current facts. As such, case law develops over time, often by adding new elements to a rule or applying exceptions to existing rules. At times, however, courts do overtly overrule previous decisions. When they do so, the courts often justify these rulings based on changes in circumstances or societal values.

Stare decisis has both vertical and horizontal limitations. On a horizontal level, a court is bound only by decisions of other courts within its jurisdiction. For example, the state of New Jersey is not bound by cases from North Dakota. Likewise, except in certain situations, state courts are not bound by cases from federal courts nor are federal courts bound by state courts opinions.

🔍 ➥ **Federalism**

On a vertical level, courts are bound only by decisions from courts from a higher level. Thus, trial courts are bound by appellate court decisions within that jurisdiction, but appellate courts are not bound by decisions from their trial courts.

Cases that must be followed under stare decisis are referred to as binding or mandatory case law, while cases that are not binding are called persuasive.

In addition, within binding case law, some cases carry more weight than others.

🔍 ➙ **Case Analysis**

Research Strategies — Binding Law vs. Persuasive Law

Primary authority is the law that is "on the books," such as statutes, rules, cases, and regulations. Statutes are usually the starting point in analyzing primary law. Cases interpret the meaning of a statute or deal with areas of law not addressed by statutes. (This is called common law.) Often legislatures will codify common law by creating a statute that synthesizes the prior law into an enacted code. In addition, when courts interpret statutes incorrectly, the legislature can rewrite the statute.

An important distinction in primary law is mandatory or binding law versus law that is merely persuasive.

Mandatory or binding law is law that is binding in that jurisdiction; it must be followed under the principle of stare decisis. For example, a trial court in Maryland must follow Maryland state codes and decisions from higher Maryland courts because they are binding authorities.

Persuasive law is law from a lower court or a different jurisdiction that that gives guidance but does not have to be followed. For example, a New York court does not have to follow a California court's decision. Likewise, a justice who sits on the Supreme Court of California, that state's highest court, is not required to follow a California trial judge's opinion.

The distinction between mandatory and persuasive law is important when deciding the best cases to rely on when writing a legal document. Usually, you want to show the judge that she is bound by certain law. However, at times, you will need to rely on persuasive authority. For example, although an opinion from the same level court is not binding on that court (one trial court judge is not bound by his colleague's opinion) because it is technically only persuasive authority, an opinion from the same level court would be extremely relevant to the judge making the decision. In addition, when no binding authority exists on an issue, you will need to use persuasive authority to make your argument.

👥? ➙ **Binding vs. Persuasive Quiz**

Research Strategies — Book Research vs. Online Research

Legal research can be accomplished through traditional law books as well as through modern computer resources. Historically, the law has developed through an organizational scheme modeled around legal books. However, computer resources are changing some research methods and ways of thinking about legal organization. This section first provides historical background for context about legal thinking and the development of computer researching. Next, it provides strategies for researching using legal books, specifically using West's key number system, as well as strategies for using computer research, mainly through Lexis and Westlaw.

THE HISTORICAL DEBATE

U.S. law, modeled on the British legal system, started as a common law system where cases were reported by individual members of the bar who sat in courtrooms, kept notes, and compiled reporters that were neither systematic nor structured. In the early nineteenth century, "official reporters" developed but remained similar to the unofficial reporters in that they had no organizational scheme and published only selected cases. As a result, lawyers used their memories to find law as opposed to any external system.

In the mid-nineteenth century, industrialization caused a dramatic increase in legal activity. Some publishers wanted to continue publishing selected decisions only; others, including John West, who was a salesman, not a lawyer, decided to publish most cases instead of selected ones. As a result, lawyers were unable to use memory to recall the huge number of cases now being reported.

To meet demand for a system to access the plethora of cases, West developed the American digest system, an organizational system of classification of law. The digest classified all areas of law into seven major categories: persons, property, contracts, torts, crimes, remedies, and government. These areas mirror the current traditional first-year law school curricula, which was simultaneously developed at Harvard Law School by Dean Langdell. Each of the seven categories was further subdivided into 430 key numbers – "the key number system." These key numbers were further subdivided. West editors became the primary classifiers. As they read cases, they decided which categories of law and key numbers to assign to the cases.

The digest with its key number system became the primary method for lawyers to locate case law. As a result, lawyers began to organize the law into the scheme developed by West and followed by law schools adopting Harvard's Langdellian curriculum. The West system became a national system with reporters spanning the country. As a result, the national legal structure has developed around the categories of the digest, and American lawyers now rely on the organizational paradigm developed by West to find law using the books.

The computer age has thrown a wrench into the digest system. Although the digest is based on organization, computer searching, by nature, has no organizational scheme at all. Instead, it is based on text searching. Words and facts are the basis for computer searching, not ideas and legal concepts. Lexis and Westlaw have become the primary services for legal online searching. These cost a fee for practicing attorneys, but are free for law students. Some free sites are located on the Web, such as ➥findlaw.com. In addition, many courts have websites where local decisions and dockets are searchable. One of the widely recognized advantages to online searching is that the law is updated frequently. Some legal researchers are liberated by the computer system as they can find cases based on judge, opposing counsel, or date. Others are still uncomfortable on the computer system because the nationally developed organizational scheme is not readily apparent, context is missing, and endless screens are hard to bring to internal order. The best researchers are those who can combine the organizational scheme of the book world with the text-based searches online. Strategies for both types of research are provided below.

To read an article by this author discussing more of the differences in online vs. book research, go to ➥teachinglaw.com.

Research Strategies — Key Number System

The key number system was developed by West as a method to organize the growing number of published cases. The system breaks all possible legal categories into seven major categories:

- Persons
- Property
- Contracts
- Torts
- Crimes
- Remedies
- Government

These large categories are then subdivided into over 430 topics.

Each topic is further subdivided into a more detailed outline, using specific numbers.

The result is a **key number**, which includes a topic and a number.

The editors at West (and Westlaw) use the key number system to categorize cases. Thus, a case may fit into a number of key numbers and is cataloged accordingly in multiple key number locations. The key numbers appear in case digests as well as on the Westlaw site and are arranged in both places alphabetically.

➥Key Number in Digests

In addition, each case published by West (or Westlaw) contains headnotes located at the beginning of the opinion. A headnote provides a key number along with an annotation explaining the key number. Any one case may have multiple headnotes for multiple key numbers. In addition, the headnote provides a paragraph number where that legal issue is discussed in the case. The headnote number can make reading a case more efficient as you can turn (or link) directly to the paragraph in the text listed in the headnotes.

➥Key Number in Cases

Research Strategies — Strategies for Book Research

1. **Think Like a Legal Editor:** Because the books are organized around legal subjects organized over one hundred years ago, it is helpful for the legal researcher to think like a legal editor. A legal editor reads recent law and tries to classify it into preexisting categories. Therefore, a legal researcher can find law more easily if she tries to determine how her issue would be classified under these categories, starting from a broad topic, such as contracts, and then narrowing the subject, such as offer or acceptance.
2. **Use Legal Terms of Art:** When using book sources to search for law, use legal terms of art. Therefore, while the word "Walmart" is not a useful research term, the word "employer" might be very useful to find cases on point. "Master-Servant" could also prove to be a helpful term of art when looking for cases involving Walmart. It is often useful for the novice researcher to scan the indexes of legal sources to determine legal terms of art that might be helpful.
3. **Use the Indexes and Digests:** Book sources are organized extremely well with thorough indexes. The cases are organized through the digest system, which also has an index. Using the indexes and digests saves time and money when using the books.
4. **Look at Pocket Parts and Supplements:** Because the books are not updated daily, it is important to check for supplements and pocket parts for recent law. Each set of legal resources should either have a supplement, usually located at the end of the volumes, or a pocket part, which is a paperback pamphlet located at the back of each book. These updates contain recent law. Therefore, if you check a source but do not look in its pocket part, you might miss an important part of the law.
5. **Determine a Research Path:** Heading to the library without a game plan is going to be frustrating and time consuming. Therefore, before you begin your research, determine which sources you think would be most helpful, list a number of legal terms of art that might prove to be productive, and devise a method for note-taking so that you do not repeat research.

1. **If You Know Nothing About Your Legal Topic**, consider researching first in a ➞**secondary source** for background and context. Often, the secondary source will provide you with a crash course in the subject area and help you narrow your focus.

2. **If You Know Your Jurisdiction**, go right to that section of your library and focus on the books from your jurisdiction. Do not waste your time with persuasive authority, especially in the initial stages of your research.

3. **If You Have One Known Source** and have read it carefully, look for other cites referenced in that source and then shepardize or key cite that source to find other sources.

🔍 ➞**Introduction to Legal Research—Overview of Process**
🔍 ➞**A Research Plan Example: From Start to Finish**

Research Strategies — Strategies for Online Research

Usually, your best bet with online legal research is to use one of the two commercial legal services, Lexis or Westlaw. Both charge practicing attorneys, but they are typically free for law students. The trick is to spend time as a student learning how to use these services efficiently and effectively so that when you start practice, you can be cost-effective in your research.

1. **What Is Online Research?**

   Online research includes logging onto a subscription database, such as ➞**lexis.com** or ➞**westlaw. com.** The editors at Lexis and Westlaw compile primary and secondary legal sources, organize them by type, and publish them on their online databases. Because the full text of thousands of publications is online, users can search the text for key terms to find the documents they need. In addition, the online services are updated frequently so that a user can access recent law. Online research can also refer to other websites that do not include Westlaw or Lexis. Legal websites such as ➞**findlaw.com** and ➞**loislaw.com** provide legal search engines on the Web. Traditional search engines such as ➞**google.com** can also be helpful for certain types of legal research.

2. **Strategize Before You Log On**

   As in book research, it is important to develop a strategy before logging onto Westlaw, Lexis, or Google. Unlike traditional web surfing, surfing for legal research can be a costly time waster. Getting to know your way around the legal databases and other online legal sources will help save time.

⬌ ➞**Westlaw - Basic Navigation Tutorial**

- Accessing Westlaw
- Getting Started with Westlaw.com
- Finding Documents by Title or Citation
- Find and Print
- Searching with Terms and Connectors
- Searching with Natural Language
- Searching with KeySearch

⬌ ➞**Lexis - Basic Navigation Tutorial**

- Basic Research Skills
- Basic Shepards Skills

- Retrieving a Document
- Statutory Research
- Terms & Connectors Searching
- Topical Research
- Advanced Research Skills

Use the tips below to help plan your online time.

1. **Narrowing the Database:** When on Lexis or Westlaw, search efficiently by narrowing your database. If you want only cases from Missouri state court, use the Missouri State Cases database rather than the All Cases database. Databases can be narrowed by topic and by jurisdiction. For example, suppose you want to research tax amnesty. There is a specific tax-related Law Reviews database on Westlaw. If you simply used the All Law Reviews database to search for "amnesty," you would find a lot of irrelevant articles.

2. **Brainstorm Search Terms:** After you find a narrow database that covers your sources, think of narrow search terms that would be found in a useful document. This process is like looking in an index in the library. Start with the general topic and write down some of the key legal terms. Then try to narrow the topic into subtopics with key words for each subtopic. Remember to include synonyms in your list. If you do not know enough about a topic to make a list of search terms, you may need to go back to the library and look up your topic in a ⇥**secondary source**.

3. **Translate Search Terms into a Search using Natural Language or the Boolean Language:** Once you have the correct database and relevant search terms, your objective is to find a manageable number of documents that discuss the topic that interests you. Input search terms using either natural language or terms and connectors.

   - **Natural language** searching provides documents that include the language you specify most often. Natural language searching is useful when your search terms are broad; it is like surfing on the Web. It often leads to more search terms, which can then be used in terms and connectors searching.

   - **Terms and connectors** searching provides all of the documents in the database that meet the specifications of the search. Terms are the words the computer searches for, and connectors are the symbols that show the relationships between the terms. Terms and connectors work together to link search terms using the Boolean language. For example, you can specify that one term be in the same sentence as another. You can limit by date. You can search only within specified fields, such as title or author for an article, or judge or party name for a case. To learn some basic terms and connectors, see ⚲ ⇥**Terms and Connectors.**

     ⚲ ⇥**Comparing Westlaw and Lexis Connectors and Functions**

   - **Segment and field searches:** Each document is divided into different sections, i.e., title, author, date. Lexis refers to these sections as segments and Westlaw refers to them as fields. You can use them to make your terms and connectors more specific by searching for just that one part of the document.

     ⚲ ⇥**Field Search on Westlaw**
     ⚲ ⇥**Segment Search on Lexis**

4. **Viewing Documents in Lexis and Westlaw:** There are different ways to display your search results.

   - **Lexis** offers the following displays:
     - **Cite:** Lists all the documents retrieved through the search

- **KWIC** (Key Words in Context): Shows excerpts from the current document where search terms appear
- **Full:** Displays the full text of the document
- **Custom:** Permits selection of certain segments
- **Westlaw** offers the following displays:
  - **Result screen:** Appearing on left, lists documents retrieved. Each entry includes excerpts from document showing where search terms appear. (Click Hide Terms to make these disappear.)
  - **Full Text:** By clicking on the name in the result screen, you will retrieve the full text of the document on the right screen. Your terms will be highlighted.
  - **Doc button:** Takes you to the next document retrieved
  - **Term button:** Takes you to the next search term in that document

5. **Use Online Databases to Update the Law**

   It is always necessary to update the law, that is, to determine whether a source you would like to cite represents current law. Lexis uses the Shepard's system for its updating database, and it has purchased the Shepard's trademark. Westlaw uses a similar system called KeyCite, which uses multicolored flags and other symbols to indicate whether a source has been overruled, discussed, or simply cited. See ⮑**updating** for a more complete discussion on how to update the law.

6. **Searching for Particular Legal Sources.** As a legal source is introduced throughout this ebook, specific strategies are provided for searching in Lexis and Westlaw.

   ⮑**Constitutions**
   ⮑**Statutes**
   ⮑**Cases**
   ⮑**Secondary Sources**
   ⮑**Administrative Law**
   ⮑**Legislative History**

7. **Evaluate the Credibility of Internet Sources**

   A source found on Lexis or Westlaw is reliable because it is a primary source or editor-reviewed secondary source. However, other websites can be less reliable. It is important to determine whether a source is credible before citing to it. Look to see who has published the cite; .gov or .edu sites are usually much more reliable than .coms.

   ☑ ⮑**Web Evaluation Checklist**

Research Strategies — Free Internet Sources: Save Time and Money

Before logging onto Lexis or Westlaw, consider whether there are any free sources that you can use instead. Often, an Internet site is the easiest way to find information and many of them are linked throughout this ebook. This page gathers those sites in one place.

Cases: Finding cases online is still probably best on Lexis and Westlaw. However, more and more courts are posting opinions on their Web sites and providing access to their dockets. As a practicing lawyer, you will probably e-file many of your court documents. To look for cases in particular jurisdictions:

➥**Federal District Courts** (click on particular district)
➥**Federal Circuit Courts** (click on particular circuit)
➥**United States Supreme Court**
    ➥**Oyez to hear oral arguments**
    ➥**Law Prose to Listen to Justices discuss writing**
➥**State Cases** (click on particular state)

Statutes and Legislative Information: Finding statutes online is easier than finding cases. Most codes are now available online:

➥**United States Code**
➥**United States House of Representatives**
➥**United States Senate**
➥**State Codes** (click on particular state)

Administrative Law, Administrative Agencies, and Executive Materials:

➥**Code of Federal Regulations (C.F.R.)**
➥**Federal Register**
➥**Agency Index**
➥**First Gov**
➥**GPO Access**
➥**Environmental Protection Agency**
➥**Federal Trade Commission**
➥**The White House**

Legislative History:

➥**Thomas**

Other Government Material:

➥**United States Constitution (through archives)**
➥**United States Constitution (through Findlaw)**
➥**Bill of Rights**
➥**Declaration of Independence**

Law School Sites: Many law schools also compile legal materials. These are extremely useful because these Web sites are usually developed by law librarians — the experts at legal research.

➥**Cornell Law School**
➥**Georgetown's Law Library**
➥**Washburn University School of Law**

Search Engines: Using traditional search engines and legal search engines can also yield results. However, consider using sites such as Google for fact investigations and broad legal issues instead of for specific law in a particular jurisdiction.

➥**American Bar Association's Legal Research**
➥**Blawg** (legal blog)
➥**Find Law**
➥**Google**
➥**Law Crawler**
➥**Law Guru**
➥**LLRX**
➥**Loislaw** (fee-based)
➥**Martindale-Hubbell**
➥**VersusLaw** (fee-based)
➥**Yahoo**

Research Strategies — Strategies for the Research Process

🔍 ➥**Introduction to Legal Research: Overview of Process and Strategy**
🔍 ➥**A Research Plan Example: From Start to Finish**

Asking the Right Questions

Most assignments are given orally by busy supervising attorneys. Therefore, when a supervisor presents you with an assignment, you should assume he has not provided you with all the details necessary to answer the legal question. It is imperative that you ask the right questions before you leave his office. While there is no set list of exact questions that must be asked in each situation, there are a number of categories that will help your research:

1. **Asking fact questions:** Ask the supervisor for details about the factual situation of the client. Often, the attorney has met with the client, but you have not. Filling in the facts will help you understand the issue.

2. **Framing the issue:** Often the supervisor has not fully thought out the legal issue he wants you to address. Therefore, repeating the issue to the partner to ensure that you understand it often helps the partner think it through as well. Before you leave the office, you and the partner should be very clear on the issue that is to be addressed.

3. **Brainstorming research strategies:** Because supervising attorneys have had years of research experience and are often specialists in their fields, it is a good idea to ask your supervisor for any research strategies she might have to begin the project. Often, the supervisor will be a gold mine for resources, save you time, and be thankful that you thought to solicit her advice.

4. **Taking notes:** It is imperative to take copious notes throughout these assignment meetings for a number of reasons: (a) you cannot remember all the details; (b) you want to refer back to the issue you and the partner have framed; (c) you want your notes to memorialize the facts as they exist at the time as they might change or expand as discovery proceeds (a change in facts could change your analysis).

The items on the above list should be addressed in the supervisor's office. Once you leave the office, you need to immediately take notes on your notes. If you focus your attention on another matter or attend another meeting, you will waste time later trying to recreate your conversation with the supervisor. Therefore, when you return to your office, take five to ten minutes to reconstruct the assignment to stay focused.

Research Strategies — Staying Focused

When you return to your office with a new assignment from a supervising attorney, be sure to focus on the assignment while the information is fresh:

1. **Write down the issue statement:** You and the supervisor have framed the issue; now, write it down in a lucid manner. A question presented, a one-sentence issue, or a brief paragraph will work. This issue statement will serve as a crutch as you find tangential arguments and issues throughout your research. Carry it with you to the library or tape it onto your computer as you do your online research.

2. **Ask yourself about the assignment:**

   1. Who is your **audience**? Are you writing for a judge, a client, the supervising attorney, the other side? Your answer will dictate the way in which you draft your document.

   2. What is the **purpose**? Are you writing to inform or to win or both? Are you writing with the idea of settlement or to litigate? What is your strategy?

   3. What is the **scope** of your document? How long should it be? How much time and money are you permitted to spend on this assignment?

   4. When is the **document** due? Time management is an important part of being a lawyer. Consult your calendar for every assignment and make sure you have time to meet your deadline.

3. **Create a list of key words:** Whether you are using the books or computer sources, you will be more efficient if you create search terms or key words before you begin to research.

4. **Devise a research sources strategy:** You should not dive into research without deciding on a strategy. What sources would be the best starting points? If you list research sources in the order you think will be most helpful, you will be more efficient when you begin your research. The least efficient researcher is the one who roams the library or cyberspace without a game plan.

Research Strategies — Taking Notes

Once you begin your research, taking notes is imperative for a number of reasons:

1. **Take Notes to Keep a Record of Where You Have Researched.** As you gather information, you will find sources that are both useful and not useful. Keep track of both. Invariably, you will need to go back and find more law. If you have kept notes on the sources that were not helpful, you will not waste time repeating research. In addition, if your notes indicate which sources were most helpful, you can focus your energy on those sources when you continue researching.

2. **Take Notes to Keep a Record of What You Have Found.** As you are researching, you will need to keep track of the law that you think is relevant. Be sure to note the citation as well as the name of the case or statute or source. Locating the source later will be just as important as finding its full name. **Note:** Just because a source has cited the law, do not assume it is the official cite. You will still need to check the Bluebook or ALWD before filing a document with citations.

3. **Take Notes on the Law You Have Read.** As you read the law, take notes — either by hand or on the computer. Note the facts as well as the law. Try to categorize each piece of law you read; sometimes a case might fall into more than one category. Some people use charts, graphs, or separate computer files to take notes as they read the law to easily find information later in a useful, organized fashion.

➥**Quick Reference: Note-Taking Chart**

Research Strategies — Deciding When to Stop

In practice, stopping your research is often dictated by time constraints (an hour lunch break in the courtroom), client's financial restraints (a small budget), or a deadline. In an ideal world, you would stop researching when you know you have found the law. However, oftentimes it is difficult to tell whether you have found all or enough of the relevant law. Some cues will tell you that your research has been thorough:

1. You start finding the same cases cited over and over.
2. You Shepardize or KeyCite the law and no new citations appear.
3. You read a secondary source about your issue and it all makes sense.
4. You have followed your research strategy list and checked every source.
5. You have researched online and in the books and the research is redundant.
6. You are able to write a logical document without any holes in legal reasoning.
7. Your opponent's document cites the same law (or less).

🔍 ➥**A Research Plan Example: From Start to Finish**
🍸 Research Testimonials

Research Strategies — Strategies for Particular Sources

The following section provides various strategies for finding particular sources. Try to learn all the strategies and then determine which strategy is most efficient and effective for you.

Finding Constitutions and Statutes

🔍 ➥**Sources: Constitutions and Statutes**
▦ ➥**Anatomy of a Statute**

Constitutions are usually found in the first volume of the federal code (U.S.C.) or state code. Each set of volumes for the code has an index; therefore, you may access parts of the Constitution using the code's index. The U.S.C.A. and U.S.C.S. as well as state annotated codes provide annotations to cases and other sources that interpret particular parts of the Constitution. In addition, you can search the full text of the ➥**Constitution online.**

Statutes are usually easier to find in the books than online. To find them using book sources, you need to find the particular set of volumes for your statute's code. Each state has its own statutory code. The federal code is found in one of the following resources:

1. United States Code (U.S.C.), the official version printed by the government
2. United States Code Annotated (U.S.C.A.)
3. United States Code Service (U.S.C.S.).

Each statutory code has its own index, usually located at the end of the set. State statutes are arranged in a similar fashion. There are a number of ways to search statutes:

1. **By number**
2. **By name**
3. **By subject**

1. **By number:**

    1. **Books:** If you have a specific cite to a statute, e.g., 12 U.S.C. § 323, you would go to the volume that contains title 12 and find section 323 in numerical order.

    2. **Online:** ➙**Westlaw**: Type the citation under Find. ➙**Lexis**: Type the citation under Get A Document.

2. **By name:**

    1. **Books:** Some codes have popular names (such as the Civil Rights Act). The U.S.C., U.S.C.A., U.S.C.S., and many state codes have alphabetically arranged popular names tables, usually located at the end of the set. Here, you can look up the statute's name to retrieve its citation.

    2. **Online:** Lexis and Westlaw both have popular names table links.

        1. ➙**Lexis** – Under Find a Source, type "popular names."

        2. ➙**Westlaw** – Look in the directory under "USCA-POP".

3. **By subject:**

    1. **Books:** If you do not know the citation or the name of the statute, but have only a general idea of the subject matter, you will need to brainstorm descriptive words to search the index to the code, usually located at the end of each volume set.

        For example, to find a particular New York statute on retaliatory action by an employer using descriptive words, you would do the following:

        1. Look through 🖳 ➙**New York's Code's index** for key words that would relate to the relevant law. Here, you need to think like a legal editor. Terms such as "Labor and Employment" or "Master and Servant" might be useful. For example, under "Labor and Employment," you will find "Retaliatory action by employers" and a reference to Labor § 740.

        2. Next, find the 🖳 ➙**Labor volume of the New York code** (which is arranged alphabetically). Within that volume, find Labor § 740. This will lead you to the relevant statute.

        3. If you are using an 🖳 ➙**annotated code**, you will also find other sources that reference that particular provision. These annotations are important in your research since they provide legislative histories, cases, and other sources that analyze your statute. You should look up these other sources to thoroughly analyze the statute.

        4. For all above book methods, be sure to check the pocket parts or supplements in the books to determine if the statutes have been recently updated, amended, or discussed.

        5. Be sure to ➙**update** your statute to make sure it is still good law.

    2. **Online:** Although searching for statutes is usually easier in the books, there are times when online searching is more efficient. For example, if asked to find similar laws in multiple jurisdictions, online searching is easier. Both Lexis and Westlaw have the full text of the U.S. Code, all the state codes, and a single database of all 50 states.

        1. ➙**Lexis**: To search the U.S. Code, go to

            "Federal Legal – U.S. – United States Code Service 1-50".

            Here, you can either browse the table of contents or create a search using descriptive words.

            To search the N.Y. Code, go to

            "State Legal – N.Y." See what words lead you to Labor § 740.

        2. ➙**Westlaw**: To search the U.S. Code, go to

            "Directory – U.S. Federal Materials – Statutes – United States Code Annotated" (or other options).

Click on the search box and use descriptive word searching.

To search the N.Y. Code, go to

"Directory – U.S. State Materials – Statutes – Statutes Annotated – Individual States – N.Y." (or other options such as "All States").

Click on the search box and use descriptive word searching. See what words lead you to Labor § 740.

Research Strategies — Finding Cases

🔍 ➥**Sources: Federal Cases**

🔍 ➥**Sources: State Cases**

🗔 ➥**Anatomy of a Case**

Getting Started

There are a number of factors to consider before you start researching case law.

1. It is important to focus on a particular **jurisdiction** whenever possible. Are you looking for cases in a particular federal circuit or a particular state? Knowing your jurisdiction will substantially limit the number of cases found.

2. It is important to understand the **hierarchy** of courts and the difference between ➥**mandatory and persuasive law.** (Bluebook Table 1 and ALWD Appendix 1 list the hierarchy for each jurisdiction.) A case from a higher court in your jurisdiction carries greater weight than a lower case in your jurisdiction or one from a different jurisdiction.

3. The **date** of a decision is important. Recent decisions carry great weight. Older decisions that have been followed over long periods of time also carry great weight. On the other hand, be wary of relatively old decisions that are rarely followed or new decisions that contradict overwhelming precedent.

4. Cases do get overturned. Therefore, it is imperative that you ➥**update** your cases before you rely on them as good law.

Cases are found in a number of different locations.

Federal Case Law

SUPREME COURT CASES

United States Reports (U.S.)
Supreme Court Reporter (S. Ct.)
United States Supreme Court Reports, Lawyers' Edition (L. Ed., L. Ed. 2d)

CIRCUIT COURT CASES

Federal Reporter (F., F.2d, F.3d)
Federal Cases (F. Cas.)

DISTRICT COURT CASES

Federal Supplement (F. Supp., F. Supp. 2d)
Federal Cases (F. Cas.)
Federal Rules Decisions (F.R.D.)

State Case Law

REGIONAL REPORTERS

1. **Atlantic Reporter** (A., A.2d): Connecticut, Delaware, District of Columbia, Maine, Maryland, New Hampshire, New Jersey, Pennsylvania, Rhode Island, Vermont
2. **North Eastern Reporter** (N.E., N.E.2d): Illinois, Indiana, Massachusetts, New York, Ohio
3. **North Western Reporter** (N.W., N.W.2d): Iowa, Michigan, Minnesota, Nebraska, North Dakota, South Dakota, Wisconsin
4. **Pacific Reporter** (P., P.2d): Alaska, Arizona, California, Colorado, Hawaii, Idaho, Kansas, Montana, Nevada, New Mexico, Oklahoma, Oregon, Utah, Washington, Wyoming
5. **South Eastern Reporter** (S.E., S.E.2d): Georgia, North Carolina, South Carolina, Virginia, West Virginia
6. **South Western Reporter** (S.W., S.W.2d): Arkansas, Kentucky, Missouri, Tennessee, Texas
7. **Southern Reporter** (So., So. 2d): Alabama, Florida, Louisiana, Mississippi

State Reporters: Most states also have their own reporters. See Bluebook Table 1 (T.1) or ALWD Appendix 1.

Strategies

There are a number of strategies for finding federal and state case law. The strategy that works best for you will be determined not only by your preferences, but also by the resources available and the starting point for your research. Your starting point might be any one of the following:

1. **Case citation**
2. **Case name**
3. **Subject matter**

1. **Case Citation:** To find a case using its citation is relatively easy.
    1. **Books:** First, you need to find the correct set of reporters (see locations of law above). Second, find the correct volume and page number in the reporter to locate the case itself. For example, 212 S. Ct. 301 is found in the 212th volume of the Supreme Court Reporter on page 301.
    2. **Online:**
        1. →**Westlaw** – Go to Find and type the citation.
        2. →**Lexis** – Go to Get A Document and type the citation.
2. **Case Name:**
    1. **Books:** To find a case using its name, go to the end of the reporter set where you will find a digest. Each digest has a volume labeled "Table of Case Names" that lists cases and their cita-

tions in alphabetical order by first party name. Some tables also have a "Defendant-Plaintiff Table" that lists cases and their citations in alphabetical order by defendants' names. Remember to check pocket parts.

2. **Online:**
   1. ➥**Lexis** – Go to Get A Document and choose By Party Name.
   2. ➥**Westlaw** – Go to Find and search by case name.

3. **Subject Matter: Using the Books:** Finding cases by subject matter is a bit trickier and requires multiple strategies, depending on the circumstances. A thorough researcher uses a variety of strategies and multiple sources. Below, you will read strategies for finding cases by subject matter using both book sources and online sources. But before you begin, you need to be familiar with the ➥**key number system** developed by West.

1. **One Good Case:** Oftentimes, a supervising attorney will provide you with one case on point. This case can be a gold mine if used properly. First, it will cite to other helpful sources, such as cases, statutes, rules, or secondary sources. Second, if it is a case published by West, it will provide key numbers, the system designed by West to arrange the law into topics. If, for example, your supervisor gives you the case, <u>Remba v. Federation Employment & Guidance Serv.</u>, 545 N.Y.S.2d 140 (App. Div. 1989), as a starting point or for background information, you could use this case to

   1. 🖳 ➥**Find other law on point.**
   2. 🖳 ➥**Find key numbers that would lead you back to the digests for more cases on point.**

2. **Statutes Annotated:** If there is a statute on point, often cases have cited to the statute. To find these cases, you should research annotated statutes in your particular jurisdiction. For example, if you were looking for cases on retaliatory action taken by employers in New York State, you could do one of the following:

   1. 🖳 ➥**Search the index** for the N.Y. State Annotated Code or Consolidated Laws Service. Under "Labor and Employment" you will find "retaliatory action by employers" and a cite to Labor § 740.
   2. Within the volumes of the annotated code, you would find Labor § 740. Here, you find (1) the statute, (2) its history and research references, and (3) case notes, called Notes of Decisions, which provide annotations to cases that have cited the statute. 🖳 ➥**Read the annotations to find relevant citations.**
   3. Remember to check the pocket parts of the book to look for more recent annotations.

3. **Case Digests:** A case digest arranges case annotations by topics. To use the digest to find New York cases on retaliatory action taken by employers, you could do one of the following:

   1. Search the 🖳 ➥**index to the New York digests**, usually located at the end of the digest volumes. Under "Employment Law," you will find "Retaliatory discharge or discipline" and a reference to "Mast & S Key Number 30 (6.5)." This reference is a key number under the West key number system. It refers to the topic "Master and Servant," and its subsection 30 (6.5).
   2. Next, you find the 🖳 ➥**Master and Servant digest** and look up number 30 (6.5) Here, you will find a number of case annotations on your topic. Read through them to find relevant cases and note the citations. Be sure to read the key numbers surrounding your key number because they are often on the same topic or related ones.
   3. In addition, each digest topic will have a table of contents at the beginning of the section. So, if you turn to the beginning of the "Master and Servant" section of the digest, you will find a 🖳 ➥**table of contents** for the key numbers of that topic. These will help you further refine your research.

4.   Remember to check the pocket part of the digest for recent annotations.

5.   Once you have noted relevant cases, you can go to the reporters and look up those cases.

6.   Be sure to ➥**update** all the cases you cite to make sure they are good law.

4.   **Subject Matter: Online**: Many of the same strategies for finding cases using books also work with online sources.

1.   **One Good Case:** If you have a good case on ➥**Westlaw** or ➥**Lexis**, you can link to other cases cited within that case. Also, you can click on the key numbers on Westlaw, located in the beginning of the case before the judicial opinion, to link directly to the key number system to find other cases listed under that key number. This method is very effective for finding cases that West editors have categorized under that key number. Be careful to take notes as you research using this strategy as you can become looped within a key number as you find case after case; keep track of the cases you have read.

2.   **Key Numbers:** In ➥**Westlaw**, you can access the key number system directly by clicking on the More menu, located at the top of the Westlaw screen. Click on the arrow to scroll down to Key Numbers and Digests; here the key numbers will be listed in alphabetical order so that you can find a relevant key number for your cases.

3.   **Searches:** Within a specified directory, you can use key terms to search for cases. The tricks here are to search in a specific directory and to create your search terms and connectors carefully. 🔍 ➥**Word Searches**

Research Strategies — Finding Legislative History

Legislative history refers to the documents that are made as Congress transforms a bill into a law. These documents can be important in determining congressional intent of a particular law. However, there is an ongoing debate about the relevance of legislative history as political motivations come into play when laws are made. Legislative documents are only persuasive authority.

Legislative history is made by the federal Congress as well as by state legislatures. Below are strategies for finding federal legislative history. Finding state legislative history is not as easy. Often, you must visit the state itself to access the legislative history from that particular branch of government. Some states have placed their legislative histories on their ➥**state home pages**, but not all states have done so.

If you are asked to find the legislative history of a particular federal law, there are many sources available:

1.   First, you should have a basic understanding as to how laws are made. See 🖳 ➥**How a Bill Becomes a Law** for background information.

2.   **Compiled Legislative Histories:** Compiled legislative histories — histories that someone else has taken the time to put together, often on major legislation — are excellent sources if they include your bill. Check the Sources of Compiled Legislative Histories, a book that lists all available published legislative histories by public law number.

3.   If your law does not have an already compiled legislative history, you will need to create your own. You can use book sources and online services. The following is a list of book sources and online sources, as well as a list of most useful legislative history documents.

4.   **Book Sources:** There are three print sources that are most useful for finding federal legislative history:

1.   **USSCAN:** This source publishes selected committee reports for legislation enacted since 1949. Committee reports are often the most useful documents for determining congressional intent. Although USSCAN provides the full text for only select reports, it provides

the bill number, date of enactment, and list of all committee reports for every law passed. It also provides the full text of public laws, presidential messages, and cites to the Congressional Record. To use USSCAN, you should find the public law number and year your bill was enacted into law. (You can find this information through the U.S. Code.) Then, you can find the full text of your public law through the relevant volume of federal legislative histories. This source references page numbers for the selected legislative history documents, which can be found in the legislative history volumes of USSCAN. Thus, you will need to use two different volumes of USSCAN to find your bill and legislative history.

2. **CIS (Congressional Information Service):** Instead of providing full text of selected documents like USSCAN, CIS provides comprehensive legislative histories. However, finding each source is not as easy as in USSCAN. You can search CIS by subject, name, committee, public law number, bill number, or document number, but you are usually provided only an abstract of that piece of history. To find the full text, you will need to go to another source, such as CIS microfiche or Congressional Universe on the Web.
3. **Congressional Record:** This hefty set of books contains the text of the congressional debates of both houses. The daily edition is published every day Congress is in session. Page numbers begin with S for Senate, H for House, E for Extension of Remarks, and D for Daily Digest. A permanent bound edition is also published, but the volumes are published very slowly and have a different numbering system from the daily edition. Therefore, you will need to use the Index or Daily Digest to find relevant pages to the bound edition.

5. **Online Sources:** The most useful online sources for legislative history are ➥Thomas, ➥Lexis, and ➥Westlaw.

The following are the most significant pieces of legislative history and how to find them online:

1. **Bills:** Bills are often amended during the legislative process; thus, comparing the different versions of a bill may help determine its intended meaning. The bill number is often the best way to trace legislative history. To find bills online, follow any of these links:

   ➥Thomas, which allows access to bills from 1989 to present.

   ➥Lexis:

   For current Congress: Short Name – Legis; Bills

   For previous Congresses starting in 1989: Short Name – Legis; BTX101-BTX109

   ⟷ ➥**Tutorial on Legislative History in Lexis**

   ➥Westlaw:

   For current Congress: Cong-BillTXT database

   For previous Congresses starting in 1995: Cong-BillTxt104-Cong-BillTxt109 databases
2. **Hearings:** Subcommittee hearings (either House or Senate) provide the views of various groups, individuals, or organizations interested in the bill and thus are not as relevant to legislative intent. To find hearings online, follow any of these links:

   ➥Lexis: Short Name – Legis: Hearing (July 1993 – date)

   ➥Westlaw: USTestimony database (January 1993 – date)
3. **Committee reports:** These reports may be created by the House, Senate, or Conference Committees and are the most important source of legislative history. They usually reprint the bill, explain its purpose, and provide reasons for the recommendation of the committee. To find committee reports online, follow any of these links:

   ➥Thomas (1995 – date)

   ➥Lexis: Short Name – Legis; CMTRPT (1990 to date)

➡**Westlaw**: LH database (1990 to present comprehensive)
(reprinted USCCAN reports from 1948–1989)

4. **Congressional debates:** Congressional debates are published in the Congressional Record and are the proceedings of the debates on the Senate and House floors. These are not as helpful for legislative history as they might show the intent of one congressperson but not necessarily the intent of the legislative body. To find the Congressional Record online, follow any of these links:

➡**Thomas** for the daily edition.

➡**Lexis**: Short Name – Legis; Record - for the daily edition.

➡**Westlaw**: LH database for the daily edition

Research Strategies — Finding Administrative Law

🔍 ➡**Sources: Administrative Law**

Administrative law consists of rules, regulations, and decisions created by federal or state agencies. While this section focuses mainly on finding federal administrative law, parallel methods of research apply within each state.

There are many ways to research administrative law depending on your starting point. If you are working with a particular statute and want to find regulations that implement that statute, you would start with the code provision itself. For finding regulations by topic, you usually will begin with the ➡**Code of Federal Regulations (C.F.R.)** rather than the ➡**Federal Register** because the C.F.R. is a topical compilation of all the regulations and is updated each year. If you were looking for a recent regulation, the Federal Register would be the best place to start. A specific agency's website is also a good starting point.

1. Starting with a **code section** to find regulations that implement it:

    1. Start with the annotated code, either U.S.C.A. or U.S.C.S., for federal law or your state's annotated code. In the annotations, you will find references to regulations and their citations. You can either use the books for these sources or log on to ➡**Lexis** or ➡**Westlaw**.

    2. You can also use the ➡**C.F.R. table of authorities**, which contains a numerical list of the regulations arising out of each U.S.C. section. This source is also available in book form (usually located next to the C.F.R.) and online for free at the ➡**C.F.R.**

    3. Once you find your regulation cite, simply look it up in the ➡**official C.F.R.**, the ➡**eCFR.**, or in the ➡**Federal Register**.

2. Starting with a **topic** to find regulations about the topic:

    1. **Books:** You can start your topic search in the C.F.R. index, which is not very effective because it contains only broad terms. A better source is the CIS Index to the Code of Federal Regulations, which is more comprehensive than the C.F.R. index; it is usually located near the C.F.R. itself.

    2. **Free Online Site:** You can directly search the ➡**C.F.R. online**.

    3. **Lexis** and **Westlaw** both allow you to access and search the Federal Register (issues since 1980) and the C.F.R.

        • ➡**Lexis**: Go to the "Search"; "By Source" tab and scroll to "Federal Legal U.S." Click on FR-Federal Regulations

        • ➡**Westlaw**: Go to "Administrative Materials."

3. Starting with the **Federal Register** if you are looking for a recent rule, regulation, proposed rule, or commentary:

   1. Federal Register Index: This index is issued monthly and is arranged alphabetically by agency. Each issue is cumulative, so the December issue covers the year.
   2. CIS Federal Register Index: This index is issued weekly with cumulative volumes issued periodically and permanent bound volumes issued twice a year. It indexes each issue of the Federal Register either by subject, name, C.F.R. section numbers affected, federal docket numbers, and Calendar of Effective Dates and Comment Deadlines.
   3. ➥**Federal Register online**: Log on and follow the instructions for searching on this free website.

4. Starting with a **particular agency** and looking for regulations and administrative decisions created by that agency:

   1. Click on ➥**Administrative Agencies**. Here, you can locate particular agencies' websites.
   2. Each agency has its own method of searching for regulations and administrative decisions. Therefore, it is important to spend some time browsing your particular agency's website.

Updating Regulations

Because the C.F.R. is reissued in quarterly installments each year, there are always volumes of the C.F.R. that are not up to date. It is important to update administrative law because regulations can change often, and new rules may be proposed that affect your regulation.

Before you update a regulation to ensure that it is still being enforced, you need to know the date of the regulation. If you are using an online version, look for the "currency date," usually located near the top of the document. If you are using the book form of the C.F.R., check the date on the cover of the volume.

The next thing you need to do is check to see if there have been any changes to your rule or regulation published in the Federal Register since the currency date you found above. If you are using an online version (C.F.R., Lexis, or Westlaw), simply search in the Federal Register for your particular C.F.R. citation or log onto ➥**List of Sections Affected (LSA)**. If you are using the books, you will need to find the book version of the LSA, usually located at the end of the C.F.R. set and in the last Federal Register issue of each month. Once you have found the correct date of the LSA, you will need to look at each subsequent LSA to ensure that nothing has changed since your currency date. The LSA does not bring a search completely up to date, however. For a thorough search, you must consult a similar list found in the last Federal Register issue of each month.

Administrative Decisions

Regulations may have been challenged in court. First, the case would be litigated before an administrative judge. This administrative decision may be appealed to the federal courts. To research the judicial treatment of regulations, you should check in Shepard's C.F.R. Citations, which is found in book form as well as in Lexis. Westlaw also posts some administrative decisions; click on Directory; Topic Practice Areas; a specific topic; Federal Administrative Materials. In addition, an agency's website often posts administrative judicial opinions.

Research Strategies — Using Looseleaf Services

What: Looseleaf services are research sources arranged by topic and issued in looseleaf binders. The benefit to the binders is that information can be easily added, omitted, or exchanged as the law changes. Thus, the publication is in a constant process of revision and is very current. The advantage of the topical arrangement is that practicing lawyers can subscribe to a looseleaf service in a specialized practice area and closely follow the developments in that field.

Looseleaf services vary in content and organization, depending on the publisher and the subject area. However, most of them contain up-to-date coverage and information regarding court decisions, statutes, administrative regulations, practice tips, forms, and developing legal trends. In addition, they contain user guides and various indexes and finding tools.

Why: Most practitioners, especially those in the regulatory field, rely heavily on looseleaf services. Oftentimes, a practitioner will rely on a looseleaf service as a total library for his practice since it contains the code, regulations, cases, and commentary in a particular area of law in an up-to-date, organized fashion. Looseleaf services are often expensive because their publishers spend enormous amounts of time bringing together primary sources from disparate places into one organized unit.

Where and How: Commerce Clearinghouse (CCH) and the Bureau of National Affairs (BNA) are two of the major looseleaf publishers. To use a looseleaf service, you should (1) be sure you have found the most useful looseleaf service, and (2) be sure to read the directions.

1. **Finding your looseleaf service:** Looseleaf services are used mainly by practicing lawyers, and certain looseleafs have become the bibles of their fields. Therefore, it is always a good idea to check with a supervising attorney for the most relevant service; at times, you may see the set sitting on the attorney's shelf. As a student, you should check with your local librarian to find the looseleaf preferred in your field. Typical subjects for looseleaf reports are criminal law, tax, evidence, and bankruptcy. Another source is a book called Legal Looseleafs in Print. Every law library should subscribe either to the print or the online version.

2. **Using your looseleaf service:** Read the directions. All looseleaf services have a section on how to use the service. You will save time by reading this section. It explains the information included in the set, the indexing tools, the finding aids, and the format of the service. The more in-depth a service, the more necessary it is that you read the "how to" section.

➡ **Looseleaf Service**

Research Strategies — Updating the Law

Before you rely on any law by citing to it in a legal document, you must determine whether it is still good law through "updating." Updating is essential because the law is fluid: statutes are amended, cases are reversed, and laws are massaged through time. A fatal mistake is to rely on a case that is no longer good law.

➡ **Case on Importance of Updating**

Historically, updating was performed through a set of books called Shepard's Citations, which was started in 1873 by a man named Frank Shepard. *Shepardizing* became the term lawyers used to refer to updating the law.

If you went to law school ten years ago or more, you would have been taught to use the bulky, maroon volumes of Shepard's, which was a tedious and intimidating process. However, Shepard's is now available online through Lexis. In 1997, Westlaw introduced its own online citator, KeyCite.

Shepard's and KeyCite are now the main citator tools for lawyers. They are used for a number of purposes: (1) to update the law; (2) to indicate the law's frequency of citation and treatment by other sources; and (3) to find other sources that have referred to your law. When used to research law, Shepard's and KeyCite can prove very useful since they not only provide links to all sources that have cited your law, but they also break down those sources by headnote, date, jurisdiction, and depth of discussion.

Currently, most lawyers use the online version of the citators, either KeyCite or Shepard's. However, you should also be somewhat familiar with the intimidating version of Shepard's in case you ever need to refer to it.

🔍 ➥ Shepard's in Print

KEYCITE

KeyCite was developed by West to compete with Shepard's. It is found only online on Westlaw, and it provides up-to-date information on cases, statutes, and administrative materials.

To access KeyCite in ➥ **Westlaw**, you can click on the KeyCite tab and enter a citation or simply click on the colored flag that appears next to the law you are reading. The colored flag system in KeyCite signals the type of treatment of your law. For example, if you are reading a case and you see a red flag next to that case, you should be wary of its precedential value as it might have been reversed or overturned.

🔍 ➥ KeyCite Flags and Symbols

Once you have accessed KeyCite, you will be given a full citation and history of your law. After the direct history, any negative history will be listed. Be sure to read the cases listed for negative treatment; at times, only part of the case might be overturned. By clicking on Citing References, you will be provided a list of sources that have cited your law and the symbols for the treatment by these sources. You may search these references through the popup menu at the bottom of the page by the following "segments":

- Jurisdiction: You can locate all sources in Hawaii, for example, that have cited your law.
- Headnote: You can search for sources related to specific headnotes in your law.
- Date: You can search by date.
- Document type: You can search, for example, for cases, administrative law, or secondary sources.
- Depth of treatment: Westlaw uses star symbols for depth of treatment. The more stars, the more treatment from that citing source. (See the **KeyCite Flags and Symbols** link above for more about star symbols.)
- Locate: You can enter search terms to further narrow your search.

Furthermore, you can search by key number by clicking on the link at the bottom of the page.

🔍 ➥ KeyCiting Tips

SHEPARD'S ONLINE

Using Shepard's on Lexis is also convenient. Shepard's provides up-to-date citations to statutes, cases, and administrative materials.

To access Shepard's on ➥**Lexis**, you can click on the Shepard's link or click on the Shepard's signal for the treatment of the law you are reading. For example, if a case you are reading has a red stop sign, you should be wary of its precedential value.

⟷ ➥**Tutorial on Shepard's**
🔍 ➥**Shepard's Symbols**

Once you have accessed Shepard's, you will be given the law's direct history and citations to later sources. Be sure to read the cases listed for negative treatment; at times, only part of the case might be overturned. These citations in Shepard's will include an editor's assessment of this source's treatment of the case. So, for example, if a source distinguishes or criticizes your law but does not reverse it, you will see a yellow triangle located next to that source. (See the **Shepard's Symbols** link above for more about Shepard's symbols.) You may organize these sources by their treatment, their kind of law (e.g., statutes, secondary sources), and by headnote number.

Research Strategies — Quick Reference — Binding vs. Persuasive Law

Binding law is law that must be followed in that jurisdiction.

Persuasive law is law that a jurisdiction may look to for guidance but is not obligated to follow.

Ordinarily, if there is sufficient binding law to support your position, persuasive authority is not necessary. However, if you are attempting to convince a court to adopt a new approach that is supported in persuasive authority from other jurisdictions, using that authority may be helpful.

STATE COURTS

On matters of state law in state trial court, precedents from higher state courts are binding. For example, a California trial court must follow precedent from the California Supreme Court. Precedent from other courts at the same level (e.g., another trial court) is usually only persuasive, not binding.

FEDERAL COURTS

Federal district courts must follow the precedents from that particular circuit's court of appeals. For example, a federal district court in North Carolina must follow precedent from the Fourth Circuit Court of Appeals and the U.S. Supreme Court. However, a federal district court is bound only by the court of appeals for the circuit in which it is located. For example, precedent from the D.C. Circuit is only persuasive in a federal district court in Wyoming. Precedent from the U.S. Supreme Court is binding in all courts. As in the state courts, precedent from other courts at the same level (e.g., another circuit court) is usually only persuasive, not binding.

SECONDARY SOURCES

Secondary sources, such as law review articles, are only persuasive authority.

STATUTES

A statute is considered to be binding law within the jurisdiction in which it was enacted. For example, a state statute in California is binding in California, but only persuasive in other states.

Research Strategies — Quick Reference — West's Key Number System

West Publishing and Westlaw use their key number system to categorize every case they publish. Cases often fit into a number of different key numbers and are catalogued accordingly in multiple key number locations.

All legal topics are divided into the following categories:

- Persons
- Property
- Contracts
- Torts
- Crimes
- Remedies
- Government

These larger categories are then subdivided into over 430 topics. Each topic is divided into a more detailed outline, using specific numbers. This results in the creation of a key number — including both a topic and a specific number.

If you can identify one or more key numbers relevant to your research topic, they can be a helpful tool for finding related cases.

Research Strategies — Quick Reference — Finding Statutes

Finding statutes is usually easier in the books than online. Each state has its own statutory code; the federal code is found in the United States Code (U.S.C., the official government-published version), the United States Code Annotated (U.S.C.A.), or the United States Code Service (U.S.C.S.). Statutes are also found on Westlaw and Lexis.

Constitutions are typically found in the first volume of the code. The index is usually located at the end of the set. The full text of the U.S. Constitution can also be searched at http://www.findlaw.com/casecode/constitution/.

Statutes can be searched in three ways:

1. **By number**
   - **Online:** Westlaw: Type the citation under Find. Lexis: Type the citation under Get A Document.
   - **Books:** If you have a specific cite to a statute, e.g., 12 U.S.C. § 323, you would go to the volume that contains title 12 and find section 323 in numerical order.
2. **By name**
   - **Online:** Lexis and Westlaw both have links to popular names tables. In Westlaw, look in the directory under "USCA-POP." In Lexis, under Find A Source, type "popular names."
   - **Books:** Some codes have popular names (such as the Civil Rights Act). The U.S.C., U.S.C.A., U.S.C.S., and many state codes have popular names tables, usually located at the end of the

set. Here, you can look up the name alphabetically to retrieve the citation to the statute itself.

3. **By subject**
   - ***Online:*** Although searching for statutes is usually easier in the books, there are times when online searching is more efficient. For example, if asked to find similar laws in multiple jurisdictions, online searching is easier. Both Lexis and Westlaw have the full text of the U.S. Code, all the state codes, and a single database of all fifty states. In Lexis, to search the U.S. Code, go to **"Federal Legal – U.S. – United States Code Service 1-50."** Here, you can either browse the table of contents or create a search using descriptive words. In Westlaw, to search the U.S. Code, go to **"Directory – U.S. Federal Materials – Statutes – United States Code Annotated (or other options)."** Click on the Search box and use descriptive word searching.
   - ***Books:*** If you do not know the citation or the name of your statute, but only have a general idea of the subject matter, you will need to brainstorm descriptive words to search the index to the code, usually located at the end of each volume set.

Research Strategies — Quick Reference — Finding Cases

Getting Started

There are a number of factors to consider before you start researching case law.

1. First, it is important to focus on a particular jurisdiction whenever possible. Are you looking for cases in a particular federal circuit or a particular state? Knowing your jurisdiction will substantially limit the number of cases found.
2. Second, it is important to understand the hierarchy of cases and the difference between mandatory and persuasive law. (Table 1 in the Bluebook lists the hierarchy for each jurisdiction.) A case from a higher court in your jurisdiction carries greater weight than a lower case or one from a different jurisdiction.
3. Third, the date of a decision is important. Recent decisions carry great weight. Older decisions that have been followed over a long period of time also carry great weight. On the other hand, be wary of relatively old decisions that are rarely followed or new decisions that contradict overwhelming precedent.
4. Cases do get overturned. Therefore, it is imperative that you update your cases before you rely on them as good law.

Strategies

Your starting point could be any of the following:

A case citation:

- ***Books:*** First, you would need to find the correct set of reporters (see locations of law above). Second, find the correct volume and page number in the reporter to locate the case itself. For example, 212 S. Ct. 301 would be found in the 212th volume of the Supreme Court Reporter on page 301.
- ***Online:*** In Westlaw, enter the citation in the Find field. In Lexis, type the citation under Find A Document.

A case name:

- *Books:* To find a case using its name, go to the end of the reporter set where you will find a digest. Each digest has a volume labeled "Table of Case Names," which lists cases and their citations in alphabetical order by first party name. Some tables also have a "Defendant-Plaintiff Table," which lists cases and their citations in alphabetical order by defendant's names. Remember to check pocket parts.
- *Online:* In Westlaw, go to Find, by title. In Lexis, under Get A Document, choose By Party Name.

Subject Matter:

The following are several strategies for finding cases by subject matter.

- *One Good Case:* Oftentimes, a supervising attorney will provide you with one case on point. This case can be a gold mine if used properly. First, it will cite to other sources, either other cases or statutes, rules, or secondary sources that might also provide other relevant law. Second, if it is a case published by West, it will provide key numbers, the system designed by West to arrange the law into topics.
- *Statutes Annotated:* If there is a statute on point, often cases have cited to the statute. To find these cases, you should research annotated statutes in your particular jurisdiction. Remember to check pocket parts of the books for more recent annotations.
- *Case Digests:* A case digest arranges case annotations by topics. The index is usually located at the end of the volumes. Each digest topic also has its own table of contents at the beginning of the section. Remember to check pocket parts for more recent annotations. Once you have found relevant cases, look them up in the reporter. Remember to update all cases to make sure they are still good law.

Subject Matter — Online:

A number of strategies for finding cases using books also work with online sources:

- *One Good Case:* If you have a good case on Westlaw or Lexis, you can link to other cases cited within that case. Also, you can click on the key numbers on Westlaw, located in the beginning of the case before the judicial opinion, to link directly to the key number system to find other cases listed under that key number. This method is very effective for finding cases that West editors have categorized under that key number. Be careful to take notes as you research using this strategy as you can become looped within a key number as you find case after case; keep track of the cases you have read.
- *Key Numbers:* In Westlaw, you can access the key number system directly by clicking on the More menu, located at the top of the Westlaw screen. Click on the arrow to scroll down to Key Numbers And Digests; here the key numbers are listed in alphabetical order so that you can find the relevant key numbers for your cases.
- *Searches:* Within a specified directory, you can use key terms to search for cases. The tricks here are to search in a specific directory and to create your search terms and connectors carefully.

Research Strategies — Quick Reference — Finding Legislative History

WHAT IS LEGISLATIVE HISTORY?

Legislative history is the collective term for all the documents produced as a bill becomes a law in Congress. It can include the text of the bill itself and any versions and amendments, the text of congressional debates, the text of committee hearings, and committee reports. These documents can be important in determining the legislative intent behind a particular law, but there is an ongoing debate as to the usefulness of legislative history. Legislative history is only persuasive authority.

HOW DO YOU RESEARCH FEDERAL LEGISLATIVE HISTORY?

When researching the legislative history of a bill or law, first check to see if there is already a **compiled legislative history** on that particular piece of legislation. Check the Sources of Compiled Legislative Histories, a book that lists all available published legislative histories by public law number. If there is not already a compiled legislative history available, you will have to create your own. There are a number of sources for legislative history.

BOOK SOURCES

- **USSCAN:**

  What it provides: USSCAN provides the full text for selected committee reports; it also provides the bill number, date of enactment, and list of all committee reports for every law passed. Additionally you can find the full text of public laws, presidential messages, and cites to the Congressional Record.

  How to use it: First, find the public law number for your bill and the year it was enacted into law; you can find this information using the U.S. Code. Then, you can find the full text of your public law in the relevant volume of federal legislative histories. This source references page numbers for the selected legislative history documents, which are found in the legislative history volumes of USSCAN. You will need to use two different volumes of USSCAN to find your bill and legislative history.

- **CIS (Congressional Information Service):**

  What it provides: Unlike USSCAN, CIS does not provide the full text of pieces of legislative history. Instead, it gives a comprehensive legislative history for a particular piece of law, but it provides only a brief abstract of each piece of history.

  How to use it: You may search CIS by subject, name, committee, public law number, bill number, or document number. To find the full text of a given piece of history, however, you will have to go to another source, such as CIS microfiche or Congressional Universe on the Web.

- **Congressional Record:**

  What it provides: This hefty set of books contains the text of the congressional debates of both houses.

  How to use it: The daily edition is published every day Congress is in session. Page numbers begin with S for Senate, H for House, E for Extension of Remarks, and D for Daily Digest. A permanent bound edition is also published, but the volumes are published very slowly and have a different numbering system from the daily edition. Therefore, you will need to use the Index or Daily Digest to find relevant pages to the bound edition.

ONLINE SOURCES

- **Thomas:**

  What it provides: For free, Thomas provides the text of bills from 1989 to the present, committee reports from 1995 to the present, and congressional debates from the daily edition.

  How to use it: Go to http://thomas.loc.gov/ and enter the bill number for your piece of legislation.

- **Lexis**

  What it provides: Bills (1989 to the present), hearings (July 1993 to the present), congressional debates, and committee reports (1990 to the present).

  How to use it: To find bills for the current congress, go to "Short Name – Legis; Bills." To find bills for previous congresses starting in 1989, go to "Short Name – Legis; BTX101-BTX106." To find hearings, go to "Short name – Legis; Hearing." To find committee reports, go to "Short Name – Legis; CMTRPT." To find congressional debates, go to "Short Name – Legis; Record."

- **Westlaw**

  What it provides: Bills (1985 to the present), hearings (Jan. 1993 to the present), congressional debates, and committee reports (1990 to the present).

  How to use it: To find bills for the current Congress, go to the Cong-BillTXT database. To find bills for previous Congresses starting in 1985, go to the Cong-BillTxt104-Cong-BillTxt106 databases. To find hearings, go to the USTestimony database. To find committee reports, go to the LH database. To find congressional debates, go to the LH database for the daily edition.

Research Strategies — Quick Reference — Finding Administrative Law

Administrative law consists of rules, regulations, and decisions created by federal or state agencies. When searching for administrative law, your research process will differ, depending on your starting point. You can start with any of the following:

Start with a **code section** to find regulations that implement it.

- Start with the annotated code, either U.S.C.A. or U.S.C.S. for federal law or your state's annotated code. In the annotations, you will find references to regulations and their citations. You can either use the books for these sources or log on to Lexis or Westlaw.
- You can also use the C.F.R. table of authorities, which contains a numerical list of the regulations arising out of each U.S.C. section. This source is also available in book form (usually located next to the C.F.R.) and online for free at http://www.gpoaccess.gov/cfr/index.html.
- Once you find your regulation cite, simple look it up in the C.F.R. or in the Federal Register.

Start with a **topic** to find regulations about that topic.

- **Books:** You can start your topic search in the C.F.R. index, which is not very effective because it only contains broad terms. A better source would be CIS Index to the Code of Federal Regulations, which is more comprehensive than the C.F.R. index; it is usually located near the C.F.R. itself.
- **Free Online Site:** You can directly search the C.F.R. online at http://www.gpoaccess.gov/cfr/index.html.
- **Lexis and Westlaw:** Both online services allow you to access and search the Federal Register (issues since 1980) and the C.F.R.

Start with the **Federal Register** if you are looking for a recent rule, regulation, proposed rule, or commentary.

- **Federal Register Index:** This index is issued monthly and is arranged alphabetically by agency. Each issue is cumulative so that the December issue covers the year.
- **CIS Federal Register Index:** This index is issued weekly with cumulative volumes issued periodically and permanent bound volumes issued twice a year. It indexes each issue of the Federal

Register either by subject, name, C.F.R. section numbers affected, federal docket numbers, and Calendar of Effective Dates and Comment Deadlines.

- **Free Online Site:** Go to http://www.gpoaccess.gov/fr/index.html and follow the instructions for searching on this free website.

Start with **a particular agency** to look for regulations and administrative decisions created by that agency.

- Locate your particular agency's website using a search engine or linking from another site. The following sites provide links to agency sites:

  Washburn University School of Law Agency Index: http://www.washlaw.edu/doclaw/executive5m.html

  Federal Web Locator (The Villanova Center for Information Law and Policy): http://www.lib.auburn.edu/madd/docs/fedloc.html

  FirstGov: http://firstgov.gov/Agencies/Federal/All_Agencies/index.shtml

- Each agency has its own method of searching for regulations and administrative decisions, so spend some time browsing your particular agency's website.

UPDATING REGULATIONS:

Remember that it is essential to update administrative law because it changes frequently. First, find the date of the regulation you have found. In online sources, this will be the "currency date" near the top of the document; in print sources, this will be the date on the cover of the volume. Next, check to see if any changes to your regulation have been published in the Federal Register since the date you found. In online versions, simply search using your regulation's citation or look in the List of Sections Affected (LSA). If you are using the books, find the book version of the LSA, usually located at the end of the C.F.R. set and in the last Federal Register issue of each month. Once you have found the correct date of the LSA, you will need to look at each subsequent LSA to ensure that nothing has changed since your currency date. The LSA does not bring a search completely up to date, however. For a thorough search, you must consult a similar list found in the last Federal Register issue of each month.

ADMINISTRATIVE DECISIONS:

To research the judicial treatment of regulations, check in Shepard's C.F.R. Citations, which is found in book form as well as in Lexis. In addition, agency websites often post administrative judicial opinions.

Research Strategies — Quick Reference — Using Looseleaf Services

Looseleaf services are research sources arranged by topic and issued in looseleaf binders. They vary in content and organization, depending on publisher and subject area. However, most of them contain up-to-date coverage and information regarding court decisions, statutes, administrative regulations, practice tips, forms, and developing trends in the law. In addition, they contain user guides and various indexes and finding tools. Looseleaf services tend to be most useful in heavily regulated, highly technical areas of law, such as tax law. Commerce Clearinghouse (CCH) and the Bureau of National Affairs (BNA) are two of the major looseleaf publishers.

When presented with a topic of research that you believe may be covered in a looseleaf service, the first task is to identify the appropriate one. The easiest way to do this is to ask your supervising attorney; the relevant looseleaf service is likely on the bookshelves in his or her office. As a student, you should ask a reference librarian which looseleaf service is appropriate for your field. A source called *Legal Looseleafs in Print* is also helpful; most libraries have this either in book form or online.

When you have found the appropriate looseleaf service, read the directions section to learn how to use it. All looseleaf services have this section, which explains the information included in the set, the indexing tools, the finding aids, and the format of the service.

Research Strategies — Quick Reference — Updating the Law

Before relying on any piece of law by citing to it in a legal document, you must update it to make sure it is still good law. The process of updating a piece of law through Shepard's or KeyCite can also aid you in your research by identifying other sources that have cited that particular piece of law. For example, by using either Shepard's or KeyCite on a statute, you can identify all other cases and secondary sources that have cited that statute. They also break down those sources by headnote, date, jurisdiction, and depth of discussion.

Updating the law was traditionally a lengthy process using the book form of Shepard's. Most lawyers today, however, use the online version of Shepard's, found on Lexis, or a similar resource, KeyCite, found on Westlaw.

SHEPARD'S

To access Shepard's on Lexis, click on the Shepard's link or the Shepard's signal for the treatment of the law you are reading. Make sure to read through any sources with negative treatment; sometimes only one part of a case is overturned. Also note the court issuing any case with negative treatment; your case can be directly overturned only by courts with jurisdiction over it, so negative treatment from another state may not be significant. The citations provided by Shepard's will include an editor's assessment of this source's treatment of the case. So, for example, if a source distinguishes or criticizes your law but does not reverse it, you will see a yellow triangle located next to that source. You may organize these sources by their treatment, their kind of law (e.g., statutes, secondary sources), and by headnote number.

Shepard's also has a system of symbols to indicate the type of treatment a source has received. For example, be wary of a case displaying a red stop sign; this symbol indicates negative treatment.

KEYCITE

To access KeyCite, click on the KeyCite tab and enter your citation. If you have already pulled up a piece of law and wish to update it, simply click on the colored flag next to the case. Clicking on Citing References will provide a list of sources that have cited your law and the symbols for the treatment by these sources. You can also search these references through the pop-up menu at the bottom of the page. As discussed above, be sure to read through sources with negative treatment to determine their impact on the validity of your law.

The colored flags in Westlaw indicate the type of treatment a source has received. Make sure you understand this system so you can recognize quickly when a source is likely to be good law. The number of stars next to a source listed in Citing References indicates the depth of treatment given to your law in that source.

Research Strategies — Quick Reference — Collecting Information

WHO	WHERE	WHAT	WHY

PARTIES	JURISDICTION	OBJECTS	CLAIMS/CHARGES & DEFENSES

Research Strategies — Quick Reference — Note-Taking Chart

Name	Facts	Holding	Reasoning
Jones v. U.S. 779 A.2d 277 2001	A. After observing Jones drop two baggies on the ground, three officers approached Jones and picked up the bags, which contained a substance that later proved to be crack cocaine. B. The officers asked Jones "for his ID, if he had ID at that time, or if he didn't have his ID what is his name, address, where he lives, things like that." C. After these questions were posed to him, Jones stated that "he was holding for those two guys." D. At the time that he made these comments, Jones had not been advised of his rights under Miranda.	Not an interrogation; appellate court didn't address issue of custody	A. "Interrogation" is not only express questioning but also words or actions on the part of police that the police should know are reasonably likely to elicit an incriminating response from the suspect. B. Given the lack of the slightest logical nexus between the officer's question and the defendant's statement, it is difficult to understand how the judge could reasonably have found anything other than the statements were voluntary and spontaneous.
Clark v. U.S. 755 A.2d 1026 2000	A. Officer observed the "beginning" of a drug deal between several men, who scattered when they saw her. B. Officer asked Clark why he was on the premises of public housing complex (visitors were supposed to sign in). C. After finding that Clark wasn't a resident or a signed-in visitor, they took him, in handcuffs, to the main office to get a "barring notice", keeping him from the property in the future. D. While walking to office, Clark threatened officer, saying she would not work there again when he told the boys. E. Officer asked, "What did you say?" and defendant repeated threat. F. The officers asked Jones "for his ID, if he had ID at that time, or if he didn't have his ID what is his name, address, where he lives, things like that." G. After these questions were posed to him, Jones stated that "he was holding for those two guys." H. At the time that he made these comments, Jones had not been advised of his rights under Miranda.	Clark was in custody, but it was not an interrogation	A. Officer's question was out of surprise, rather than an intent to get Clark to incriminate himself.

| Mitchell v. U.S. 746 A.2d 877 2000 | A. Officer saw defendant parked near a "No Parking" sign. B. Officer saw "blunts" in the car and asked the defendant if he had any marijuana in the car. C. Defendant said he didn't. D. Officer asked him to get out of the car on the basis of an alcohol violation, told him he was going to search the car. E. As defendant was getting out of the car, officer asked him again if he had marijuana, and he answered that he did. F. Defendant's rights were not read to him until after he got to the police station, where he indicated that he didn't want to talk without any attorney. G. However, he continued to make incriminating statements to the officer at the police station (spontaneous statements, rather than in response to questions). | Defendant was not in custody when he admitted he had marijuana in the car. | H. In order to constitute "custody" for Miranda purposes, the suspect must be subject to "the functional equivalent of formal arrest." |
| Dancy v. U.S. 745 A.2d 259 2000 | A. Officer came to defendant's hospital room, where he saw him alone. B. Officer told D that he had an arrest warrant for him, about the police investigation (including what the police had found of defendant's role), and the penalty in the event of conviction. C. D responded by asking if "the girl" (person who drove Ds to the murder scene) was being charged and whether "Mike" (another D) was "finished." D. Officer asked D if he would be willing to talk about his involvement. E. D said that he wanted to speak to his lawyer, at which point officer read him his Miranda rights. | D was "interrogated" for Miranda purposes. | A. Officer should have known that his words were reasonably likely to elicit incriminating evidence. B. There were no other circumstances to indicate that the officer's words had any purpose other than getting the D to incriminate himself. C. Officer in this case also admitted that he made statements in an effort to get D to talk about his involvement. |

Stewart v. U.S. 668 A.2d 857 1995	A. D was convicted of murder. B. Upon his arrest, D initially waived his Miranda rights but then said that he did not want to make a statement. C. Another detective (X), who had known D since childhood and attended his church, showed up and was told that D had chosen not to give a statement. D. Inside cellblock, D and X spoke privately, with X telling D that "we all make mistakes", that members of his church would not judge him, and that D still had support. E. X also offered D a photo of their church bishop and asked if he would like to talk more with X, to which D said yes. F. Later that evening, D was brought to see X in the squad room. G. X asked, "What happened?" and D confessed.	Court found that conversation in cellblock and conversation in squad room were both "interrogations" for Miranda purposes.	A. "Any knowledge the police may have had concerning the unusual susceptibility of a defendant to a particular form of persuasion might be an important factor in determining whether the police should have known that their words or actions were reasonably likely to elicit an incriminating response from the suspect." B. X's words in cellblock were designed to "encourage" D. C. "No conversation concerning a criminal investigation between such a detective and a suspect can be said to be 'purely personal'" (as government claimed).
Wilson v. U.S. 444 A.2d 25 1982	A. D was convicted for accessory to murder. B. D was Mirandized and told police that he did not want to give a statement, although he and two officers discussed case on the way to D.C. police dept. C. At police station, officers continued to discuss case and answer D's questions about investigation. D. Officers finally, in response to D's question, told D the name of the witness against him and told him it was in his interest to make a statement, which D did.	Conversations with D after he said that he would not make a statement were "interrogation" for Miranda purposes.	A. Detectives admitted that they hoped specific information about the investigation would lead D to make a statement.

Alexander v. U.S. 428 A.2d 42 1981	A. D lived with murder victim, who had been stabbed. B. Upon being called to crime scene, officer read D her Miranda rights and directed that D be taken to police station for questioning (in handcuffs). C. After one of the victim's daughters implicated D in the murder, she was arrested and Mirandized. D. D answered "no" when asked if she would answer questions without an attorney present. E. Shortly after, the officer told D that the police knew what happened (or that the police knew she was responsible). F. During processing, officer indicated to D that she was going to jail. G. D then began to tell her version of what had happened. H. She was read her Miranda rights again and then gave a statement.	Officer's statements after D invoked right not to speak were "interrogation" for Miranda purposes.	
Miranda v. Az. 384 U.S. 436 1966	A. Officers admitted that defendant was not advised of his rights. B. Defendant was questioned for only two hours, after which officers had a signed confession.	Custody and interrogation were both present.	A. "By custodial interrogation, we mean questioning initiated by law enforcement officers after a person has been taken into custody or otherwise deprived of his freedom of action in any significant way… This is what we meant in Escobedo when we spoke of an investigation which had focused on an accused (FN4)." B. "The constitutional issue we decide in each of these cases is the admissibility of statements obtained from a defendant questioned while in custody or otherwise deprived of his freedom of action in any significant way." C. "Moreover, this warning may serve to make the individual more acutely aware that he is faced with a phase of the adversary system — that he is not in the presence of persons acting solely in his interest."

Alvarado v. Hickman 316 F.3d 841 9th Cir. 2002	A. Police contacted defendant's mother at her office. B. Parents brought defendant to the police station at police request, but both were denied permission to sit in on interview. C. Defendant was 17 years old. D. Defendant had no criminal record or experience with police. E. Interview lasted two hours. F. Defendant's initial statements did not mention crime, but after officer indicated that there were witnesses who gave information opposite that given by the defendant, he began to make incriminating statements. G. Toward the end of the interview, officer implied to defendant that he would be going home after giving statement. H. State appellate court found that the interrogation was not custodial.	9th Circuit held that the defendant was in custody.	A. Juvenile defendants more susceptible to coercion that adults, and more susceptible to the impression that they are "in custody." B. "In custody" determination requires an inquiry into whether a reasonable person would feel as if they could leave. C. Factors to be examined in custody determinations: a. Language used by officer b. Extent to which defendant is confronted with evidence of guilt c. Surroundings of interrogation d. Duration of detention e. Degree of pressure applied to detain defendant D. Defendant did not come voluntarily to police station, but as arranged by his parents. E. Defendant was denied "protective presence of his parents," which is relevant to coercive nature of the interview.
Berkemer v. McCarty 468 U.S. 420 1984	A. Officer saw car weaving in and out of traffic. B. Officer stopped car and asked driver to get out. C. Officer noticed that driver was having trouble standing. D. Officer conducted a field sobriety test (which driver failed) and asked if he'd been using any intoxicants. E. Driver told officer that he'd been drinking beer and smoking marijuana a short time earlier. F. Driver was arrested and taken to jail, where he was asked more questions and told to complete a form indicating whether the marijuana he'd smoked contained any chemicals. G. Driver was not Mirandized at any point and was later convicted of a misdemeanor traffic offense.	Persons temporarily detained during traffic stops are not "in custody" for Miranda purposes (so driver here was not in custody until he was placed under arrest).	A. Traffic stops are "presumptively temporary and brief," which differentiates them from stationhouse interrogations. B. Brevity and spontaneity of a traffic stop mitigates the danger that a driver will be tricked into incriminating himself (the danger Miranda tries to avert). C. Circumstances surrounding traffic stop differ significantly from stationhouse interrogations—traffic stops are public, there's only one officer (at most two), traffic stops are less police-dominated than other interrogatory settings. D. Custody is the "functional equivalent of formal arrest."

| R.I. v. Innis 446 U.S. 291 1980 | A. Murder victim was shot with sawed-off shotgun; another cab driver was robbed shortly afterwards by a man with a sawed-off shotgun.
B. After second victim identified photo of defendant, defendant was arrested and Mirandized several times.
C. D indicated that he wanted to speak to a lawyer, so officers were told not to interrogate him.
D. While being transported to central police station, officers in car with D discussed proximity of school for handicapped children to murder scene and worried that handicapped children might find the murder weapon and hurt themselves.
E. D then offered to show officers where the gun was buried.
F. D was Mirandized again, but said that he wanted to show officers the gun. | Defendant was not "interrogated" within the purposes of Miranda. | A. "Interrogation" for purposes of Miranda warnings is not limited to express questioning.
B. " 'Interrogation,' as conceptualized in the Miranda opinion, must reflect a measure of compulsion above and beyond that inherent in custody itself."
C. Miranda applies when a person in custody is subject to express questioning or its functional equivalent—words or actions on the part of the police that are reasonably likely to elicit an incriminating response.
D. "Reasonably likely" test focuses on perception of suspect, rather than intent of the police.
E. Police cannot be held accountable for unforeseeable consequences of their actions—only applies to words or actions that police should have known would lead to an incriminating response.
F. Nothing in the record in this case indicates that the officers knew or should have known that suspect was particularly susceptible to concerns about the safety of handicapped children.
G. Nothing in this case indicates that officers knew that suspect was "unusually disoriented or upset."
H. "This is not a case where the police carried on a lengthy harangue in the presence of the suspect."
I. Subtle compulsion is not the same as interrogation. |

More Ebook Interactivity

 Research Strategies — Quick References and Checklists

QUICK REFERENCES

- Binding vs. Persuasive Law
- West's Key Number System
- Finding Statutes
- Finding Cases
- Finding Legislative History
- Finding Administrative Law
- Using Looseleaf Services
- Updating the Law
- Collecting Information
- Note-Taking Chart

CHECKLISTS

- 1. Before Beginning Research
- 2. Initial Research
- 3. Continuing Research
- Strategies for Researching Statutes
- Strategies for Researching Cases
- Strategies for Researching Administrative Law
- Strategies for Researching Legislative History

 Research Strategies — Class Exercises

- Choosing Between Secondary Sources
- Research Exercise #1
- Research Exercise #2
- Research Exercise #3
- Research Exercise #4
- Research Exercise #5

 Research Strategies — Quizzes

- Research Strategy in General
- Updating Quiz
- Finding Cases
- Finding Statutes

Legal Documents

In this section, you will learn about legal documents. First, you will learn how to consider purpose, audience, scope, and view before you begin writing legal documents. Second, you will learn the formal requirements for each type of legal document; within each formal requirement, you should click on sample pages. Third, you can review annotated samples of each type of legal document.

Legal Documents — Memorandums of Law (Memos)

A memorandum of law, or memo, is a document written to a lawyer addressing a particular legal issue. Usually, it is written by an associate to a supervising attorney with a client's specific interest at issue. Memos are often the first type of documents written by young associates.

Purpose: A memo informs the supervising attorney of the relevant law and how it applies to the client's issue. It should be objective and show both sides of an issue so that the attorney can make an informed decision about the client's interests.

Audience: A memo is written for a lawyer, usually a supervising attorney. Assume that the attorney will be busy and expect you to apply the law to the facts of the case to analyze the issue. Legal conventions, such as proper citation format and an understanding of legal interpretation and analysis are presumed. Legalese, however, is not recommended.

Scope: A memo can vary in scope; therefore, the associate should inquire about the amount of time, money, and attention required on each memo. The associate should focus only on the particular issue that she is asked to address rather than go beyond the scope of the problem.

View: The point of view of a memo can vary greatly. Most are very formal, but the writer should consider tone. For example, some clients might read these memos, so an associate should watch for any condescending or accusatory language.

- ➥ **Annotated Memo Sample 1**
- ➥ **Annotated Memo Sample 2**
- ➥ **Annotated Memo Sample 3**

Legal Documents — Memos — Formal Requirements

Remember to consider purpose, audience, scope, and view when you receive a memo assignment from a supervising attorney.

The following are the formal requirements of a legal memo. However, many attorneys do not require all of them. For example, some prefer an introduction to replace the traditional question presented and brief answer. Therefore, before you begin writing, you should inquire as to your supervising attorney's preferences or your office requirements in general.

- ➥ **Heading**
- ➥ **Question Presented**

- ⇥ **Brief Answer**
- ⇥ **Statement of Facts**
- ⇥ **Discussion**
- ⇥ **Conclusion**

Process: Writing a memo is a recursive process. Most legal writers understand the law more when they are forced to write about it. They learn what they know, what they still need to research, and what facts they need to discover. They might not make a decision or form an opinion about the outcome until they have finished writing the analysis portion of the memo. As a result, many legal writers begin writing the discussion section instead of starting with the question presented, brief answer, or facts section. As a novice legal writer, you might be asked to write the question presented or brief answer first. This process will help you focus your analysis. However, once you are finished writing the discussion section, you should go back and rewrite the other sections of the memo t ensure they are consistent with your analysis.

Legal Documents — Memos — Heading

As in any memo, "to," "from," subject, and date lines are expected. A legal memo's subject line should include more than just a client name or number, however, because many memos likely will be written for the same client file. Include in the subject line the specific legal issue you are addressing.

Heading

TO: Partner
FROM: Associate
DATE: September 12, 2006
RE: Possibility of Protective Order for Andrea Dawson

Legal Documents — Memos — Question Presented

The question presented is one sentence that provides the reader with a quick summary of the issue addressed in the memo. It should contain (1) the jurisdiction and applicable law, (2) the legal issue presented, and (3) the most legally significant facts that are necessary to answer the question. Many legal writers use the "under-did-when" convention to ensure that the three parts of the question presented are included.

1. **Jurisdiction (under):** The jurisdiction and applicable law is covered in a simple few words that let the reader know what law applies. For example, "Under New Jersey law" might be sufficient. "Under New Jersey common law" is more specific if the writer determines that specificity is preferred. A code provision or a case name is usually too specific as the reader probably knows very little about the law. (However, Roe v. Wade or "Chapter 11 bankruptcy" would be appropriate as a lawyer would gain meaning from either of these phrases.)

2. **Legal issue (did or can or will):** The legal issue presented defines the legal scope of the memo. For example, "Did Mr. Jones assault Mr. Smith?" or "Can Mr. Jones prove libel?" Here, you need to be careful to avoid making your issue too broad and generic (Can he be convicted?) or too narrow and detailed (Can Robert Austin, a well-known actor, prove that Gail Lain, his ex-girlfriend,

made false and misleading statements regarding his three illicit affairs to The Hollywood Star Magazine . . . ?)

3. **Legally significant facts (when):** The legally significant facts are those that apply to the client and are most likely to affect the outcome of this particular issue. Here, the writer needs to choose only those facts that are most significant so that the sentence is readable. A simple "breath test"—reading the question aloud—works to determine wordiness. Also, the writer should be careful not to be one-sided in addressing these facts; often the best questions presented include facts from both sides of the argument so that the reader has a more objective viewpoint.

Some legal writers prefer to use the word *whether* to begin the question presented. This structure is an accepted legal convention, even though it creates a sentence fragment. Because this convention is used as a shorthand for the phrase "the question is whether," the sentence ends with a period instead of a question mark.

If the memo addresses more than one issue, you should include more than one question presented. Include the questions in the same order that you address them in the memo. Each question presented should have a corresponding brief answer.

Question Presented

♦ Under
  o Jurisdiction
  o Controlling law
♦ Did
  o Specific legal question
♦ When
  o Legally significant facts

▯ ↪**Question Presented**

Legal Documents — Memos — Brief Answer

The purpose of the brief answer is to inform the reader how you think the issue will be resolved. You are predicting an outcome of a legal issue – not providing a guarantee on how the judge will decide the case. However, do not include phrases such as "I think" or "I believe."

The brief answer typically contains two parts. First, it quickly answers the question presented with a simple "yes," "no," "probably," or "probably not." Next, using no more than a few sentences, the brief answer uses the terms of art from the applicable law to answer the question presented. Although you will use many of the same terms here as in your ↪**roadmap**, your brief answer does not substitute for a roadmap. Instead, the brief answer uses legal terms of art embedded within significant facts to answer the question. Keep in mind, however, that the brief answer will be read in conjunction with the question presented, so repetition of the same facts is usually not necessary. Likewise, citations usually are not necessary in a brief answer.

A brief answer should be brief. It should not analyze each element of the law. In the ↪**conclusion**, you will provide the reader with more specific reasons for your answer and you will fully analyze the law in the ↪**discussion section** of the memo.

If you provide more than one question presented, you should provide the same number of correlating brief answers.

Brief Answer

- Yes
- No
- Probably
- Probably not

- Brief response to question presented
- Summary of answer and analysis, using key legal terms
- No citations

 ⤵ **Brief Answer**

Legal Documents — Memos — Statement of Facts

The statement of facts presents the facts to the reader in a clear, concise, and objective manner. Although the supervising attorney may have provided you with the facts originally, you do not simply repeat verbatim the facts as given to you by the supervising attorney. Instead, craft a concise and objective story using the legally significant facts and background facts. In addition, do not assume your reader remembers the facts. Your supervisor might have hundreds of clients; as a result, he or she will rely on your fact statement to refresh his memory about the case. Also, facts change. Unlike fact patterns provided in your legal writing class, in real cases, lawyers discover facts as the case proceeds forward. Therefore, by writing a fact statement, you are creating a record on which you are relying to answer the legal question. If the facts change (and they often do), then your opinion may change as well.

An effective Statement of Facts should include the following:

Legally Significant Facts: Your statement of facts should focus mainly on legally significant facts. A fact is legally significant if it is considered when applying the law. Therefore, if you use a fact in your discussion section, it is legally significant. One trick to writing the statement of facts is to write it after writing the discussion section to ensure that all facts in the discussion section are included in the fact section.

Background Facts that tell a Clear and Concise Story: Your statement of facts should tell a story. Therefore, you will need to include background facts to tie the legally significant facts together. Do not use bullet points. Instead, consider the best organizational schema for presenting the facts to the reader. Chronological organizations usually work well, but there may be circumstances when you will organize your facts by topic, by client, or by causes of action.

Objective Writing: The fact section should be written objectively. Do not omit facts that might not be helpful to your client. Remember that a legal memo is confidential; the opposing side and the court do not have access to it. The supervising attorney is relying on the facts to make decisions about how to proceed with the case. Therefore, you should strive to be as accurate and honest as possible when presenting the facts. At times, you might include emotional facts because they may affect the way a judge or jury will decide the case. However, do not make arguments in the fact section and avoid partisan or qualifying language.

Do not create new facts or make assumptions in your fact section. Your opinion in the memo is based on the facts as you know them at the time. When in doubt, indicate that more facts are necessary.

Statement of Facts

♦   Legally significant facts
♦   Background facts
♦   Clear and concise story
♦   Objective writing

▢ ↪**Statement of Facts**

Legal Documents — Memos — Discussion

The discussion section is the meat of the memo. Here, the writer presents the law in an organized fashion and applies it to the client's situation. The purpose of the discussion section is to show the reader the application of the law to the facts to prove the predicted outcome. There are many other sections of this ebook that discuss the process of writing the discussion section as well as organizing and analyzing the law. Links are provided below.

Organization: The organizational schema of the discussion section should be based on the organization of the law itself. Thus, the beginning of the discussion section should set out the law for the reader with a clear ↪**roadmap**. The rest of the discussion section follows the organization of the roadmap with strong ↪**topic sentences**.

Typical Mistakes:

1.   Do not vary the terms of art in your discussion section. Instead, legal terms remain consistent as you analyze their meaning within the law. So, terms in your topic sentences should be consistent with the terms in your roadmap.
2.   Do not feel compelled to provide a history of the law. The legal reader wants to know what the law is today. Unless the history is significant for some reason, there is no need to provide the history of the law for the reader.
3.   Do not forget to cite the roadmap. The roadmap will be based on the law. Therefore, you need to cite to the appropriate legal authority in your roadmap.

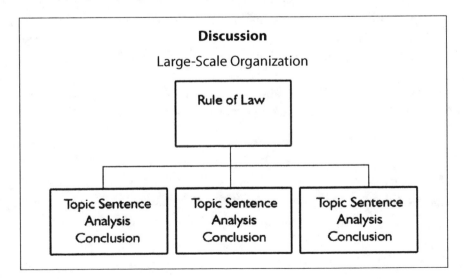

▢ ↪**Discussion**

🔍 ➙**Large-Scale Organization**

Legal analysis: The reader expects a thorough application of the law to the facts in the discussion section. Here is where you will use primary law and create policy arguments to show why you think the issue will come out the way you predict.

Typical Mistakes:

1. Not enough law. Many novice writers argue the facts but fail to prove their conclusions using the law.
2. Not enough facts. Do not force the reader to flip back to your fact section. Include the legally significant facts within the analysis.
3. Too many quotations. If you find yourself quoting the law instead of applying it, you are not writing an effective discussion section.
4. Failure to conclude. Many novice writers are afraid to conclude on an issue or element of the law. Remember that you are providing an opinion — not a guarantee. Provide the reader with enough of the logical reasoning so that he or she can disagree with your position.
5. Failure to provide counter-arguments. Because your discussion section should be objective, you need to anticipate the other side's arguments.

🔍 ➙**Legal Analysis**
🔍 ➙**Paragraph Organization and Legal Analysis**
🔍 ➙**Conciseness**
🔍 ➙**Writing Process**

Legal Documents — Memos — Conclusion

The conclusion answers the particular question but with more detail than the ➙**brief answer**. An effective conclusion usually breaks down the component parts of the law and uses specific client facts and legal reasoning to show why that element of the law is either favorable or unfavorable for the client. It should not include references to specific authorities such as statutes or cases; these specifics belong in the discussion section.

A busy reader should be able to read your question presented, brief answer, and conclusion together to have a complete summary of the issue, the law, and the effect on the client. Make sure that they are all consistent.

If you have multiple questions presented and brief answers you should have multiple corresponding conclusions.

If you believe that more investigation is necessary or that another issue should be addressed, you should consider including a separate paragraph in your conclusion addressing your concerns.

Conclusion

◆ Summarizes each main point of discussion
◆ Gives a more thorough explanation than the brief answer
◆ Provides a solid answer for attorneys reading the memo
◆ Written objectively

Legal Documents — Briefs

Briefs are persuasive documents written for appellate and trial courts. This section will address appellate briefs. For information about trial briefs, see ➥**Motions.**

Appellate briefs are carefully crafted documents that attempt to persuade a panel of appellate judges to rule in the client's favor. Appellate briefs are not a rehashing of the trial. Instead, they focus on specific errors at the trial level. Therefore, appellate attorneys must carefully choose the issues they raise on appeal and focus the court on those issues. The appellant (or petitioner) files his or her brief first and the appellee (or respondent) must respond by filing his or her brief within a certain prescribed time. The appellant has an opportunity to file a reply brief (and some courts permit reply briefs from appellees). In some instances, amicus briefs may also be filed.

Purpose: The underlying purpose of a brief is to convince the judges to affirm, reverse, or remand the case to the lower court. Thus, an appellate brief should inform and persuade. It should be written to win a particular issue or a number of issues. The best briefs seem objective and reasonable, but are subtly persuasive so that the judges feel compelled to rule for the client. The least effective briefs attempt persuasion with incendiary passages that often attack the other side's position or present a defensive posture.

Audience: The judge (or panel of judges) is the primary audience for an appellate brief. When you know which judges are assigned to your panel, you should research their prior cases to understand their leanings and reasoning in previous decisions. Often this research will give you a much better sense of your audience. You can research state judges by searching on the ➥**state map**, and you can find information on federal appellate judges by searching each ➥**circuit**. You can find cases they have written through Lexis and Westlaw.

Keep in mind that the judges' clerks are also the audience; oftentimes they are the worst critics. Other secondary audiences include opposing counsel, your client, the opposing client, and the public. Therefore, tactical considerations are also necessary.

Scope: The scope of an appellate brief turns on the errors in the court below. In most instances, an appellate attorney may request the trial court only to reconsider issues already addressed at the trial level. Therefore, the appellate attorney must scour the trial record for error and decide which issues to raise on appeal. Many briefs raise multiple issues. Appellate courts have page or word number limits on briefs filed. You should always consult your court's rules before beginning a brief. You can find these rules through the ➥**state map** or the ➥**federal circuit map.**

View: You should have a "theory of the case" or "core theory" underlying your brief. This is not the actual legal theory, but instead a writing theory that tugs at the emotions of the judges. The core theory can be based on policy arguments, emotional facts, fairness issues, logical analysis, or any creative argument that is easily understood. Think of the core theory as your "cocktail party answer" when a nonlawyer asks you about your case. For example, a bus accident case might have a legal theory of negligence, but the theory of the case for the brief might be: "The bus driver was in a rush." The theory should be subtle and interwoven throughout the brief itself, starting with the fact section and pervading every facet of the argument.

⌨ ➥**Annotated Sample Brief 1**
⌨ ➥**Annotated Sample Brief 2**
     → ⌨ ➥**Revised Brief 2**

Legal Documents — Briefs — Formal Requirements

The following are the possible formal requirements of an appellate brief. Most courts do not require all of them. You should always consult the rules in your jurisdiction before beginning to write an appellate brief. These rules not only require specific formal requirements of a brief, but they also dictate page, font, and filing requirements. (To access your court's rules, see the ➥**state law map** or ➥**federal courts maps**.) Some professors create fictional rules or require a particular jurisdiction's rules, so be sure to follow your course requirements.

- ➥**Title Page**
- ➥**Table of Contents and Pointheadings and Subheadings**
- ➥**Table of Authorities**
- ➥**Jurisdiction**
- ➥**Standard of Review**
- ➥**Statement of the Issue Presented for Review**
- ➥**Statement of the Case**
- ➥**Summary of Argument**
- ➥**Argument**
- ➥**Conclusion**
- ➥**Signature and Certificate of Service**

Process: Writing a brief is a recursive process. Don't expect to thoroughly understand all of your arguments until you begin writing them. During the writing process, you will discover gaps in your legal reasoning as well as strengths of your opponents arguments. As a result, you will need to research the law again to address these concerns.

Most legal writers begin their briefs by writing the argument section or the summary of the argument section. Some prefer to outline the arguments first by writing the pointheadings and subheadings. Others prefer to draft an issue statement to focus on the main issues or to write the facts to help create the theory of the case. Regardless of your starting point, you will need to rewrite the specific sections once you have completed the argument. An issue statement will need fine-tuning once your arguments are detailed. A fact section will need to be rewritten to include all the legally significant facts in the argument. Pointheadings and subheadings will need to be rewritten to conform to the final organizational schema. Of course, you will need to ➥**rewrite** your argument section as you discover nuances in the law and logical gaps in your analysis.

Legal Documents — Briefs — Title Page

Because a brief is filed in a court, it needs identification. Therefore, the title page contains the name of the court itself, the name of the case, the docket number and judge's name (if available), and the names and addresses of counsel. Some courts require different color pages for the title pages to distinguish appellants' briefs from appellees' briefs.

Title Page

♦   Case caption
♦   Docket number
♦   Attorney name and address
♦   Type of brief

Legal Documents — Briefs — Table of Contents and Pointheadings and Subheadings

The **table of contents** (sometimes called the index page) refers the reader to page numbers for each section of the brief. Usually, page 1 begins with the statement of issues presented for review. Previous pages, such as the table of contents and the table of authorities, are usually referenced as i, ii, iii, and so on. The table of contents page often takes a substantial amount of time to create; for instructions and programming tips, see **➥Georgetown Law's Information Systems Technology page**.

Table of Contents

♦   References page numbers for each section of the brief
♦   Shows the organization of your document by using pointheadings, which
    o   Show organization of argument
    o   Are written persuasively
    o   Use facts and law

➥Table of Contents

Pointheadings and subheadings are also specifically referenced in the table of contents. Pointheadings serve as thesis statements for each part of the argument section. They illustrate the organization and arguments of the brief.

The pointheadings and subheadings appear in two places: (1) the table of contents, and (2) the argument section. In the table of contents, the pointheadings and subheadings provide the reader with an understanding of your large-scale organization and your arguments. Therefore, it is important that they both inform and persuade the reader. In the argument section, the pointheadings and subheadings break your argument into readable sections and serve as signs for the reader that you are moving from one argument to the next. Strong pointheadings and subheadings do not substitute for strong topic sentences; your brief will need both.

Pointheadings are usually your main arguments and correlate with each issue statement. Each pointheading should be one sentence, written persuasively, and should contain the legal issue you will address in that section. Pointheadings might also reference some of your favorable facts or the standard of review. Each pointheading should answer the correlating issue statement.

Subheadings are used to break down the organization within each pointheading. They flesh out the arguments under each pointheading, providing facts and legal reasoning. You might have one sub-heading for each factor within a multi-factor test or you may combine a number of factors to create each subheading. At times, you might provide subheadings within subheadings, but rarely would you go beyond this third level of organization.

You can be very creative when designing your organizational schema. You need not provide the same number of subheadings under each pointheading. You might not have any subheadings at all under one particular pointheading. However, if you choose to write a subheading A, you should also include a subheading B. If you do not have separate sub-issues, there is no need for a subheading – just make your argument in the pointheading.

Novice writers tend to write excessively long pointheadings and subheadings. Instead, keep them read-able by focusing the reader on the main point you are making. While they should be full sentences, short headings often are the most persuasive.

Briefs filed in different courts serve different purposes; your pointheadings and subheadings should mirror those purposes. If you file a brief in the United States Supreme Court, your pointheadings and subheadings might be more general and lay out policy arguments and reasons for changes in the law. However, most briefs apply already-existing law to the client's facts and the pointheadings and sub-headings should specifically reference that law and the facts of the case.

⌨ ➥**Table of Contents and Pointheadings and Subheadings**

Legal Documents — Briefs — Table of Authorities

Sometimes called "authorities cited," this page alphabetically lists the legal authorities cited within the brief with references to page numbers. The citations provided should be complete and conform to the citation format required by that court (usually the Bluebook or ALWD). Some jurisdictions require that seminal law be cited with an asterisk (*). Various types of legal authority (constitutions, cases, statutes, regulations) are often separated when listed. The page takes a lot of time and effort to create; for instruc-tions and programming tips, see ➥**Georgetown Law's Information Systems Technology page.**

Table of Authorities

- ◆ Ordered alphabetically
- ◆ Shows authorities relied on
- ◆ May organize by types of authorities
  - ○ Constitutions
  - ○ Statutes
  - ○ Cases
  - ○ Regulations

⌨ ➥**Table of Authorities**

Legal Documents — Briefs — Jurisdiction

Not all courts require a jurisdiction section. When one is required, this section briefly states the jurisdictional basis for appeal by providing relevant facts and a specific legal foundation.

Jurisdiction

♦ Some courts require a showing of jurisdiction
♦ Provide specific law and relevant facts

→**Jurisdiction**

Legal Documents — Briefs — Standard of Review

In appellate cases, the court must apply a certain standard of review over the trial court. This standard is analogous to the burden of proof in trial cases. The appellate court determines how much deference to give to the trial court because the appellate court does not sit in the same shoes as the trial judge.

First, the appellate court does not hear witnesses or judge credibility like the trial judge; therefore, the trial judge is given great deference in deciding questions of fact. Her ruling is overturned only if it was **"clearly erroneous"** as to the facts.

On the other hand, the appellate court needs to ensure that stare decisis is preserved so that laws are followed in an equitable manner; therefore, questions of law are reviewed independently, or **de novo**, with no deference given to the trial court.

For issues that present mixed questions of law and fact, the standard is not always clear. Courts themselves seem to be confused on the standard of review. Therefore, it is important to pay attention to what standard the court says it is using, but also look at what standard the court actually applies.

Another standard, **abuse of discretion**, applies for procedural and evidentiary issues where the trial court has discretion. On appeal, the appellate court will overrule a trial judge only if he has abused his discretion on that particular issue.

Some courts require a separate section for the standard of review, while others require that you include it in the statement of the case or the argument section. Consult your appellate court rules to ensure proper placement of the standard of review.

Standard of Review

♦ The burden of proof in appellate cases.
♦ How much deference to give to the trial court.
♦ The appellate court gives more deference to trial court for questions of fact because the trial judge has the opportunity to access witness credibility.
♦ Questions of law are reviewed with no deference to trial court so that the law remains consistent and predictable in that jurisdiction.
♦ Mixed questions of law and fact often have an unclear standard.
♦ Look at what the appellate court does as well as what it says it is doing in terms of the standard of review.

→**Standard of Review**

Legal Documents — Briefs — Statement of the Issue Presented for Review

The issue statements explain the precise legal issues the court will need to address. They should be written persuasively and contain both the legal issue and some of the most persuasive facts for your side. They are usually one sentence and should pass the breath test. Although not required, lawyers often include the standard of review within the issue statement.

Many briefs include multiple issue statements if the brief itself addresses more than one issue on appeal. Each issue statement should correlate to a main pointheading. If you argue in the alternative in a brief, your issue statements should reflect those specific arguments.

This section is similar to the ↪**question presented** in a memo; however, it does not require a jurisdictional statement as one is usually provided in a separate section. Unlike a memo, the issue statement in a brief should be written persuasively so that the reader empathizes with your client. The answer should be implicit because a brief, unlike a memo, does not include a corresponding brief answer. However, be careful not to provide the actual conclusion in the issue statement.

Statement of the Issue Presented for Review

♦ Presents the issue or issues to be addressed by the court
♦ Presents the issue in a light most favorable to the client
♦ There is no brief answer, so answer should be implied

⊞ ↪**Statement of the Issue Presented for Review**

Legal Documents — Briefs — Statement of the Case (or Statement of the Facts)

The statement of the case (also called the statement of the facts) presents the facts to the reader in a clear, concise, and persuasive manner. As an appellate attorney, you will probably receive the facts in the form of a record, which usually includes a lower court transcript and a variety of documents. Your job will be to cull through the record and pull out the most relevant facts to tell the client's story.

The statement of the case is your first opportunity to tell the story from the client's perspective. There are a number of persuasive techniques that you can use to make the statement of the case persuasive:

Provide emotional facts. Unlike the objective ↪**fact section in a memo**, the statement of facts in a brief should provide the reader with emotional facts. These facts should tug at the heart strings of the reader so that the judge feels compelled to rule for your client — even before he or she understands the law.

Provide legally significant facts and background facts. In addition to emotional facts, you will need to provide legally significant facts and use background facts to tie the significant facts to the emotional facts. Facts are legally significant if you use them in your argument section.

Tell a compelling story. Here, you can use your creativity to tell your client's story. A chronological organization is often preferred, but it is not necessary. Consider whether you want to organize by claims, witnesses, crimes, or other schema.

Choose a starting point. The starting point for your story is important. It should engage the reader from your client's point of view. For example, if you represent a client who has been arrested, you might start with the scene of the arrest. If you represent the prosecution in the same case, you might start with the crime from the victim's perspective.

Choose a theory of the case. You need to decide on an overall theory of your case. It will pervade your writing and should be an integral part of your fact section.

🔍 → Theory of the Case

Highlight helpful facts. Highlight those facts that are most helpful for your position. You can focus on them by placing them at the beginning of paragraphs and sentences. Use short sentences to highlight important points.

Do not avoid harmful facts. You will lose credibility if you do not include facts that help the other side. (Remember that opposing counsel will include them in his brief.) When you include the harmful facts, you can downplay them by explaining them or including them mid-paragraph or mid-sentence.

Choose names and titles carefully. You should personalize your client and be more generic with names of the opposing party. For example, refer to your client as Mr. Jones or Michael Jones. Refer to the other party with more generic terms such as the employer, the government, or the defendant.

Use subtle persuasion. Your persuasion should be subtle. Avoid overly dramatic statements or Hollywood scripts. The key to a statement of facts is to sound objective while you subtly persuade.

Some jurisdictions distinguish between the terms "statement of the facts" and "statement of the case." In these jurisdictions, the statement of the facts is usually a general term that includes the whole fact section, while the statement of the case contains only the procedural history. Most courts have specific requirements for the procedural history sections of the statement of the case.

Statement of the Case (or Statement of the Facts)

- ♦ Includes procedural history, background facts, legally significant facts, and emotional facts
- ♦ Written in clear, precise, and persuasive language
- ♦ Develops subtle theory of case
- ♦ Tells compelling story
- ♦ Highlights helpful facts but does not avoid harmful facts
- ♦ Uses subtle persuasion

🖥 → Sample Statement of the Case from Supreme Court Briefs in <u>Rhode Island v. Innis</u>

Legal Documents — Briefs — Summary of the Argument

The summary of the argument provides the court with a snapshot of your arguments. The summary should show the court which way it should decide on each issue referring to rules of law, application of the law to the facts, and any relevant policy issues. However, specific cites to cases are usually not required.

The summary of the argument is similar to the ➥**conclusion** section of the memo in that it briefly summarizes the main legal points of the document, using key facts from the client's case. However, in a brief, this section is persuasive and designed to give a compelling overview for the very busy reader. Consider writing a paragraph or two per issue to summarize your main points for the reader; do not try to make every specific point in your summary.

Some lawyers choose to write summaries that refer only to the law while others write very fact-specific summaries, applying the law to the facts on each issue but only highlighting the most compelling arguments.

Not all jurisdictions require a summary of the argument; however, consider including this section if space permits.

Summary of the Argument

- ◆   Provides an opportunity for a synopsis of the arguments
- ◆   Should be brief and persuasive
- ◆   Should introduce your theory of the case
- ◆   May or may not include citations

⌨ ➥**Summary of the Argument**

Legal Documents — Briefs — Argument

The argument section is the "meat of the brief," complete with ➥**pointheadings and subheadings.** Here, the writer presents the law and applies it to the client's situation in a persuasive manner, applying the theory of the case and other persuasive techniques to the writing. The purpose of the argument section is to prove your arguments to the court using sound legal analysis and persuasive techniques. There are many other sections of this ebook that discuss writing the argument section, writing persuasively, and organizing and analyzing the law. Links are provided below.

Content: First, you will need to decide which arguments to include and which to ignore. You might not make some of these decisions until you actually write the argument section and discover your weak points in the analysis. Most judges prefer to read only the most compelling arguments instead of the kitchen-sink approach where the lawyer includes every possible alternative argument.

🔍 ➥**Content**

Organization: The argument section should be organized around the law in a persuasive fashion. This section usually starts with a persuasive ➥**roadmap**, which sets out the legal arguments for the court. The rest of the argument section follows the organization of the roadmap with clear pointheadings and subheadings and conclusive topic sentences. Here are some techniques to make your organization more persuasive:

1. Start with your strongest argument.
2. Combine a weak factor with a strong factor.
3. Organize your sentences with strong subject-verb combinations.
4. Create active topic sentences to focus the reader on your strong points.
5. Use passive voice to downplay an actor.

🔍 ➥**Large-Scale Organization**
🔍 ➥**Persuasive Techniques**

Legal Analysis: The reader expects a thorough analysis of the law to the facts in the argument section. You should start with the law that is most favorable to your side. If the law is not favorable, start with the facts of your case. If neither the facts nor the law provide the basis for your best argument, consider beginning with a policy argument. As you create your legal arguments, you should combine all three when possible – law, facts, and policy arguments – to make a compelling case for the reader. Here are some techniques for persuasive analysis:

1. Present the rules in a light most favorable to your client.
2. Start with the most compelling cases for your client.
3. Don't ignore the other side's counterargument.
4. Downplay the other side's counterargument but don't highlight it (You will highlight it if you state the other side's argument defensively – especially in a topic sentence.)
5. Use policy arguments to show the court why the law should apply in a certain way or why the law should be changed.

Argument

♦ Meat of the brief
♦ Presents arguments in persuasive manner
♦ Includes pointheadings and subheadings written in complete sentences to advance the arguments
♦ Includes appropriate legal citation
♦ Contains subtle persuasive techniques such as a core theory

---

🖳 ➥**Argument**

🔍 ➥**Persuasive Writing**
🔍 ➥**Legal Analysis**
🔍 ➥**Analysis and Paragraph Structure**
🔍 ➥**Conciseness**
🔍 ➥**Writing Process**

Legal Documents — Briefs — Conclusion

The conclusion in a brief differs from that in a memo. In a brief, the conclusion simply states the relief requested, usually in one sentence.

Conclusion

- ◆ Does not summarize argument
- ◆ Usually one sentence requesting specific relief, for example:
  - ○ Reverse
  - ○ Remand
  - ○ Affirm

"For the aforementioned reasons, this Court should reverse the trial court and remand for new trial."

🖳 ➥**Conclusion**

Legal Documents — Briefs — Signature and Certificate of Service

The attorney's signature, name, bar number, and address are required at the end of every brief. In addition, the court requires a short statement indicating that the writer has provided a copy of the brief to opposing counsel (indicating whether service was hand-provided, emailed, or mailed). An attorney's signature is required after the certificate of service as well.

Signature and Certificate of Service

- ◆ The lawyer's signature, bar number, and address are required
- ◆ A certificate of service is required to show that opposing counsel has received a copy

---

🖳 ➥**Signature and Certificate of Service**

➥**Annotated Sample Brief 1**
➥**Annotated Sample Brief 2**
➔ ➥**Revised Brief 2**

Legal Documents — Persuasive Techniques

In persuasive writing, such as briefs, the writer's goal is to inform and persuade. Persuasion, however, does not mean informing the reader of just one side of the argument. The best persuasive documents address the other side's arguments, but downplay or distinguish them. One of the biggest mistakes in persuasive writing is to hit the reader over the head with persuasion so that the arguments sound hyperbolic or become personal attacks against the other side. Therefore, subtle persuasion is the trick to effective persuasive writing. While there is a whole section in this ebook on ➥**persuasive writing**, below is a summary of some simple techniques to subtly convince the writer of your position.

1. **Develop a Subtle Theory of Your Case:** Each persuasive document should contain a subtle theory. This is not a legal theory; instead it is a simple theory that will help your reader empathize with your client. For example, in a bus accident case, a legal theory might be negligence, but the theory of your case might be "the bus driver was in a rush." Such a simple theory is easy to understand and goes hand in hand with the legal theory. Thus, as you develop the law of negligence in your persuasive document, you can also use facts to enhance your theory of the case, such as the speed of the bus or the bus driver not paying careful attention. By using a subtle theory that is simple and easy to understand, the reader can sympathize with your client before she even understands the law. The theory of the case should be evident throughout your document, from the fact section to the argument section.

   ➥**Sample Theory of the Case from Supreme Court Briefs in <u>Clinton v. Jones</u>**

   🔍 ➥**Designing the Theory of the Case**

2. **Fact Section:** The fact section is an opportunity to tell the story from your client's perspective. Choosing a starting point is important as it provides a focal point for your theory of the case. For example, while a prosecutor might begin a fact section with the gruesome crime, the defense brief might start with the scene of the arrest. Word choice is also crucial: the prosecutor might use the term *defendant*, while the defendant's brief would use the client's name, Mr. Samuel Jones. The fact section of a brief should not avoid harmful facts; instead, it should downplay them by discussing them in a light most favorable to the client.

   ➥**Sample Statement of Facts from Supreme Court Briefs in <u>Rhode Island v. Innis</u>**

   🔍 ➥**Crafting the Fact Section**

3. **Argument Section:** The argument section includes facts and law to persuade the judge that you should win. Here, you should make informed decisions about the order you place your issues, legal points, and primary authority. General legal wisdom is to present your best arguments first, initially using your strongest cases to prove your point. The reasoning here is that you hold your reader's attention most carefully in the beginning of your document and at the beginning of each paragraph. Sometimes, however, ordering your arguments chronologically or in another order to best introduce your theory of the case makes more sense. A typical legal writer will order and reorder a persuasive document many times before filing.

   🔍 ➥**Drafting the Argument Section**

4. **Don't Sound Defensive:** Many poor persuasive documents sound defensive. For example, an opposition to a motion might use the opponent's motion as a model for organization and counter each argument in the same order. This technique is not effective for two reasons. First, the writer loses the opportunity to make organizational decisions to help prove his argument. Instead, he accepts the carefully designed organizational decisions of his opponent. Second, the document is consistently arguing the negative and the tone of the document is "did not"—a very whiny approach to legal writing. Therefore, watch for topic sentences that begin with, "The opposing side argues ...". There is no need to present the other side's argument again as repetition helps the reader remember. Instead, present your arguments affirmatively and in the order in which you decide is best for your theory of the case.

   ➥**Samples of Defensive Writing**

5. **Don't Personally Attack the Other Side:** Oftentimes, lawyers let arguments become personal. Avoid this urge. Instead, make sure that your document addresses issues and does not attack the other side personally. Judges do not appreciate personal gripes between lawyers, and usually you will lose credibility with your audience if you become involved in such tactics.

   ➥**Samples of Personal Attacks**

6. **Use Points of Emphasis Through Your Sentences:** The choices you make in sentence structure, placement, and length can affect your persuasion. Some simple tricks will help. First, open and close your paragraphs with strong points; bury weaker points mid-paragraph. Second, use active voice to highlight the subject of your sentence; use passive voice to downplay the actor. Third, shorter sentences pack a punch; use them wisely. Fourth, make your points in independent clauses; downplay the other side by placing their points in dependent clauses.

    🔍 ↪*Using Effective Sentence Structure and Word Choice*

7. **Use Selective Word Choice:** The words you choose can make a big impact on your persuasive writing. For example, a defendant might write that the police "burst" into a room while the prosecution will state the police "entered" the room. Likewise, a drug defendant might want to call his vehicle "the car," while the prosecution would be more specific and refer to it as "the Porsche." Subtle choices like these can impact the reader.

    🔍 ↪*Using Effective Sentence Structure and Word Choice*

Legal Documents — Oral Argument

WHAT IS ORAL ARGUMENT?

If the brief is your first chance to persuade the appellate court, then oral argument is your last chance. In a typical appellate court oral argument, the two opposing counsel appear in front of a three-judge panel and argue their cases for approximately half an hour. The appellant argues first, then the appellee argues, and the appellant has a chance for rebuttal. During oral argument, the judges ask questions about the issues presented in the briefs. While the judges' levels of preparation differ, you should assume that your judges have not only read the briefs, but also done additional research. Oral argument provides you with an opportunity to answer questions the judges find important, stress issues and cases you find most compelling, and persuade the bench that you win.

Audience: You are answering questions for a panel of judges. Therefore, you must be respectful at all times, regardless of the judges' possible antagonistic tones, irrelevant questions, or apparent disregard for you or your client. Remain professional at all times; do not show your exasperation with a judge's barrage of irrelevant questions. On the other hand, do not inundate the court with unnecessary platitudes such as "As this masterful court has already decided" or "As I have read in your artfully worded opinion."

Answer questions directly, looking the judge in the eye: "Yes, Your Honor," or "No, Judge Schwelb." If a judge interrupts you, let her talk. Do not try to talk over a judge at any point in time and do not interrupt a judge on the bench. Do not tell a judge that she is wrong. Give deference to the bench at all times.

With a three-judge panel, you need to make sure two of the judges are on your side by the time the oral argument has finished. The best appellate attorney is the one who can assess which judges are for him during oral argument and win over those judges who are against him.

Your bench will usually be a "hot bench," peppering you with constant questions. Rarely will you encounter a "cool bench." Often, the cooler benches make for more difficult oral argument because it is hard to engage the judges and understand their concerns and questions if they ask very few questions.

Purpose: Oral argument is not a speech but a conversation with the court. The purpose of oral argument is to answer the judge's questions and to convince each judge on the panel that your client should win. Therefore, you should answer each question thoroughly — relying on facts, law, and policy arguments. Speak slowly, make eye contact, and avoid hand gestures or body movements that could distract from the argument.

Listen carefully to each judge's question and feel free to repeat the question if you are unsure of its meaning. Active listening is the most important tool during oral argument; you must be completely focused on the judge's question instead of thinking about your next sentence. Do not be afraid to take a moment to think about your argument before stating your answer.

Scope: Your oral argument should focus on the main, most compelling arguments of your brief. The judges might steer you into different areas of law or points made by the other side. While you need to answer these questions, you should try to steer the court back to your main arguments whenever possible. Framing the issue from your client's viewpoint is important in oral argument.

Stance: Tie your argument back to your theory of the case whenever possible. You want the judges walking off of the bench and repeating your theme to the other judges on the panel when they are deciding how to rule on the case.

HOW SHOULD I PREPARE?

To prepare for oral argument, you need to do much more than reread the briefs. While all attorneys have their own methods of preparation, a novice should prepare an outline of arguments. In addition, the law should be handy for reference. The outline and law should provide you with a flexible guideline to make sure you cover all important issues. Often, the judges will steer you away from your outline with their questions. A good attorney will be able to weave in points from the outline in answering the judges' questions.

In preparing, you should practice your argument in front of other attorneys in a "moot," or mock, oral argument. Discuss your answers and prepare better approaches to the tough questions. Also practice the level, tone, and speed of your voice. Arguments that are strong on substance can be weakened by poor delivery.

If possible, videotape yourself practicing oral argument. When you play back the video, you will notice your tone, speed, delivery, and distracting gestures. The use of a low-tech Web cam can be very helpful for practicing oral arguments. Time yourself when practicing because time will go faster than you expect.

ARE THERE CONVENTIONS FOR ORAL ARGUMENT?

Introduction: Typically, before beginning to speak, you should ask permission from the court to do so by saying "May it please the court." It is often helpful to introduce yourself (and your co-counsel if appropriate) and give an overview of the case. This overview is similar to the theory of your case in the brief. (This case is about a bus driver who was in too much of a rush.) You should memorize the introduction as judges rarely interrupt you during this short time frame.

▯ ➥**Sample Introduction**

Facts: If you have compelling facts, you should tell them to the court. If the other side has already presented the facts, you should take the opportunity to present them from your client's perspective instead of relying on the recitation of the facts by the opposing counsel. If the facts are not very helpful and you would prefer to start with the law, you are free to do so. Oftentimes, counsel will ask the court if it wants a brief recitation of the facts; be prepared to do so or to answer factual questions from the bench.

Roadmap: You should provide the court with an oral roadmap. Typically, you will argue two or three main issues or provide a number of reasons why the court should rule in your favor. List those issues or arguments up front for the court. Start with your most compelling argument to be sure the court has heard it. If the judges want to hear one of your later arguments first, they will ask. Otherwise, begin with your first argument. At this point, judges might ask you what legal authority you are relying on and what relief you are seeking.

⤏ Sample Roadmap

Main Argument: After the introduction, facts, and roadmap, you will spend the rest of your time arguing your case and answering the judges' questions.

> **Types of Questions to Expect:** You will be asked a range of questions from the panel. Typical questions include these:

>> **Softball questions:** Here, one judge will try to help you make the argument to the rest of the panel. Take these questions as a sign that at least one judge is already willing to rule in your favor. Help this judge convince his or her colleagues that your position is correct. Also, listen to this judge's questions and arguments; they will provide you with insights as to which of your arguments are compelling.

>> **Hypothetical questions:** Judges' decisions affect not only your client but also cases that arise in the future. Therefore, judges will ask you how far you think the rule should be stretched. Here, you need to sound reasonable or you will lose credibility with the court.

>> **Factual questions:** The judges might ask you about the facts of your case or pose questions regarding possible factual scenarios. Do not tell the judge that "those are not the facts of this case." You can distinguish the facts or clarify them if necessary.

>> **Legal questions:** Here the judges might ask for authority to support your argument or ask about a specific case. You need to be extremely familiar with the details of the law; know the facts, reasoning, and holding of the cases so that you can refer directly to these cases and distinguish them if necessary. If you don't know the case the judge is referencing, do not make up an answer. Instead, be honest and tell the court you are not familiar with the case. Often, a judge will fill you in on the details of the case so that you can provide an intelligent answer to the question. At times, the judge might ask you to file a supplemental brief to address the case.

Conclusion: At the end of the argument, conclude with a brief summary of the points you made and a request for relief (for example, the reversal of the lower court's holding). In most cases, however, you will run out of time, so try to do so gracefully. If you are in the middle of answering a question when time runs out, pause and ask the court for permission to briefly answer the question and wrap up. You should never continue speaking after your time is up without the leave of the court.

WHAT SHOULD I DO WHEN OPPOSING COUNSEL IS SPEAKING?

When opposing counsel stands up to give his presentation, pay attention and take notes. The best arguments respond directly to points raised by opposing counsel. Reviewing the opposing brief beforehand can give you a preview of opposing counsel's arguments, but you must always listen to what he actually says so that you can effectively rebut him, either as the appellee in your main argument or as the appellant on rebuttal.

WHAT IS REBUTTAL?

Rebuttal should not be a rehashing of your arguments. Instead, you should address only one or two points usually as a counterpoint to one of opposing counsel's best arguments. For example, if the opposing counsel mentions a case that seems compelling, be sure to distinguish the case in your rebuttal. If you have a chance for rebuttal, you should always take the opportunity to be the last speaker.

➤Sample Oral Arguments: A Bad Example and a Good Example
➤Listen to Supreme Court Oral Arguments
➤Do's and Don'ts of Oral Arguments

Legal Documents — Pleadings and Motions

Pleadings are the documents used to initiate lawsuits. They include complaints, answers, and interrogatories. Together, the complaint and answer focus the issues of the lawsuit. The interrogatories begin the discovery process. In drafting pleadings, attorneys must investigate the facts, research the law, and make tactical decisions regarding the case. Oftentimes, young associates are asked to draft pleadings without much guidance. Therefore, this section will discuss the basics of drafting complaints, answers, and interrogatories.

Legal Documents — Complaints

Purpose: The complaint commences the legal action. It also provides notice to the defendants and stops the running of the statute of limitations on the action.

Audience: The complaint is written and served on the defendant. However, it is basically written for the legal audience as it is also filed with the court and read by the eventual counsel for the defense.

Scope: The complaint actually sets the scope of the lawsuit by alleging particular legal claims against the defense. Some complaints are only a page or two; others can be particularly lengthy if they set out a plethora of claims.

View: A complaint is a very formal document. It is usually written in bullet point form with numbered allegations.

➤Sample Complaints

Legal Documents — Formal Requirements of a Complaint

Before drafting a complaint, you should do the following:

1. Research the rules for filing complaints in your jurisdiction.
2. Research the substantive law of your case.
3. Investigate the facts for your client.

First, each jurisdiction has rules governing the content of a complaint and the procedures for filing them. Check the civil procedure rules for your jurisdiction as well as the local rules. These rules set out the appearance, content, and filing requirements for the complaint.

▦ ↪Filing Requirements for District of Columbia Superior Court

Second, you will need to research the law to determine (1) the legal causes of actions you will assert, and (2) the elements necessary to prove those causes of action. It will take some time and tactical care to determine which causes of action you will allege. For complicated cases, the causes of action can be numerous and tedious.

Third, the specific facts of the case are essential to determine if you can meet a particular cause of action. Therefore, you will need to investigate the facts before you draft your complaint. Depending on the type of case, factual investigation can include interviewing the client and potential witnesses, locating police reports, copying medical records, observing the client, and investigating the scene of an accident.

Once you are ready to draft your complaint, you should consider looking at complaints already filed by your firm or form complaints. While forms and samples are helpful, they are not end points for drafting a complaint or substitutes for researching the procedural requirements, law, or facts for your case. They should help only to determine the formal requirements of a complaint. Each complaint should be drafted for your particular client's situation as no case is exactly the same as another.

▦ ↪Form Complaint for Negligence Action

A complaint usually consists of the following elements:

- ↪**Caption**
- ↪**Commencement**
- ↪**Body or Charging Part**
- ↪**Prayer or Demand for Judgment**
- ↪**Signature and Verification**

Legal Documents — Complaint — Caption

The caption contains the name of the court and jurisdiction as well as the names of the parties. It also identifies the document as the complaint.

Caption Sample

SUPERIOR COURT FOR THE DISTRICT OF COLUMBIA CIVIL DIVISION

DAVID BRINK,	:	
Defendant	:	
v.	:	Civil Action No. _____
DR. ROBERT TAYLOR,	:	
Plaintiff	:	

COMPLAINT

Legal Documents — Complaint — Commencement

The commencement introduces the complaint, usually using some form of legalese. However, legalese is not necessary.

Commencement Samples

- Now comes David Brink by his attorney, Diana Donahoe, and herein alleges:
- Comes now plaintiff, David Brink, by his attorney, Diana Donahoe
- Comes now plaintiff, David Brink, for cause of actions allege and complaint against Dr. Robert Taylor, herein alleges:
- Plaintiff, David Brink, makes the following allegations against Defendant, Robert Taylor

---

Legal Documents — Complaint — Body or Charging Part

This is the meat of the complaint and is comprised of numbered paragraphs. Some courts require immediate allegations of jurisdiction; for example, if filing in federal court, you must allege subject matter jurisdiction, personal jurisdiction, and venue. Afterwards, the initial paragraphs often state the parties' names and addresses. The following paragraphs give notice of the legal causes of action and allege each element of those actions. You may organize these allegations by "counts," by providing headings for Count I, Count II, etc. While you need to allege sufficient facts to support those allegations, you need not include all of your evidence. Tactical considerations come into play here as you decide how much of your case you want to display. At the least, you need enough to survive a motion to dismiss. If you are requesting a jury trial, some jurisdictions require that the jury demand be made in the charging portion of the complaint or in a separate section labeled "jury demand." The last paragraphs of a complaint usually describe the plaintiff's injuries and damages.

Body or Charging Portion

- 1. David Brink, the plaintiff, an eighteen-year-old, resides at 2211 North Capital St., N.W., Washington, D.C. 20001.
- 2. Dr. Robert Taylor, the defendant, an adult, resides at 432 Nebraska Ave., N.W., Washington, D.C., 20003.
- 3. On or about August 8, 2000, the vehicle operated by the defendant, Dr. Robert Taylor, struck the vehicle owned and operated by the plaintiff, David Brink.
- 4. The defendant, Robert Taylor, was operating the vehicle in a negligent and careless manner in violation of traffic laws then and there in full force.
- 5. As a direct cause and proximate cause of the negligence, the defendant's vehicle collided with the plaintiff's vehicle.

Legal Documents — Complaint — Prayer or Demand for Judgment

Here, the plaintiff lists the relief requested, such as specific performance, special damages, punitive damages, and equitable relief. The demand for judgment is not numbered; it usually begins with "WHEREFORE" and ends with a catchall phrase requesting all other relief appropriate. You may place the demand for judgment at the end of the complaint or at the end of each cause of action if different relief is appropriate for different counts. In some courts, specific amounts must be pleaded, while in others, specific amounts may not be pleaded. Again, be sure to check your local rules.

Prayer or Demand for Judgment

♦ WHEREFORE, the plaintiff demands judgment against the defendant in the sum of five hundred thousand dollars. ($500,000)
♦ WHEREFORE, the plaintiff requests that this court:
  o   declare the defendant in breach of contract;
  o   award the plaintiff damages plus interest;
  o   award the plaintiff costs and attorneys' fees;
  o   award the plaintiff any other relief the court deems appropriate.

Legal Documents — Complaint — Signature and Verification

The attorney's signature, bar number, and address are required at the end of the complaint. (If the plaintiff is filing *pro se*, he must sign his own name and provide an address.) Your signature states you have read the document and believe it is not a frivolous claim. Federal rules and some state rules require verification of the complaint by the party or an affidavit accompanying the complaint. In the verification clause, the party swears under oath that the allegations are believed to be true.

Signature Sample

By: _____

    Diana R. Donahoe Bar # 111-111
    Donahoe & Associates, L.L.P.
    600 New Jersey Ave., N.W.
    Washington, D.C. 20001

Attorney for Plaintiff

Verification Sample

On March 30, 2003, David Brink, being duly sworn, claims he is the plaintiff in the above action and that the facts set forth above are true except for those statements made upon information and belief, which he believes to be true.

_____
Plaintiff's signature   date

_____
Notary's signature   date

Legal Documents — Answers

Purpose: The answer responds to the complaint by indicating whether the defendant admits, denies, or is unable to answer each allegation.

Audience: The answer is written for the plaintiff, but its primary audience is the plaintiff's attorney and the court.

Scope: The scope of the answer is related to the scope of the complaint as the answer must admit or deny each of the plaintiff's allegations.

View: An answer is a formal document. It usually follows the numbered paragraphs in the complaint and adds additional numbered paragraphs for affirmative defenses and counterclaims.

⬛ ➥**Sample Answer**

Legal Documents — Formal Requirements of an Answer

An answer responds to the complaint by indicating which of the plaintiff's allegations the defendant admits, denies, or is unable to answer due to insufficient information. An answer also raises affirmative defenses and possible counterclaims. You should consult the rules in your jurisdiction for affirmative defenses as well as for procedural filing requirements.

⬛ ➥**Sample Requirements for Filing Answers in District of Columbia Superior Court**

An answer usually contains the following elements:

- Caption and Introductory Sentence
- Admissions in Answer
- Denials in Answer
- Affirmative Defenses
- Affirmative Claims and Demands for Judgment
- Signature and Verification

Legal Documents — Answers — Caption and Introductory Sentence

The caption is identical to the one in the complaint except that it is labeled "Answer." An introductory sentence can be used before the answer.

Caption Sample

SUPERIOR COURT FOR THE DISTRICT OF COLUMBIA CIVIL DIVISION

DAVID BRINK,   :

    Defendant   :

    v.   :   Civil Action No. _____

DR. ROBERT TAYLOR,   :

    Plaintiff   :

<u>Answer</u>

In response to the plaintiff's allegations, defendant states the following:

Legal Documents — Answer — Admissions in Answer

Some rules require defendants to admit portions of the complaint that are true so that the attorneys are acting in good faith. In addition, by admitting portions of the complaint, the defendants help to narrow the issues. You can admit specific paragraphs individually, group admissions together, or admit only parts of paragraphs.

Admissions in Answer Samples

- Defendant admits allegations in paragraph 1.
- Defendant admits allegations in paragraph 2.
- Defendant admits allegations in paragraphs 3, 5, 7, and 10.
- Defendant admits that she owned and operated a vehicle on September 21, 2000, but denies that she was operating it negligently.

Legal Documents — Answer — Denials in Answer

The defendant may make a general denial, which denies the whole complaint, or a special denial, which denies only certain paragraphs or parts of paragraphs. In addition, the defendant may state that there is insufficient evidence to deny or admit certain parts of a complaint, which, in effect, acts as a denial.

Denials in Answer Samples

- ◆ Sample General Denial:
  - • The defendant denies each allegation in the plaintiff's complaint.
- ◆ Sample Special Denial:
  - • The defendant denies paragraph 1.
  - • The defendant denies paragraph 2.
  - • The defendant denies the allegations in paragraphs 11, 12, 14-21, and 23.
  - • The defendant denies the allegations in paragraph 5 except to state that he does own a 1999 Honda Accord.
  - • The defendant is without sufficient information to admit or deny the allegations in paragraph 15.

Legal Documents — Answer — Affirmative Defenses

Some jurisdictions require certain affirmative defenses to be raised in an answer or they are waived. For example, the federal rules require the following affirmative defenses to be raised in an answer: lack of personal jurisdiction, improper venue, insufficient process or insufficient service. When writing affirmative defenses, you can separate them by headings or by count.

Affirmative Defenses Samples

- • The complaint fails to state a cause of action upon which relief can be granted.
- • First Affirmative Defense: The plaintiff's claims are barred for lack of personal jurisdiction.
- • Affirmative Defenses to Count II: The plaintiff's claims are barred by his assumption of the risk.

Legal Documents — Answer — Affirmative Claims and Demands for Judgment

Counterclaims, cross-claims, and third-party claims are made in the same form as the ➥**complaint**, using numbered paragraphs with separate headings to label each claim. If a defendant alleges a claim, he should also include a demand for judgment.

Legal Documents — Answer — Signature and Verification

Similar to the complaint, a signature and verification are usually required in an answer.

Signature and Verification Samples

By: _____

Diana R. Donahoe Bar # 111-111
Donahoe & Associates, L.L.P.
600 New Jersey Ave., N.W.
Washington, D.C. 20001

Attorney for Defendant

On March 30, 2003, Robert Taylor, being duly sworn, claims he is the defendant in the above action and that the facts set forth above are true except for those statements made upon information and belief, which he believes to be true.

_____
Defendant's signature   date

_____
Notary's signature   date

Legal Documents — Interrogatories

Purpose: Interrogatories are used in the discovery process to ask questions of the other side. They should not be used to overwhelm opposing counsel or to overload the litigation process.

Audience: Interrogatories are written for a layperson and a lawyer. Typically, the lawyer will ask the layperson, or client, to answer the interrogatories. Then, the lawyer will review the interrogatories and the answers with the client.

Scope: Many jurisdictions limit the amount of interrogatories permitted. While some jurisdictions impose number limits, others prohibit certain types of interrogatories, such as those that cause "annoyance, embarrassment, oppression, or undue burden or expense."

View: Interrogatories should be written clearly and precisely. They are numbered and often arranged by subject matter.

Legal Documents — *Formal Requirements of an Interrogatory*

Interrogatories are the questions posed by one party to another during the discovery process. They are usually used early in the litigation process to begin discovery and to prepare for depositions. However, they can also be used to fill in gaps from depositions or obtain information later in the process. Interrogatories are served on opposing counsel and also filed with the court. They must be answered within a prescribed amount of time, depending on your jurisdiction's procedural rules.

Before you begin drafting interrogatories, you should research the procedural rules controlling interrogatories in your jurisdiction as well as the substantive law on the legal issues involved. First, the procedural rules will notify you of any limits on number or types of interrogatories permitted. For example, the Federal Rules of Civil Procedure permit only 25 interrogatories, see ➡**Fed. R. Civ. P. 33**, while the trial court in the District of Columbia limits parties to 40 interrogatories, including subparts. See

➥**Super. Ct. Civ. R. 33**. The procedural rules also control answering interrogatories, such as format, filing, and objecting to certain questions. Second, the substantive law will help you draft your interrogatories to gain factual information regarding the elements of the cause of action and possible defenses.

When drafting interrogatories, you may review forms or previously filed interrogatories. However, because each case is factually different, you should draft interrogatories for your specific case.

Interrogatories usually contain the following elements:

- ➥**Preface**
- ➥**Definitions**
- ➥**Preliminary Questions**
- ➥**Substantive Questions**
- ➥**Concluding Questions**

Legal Documents — Interrogatories — Preface

The preface usually serves as the instructions for the interrogatories; it often states the duties of the parties, the time limit for answering, and the rule under which the interrogatories are propounded.

Preface Samples

- ◆ These interrogatories are propounded under Rule 33 of the Federal Rules of Civil Procedure. You must answer them, under oath, within thirty days.
- ◆ You are requested to answer the following interrogatories pursuant to Superior Court Rule 33. These interrogatories are continuing in nature so as to require you to file supplemental answers if you obtain further or different information before trial.

Legal Documents — Interrogatories — Definitions

A definition section in a set of interrogatories helps to clearly identify certain terms so that there can be no confusion later in litigation. This section, while often written last, usually appears toward the beginning of the interrogatories.

Definitions Samples

- ◆ "You" refers to the Defendant to whom these interrogatories are addressed as well as your predecessors and successors, attorneys, and all others acting or purporting to act on the behalf of the Defendant.
- ◆ "Person" refers to any individual, association, partnership, corporation, governmental entity, or business entity.

Legal Documents — Interrogatories — Preliminary Questions

These questions usually ask for background information about the parties. Depending on your jurisdiction, they may not count as one of the permitted interrogatories. However, if they are part of the limit, you will want to keep these types of questions to a minimum.

Preliminary Questions Samples

◆   1. State your full name, age, address, marital status, social security number, and date of birth.

◆   2. State all places of residence for the past five years, including addresses and dates.

◆   3. By whom were you employed, and what were your duties and wages, at the time of the occurrence?

Legal Documents — Interrogatories — Substantive Questions

These questions are the meat of the interrogatories and provide the factual information you will need for litigation. The questions may be general or specific. Consider organizing your interrogatories based on subject matter and remember to number them.

Substantive Questions Samples

◆   General Questions:
  •   14. Give a concise statement of the facts as to how you contend that the occurrence took place.
  •   21. Describe your injuries.
◆   Specific Questions:
  •   21. List the dates you were able to do the following for the first time after your injury: 1. move your leg; 2. put pressure on your leg; 3. walk with a cane; 4. walk on your own; 5. participate in sports (please list specific sports).

Legal Documents — Interrogatories — Concluding Questions

These questions are usually catch-all questions to ask for information regarding other people who might provide information or to ask for the party's narrative of the facts. If you are in a jurisdiction with limits on the number of interrogatories, you will use these types of interrogatories sparingly.

Concluding Questions Samples

•   36. Identify all documents related to this case.
•   37. Identify all persons with knowledge of this case.
•   38. State in detail your version of how the accident occurred.
•   List all relevant details you have obtained about the case from other sources.

Legal Documents — Motions

Motions are persuasive documents written at the trial level. They can be categorized as pretrial motions, trial motions, and post-trial motions. They are similar to appellate briefs in that they inform and persuade. However, unlike appellate briefs, motions raise issues as they arise in the litigation.

Purpose: A motion is a persuasive document that requests a trial court for certain relief. Therefore, a motion should inform and persuade. It should be written to win a particular issue. The best motions seem objective and reasonable, but are subtly persuasive so that the judge wants to rule for the client. The poorest motions attempt persuasion with incendiary language that either attacks the other side's position or develops a defensive posture. Motions should not be written to harangue opposing counsel, burden the court, or improperly delay litigation.

Audience: The trial judge is the primary audience for a motion. Therefore, the writing should conform to the legal standards of your jurisdiction. However, secondary audiences include opposing counsel, your client, the opposing client, and the public. Therefore, tactical considerations are also necessary.

Scope: Unlike appellate briefs, which usually cover multiple issues from the trial litigation, motions usually only address one particular issue for the court's consideration. Similar to appellate briefs, motions are often controlled by page limits set by each court's procedural rules.

View: Your motion should be subtly persuasive. It should contain a subtle theory of the case and persuade the judge to rule for you. Because many motions are filed pretrial, you must consider how much of your case to reveal in your motion. Tactical considerations are, therefore, essential.

➥**Sample Form Motion**

Legal Documents — Formal Requirements of a Motion

If you are involved in a motions practice, you will be writing motions as well as oppositions to motions. Both of these are similar in form and content. Before you begin to draft a motion or opposition, you should consult your jurisdiction's filing requirements. For example, some courts require a notice of motion and a motion, while others require a motion and a memorandum of points and authorities in support of (or in opposition to) the motion. In addition to format, these rules control the timing of filing, page limits, and requirements for gaining consent from opposing counsel for the motion before filing.

➥**Filing Requirements for Motions in District of Columbia Superior Court**

There are a variety of motions filed with trial courts. Some examples include the following:

Pretrial motions: motion for continuances, motion in limine, motion to suppress evidence, motion for summary judgment, motion to compel discovery

Trial motions: motion for judgment notwithstanding the verdict

Post-trial motions: motion for new trial, motion for remittitur

A typical trial court requires the following for any of these motions:

- A notice of the motion
- The motion itself (often called the memorandum of points and authorities)
- A certificate of service

- Perhaps an affidavit
- An order

NOTICE OF MOTION

While some courts simply term this document "the motion," it serves the purpose of putting the court and the other party on notice of a particular motion being filed with the court. Parts of the notice include the caption, the name and address of the opposing party who receives a copy of the motion, the body of the notice, the date, and your signature. The body of the notice should specify the relief sought.

⌨ ➙**Form Motion Points and Authorities**

THE MOTION (OR MEMORANDUM OF POINTS AND AUTHORITIES)

This is the document that provides the meat of your argument. It should contain the facts as well as the legal analysis to support your motion. Motions for a continuance are going to be short and contain no legal analysis; however, motions for summary judgment or other substantive motions will be filled with legal analysis and factual support. These types of motions are basically trial briefs and are very similar to appellate briefs, but without many of the formal requirements. The motion will start with a caption and end with a signature and address. In addition, it may petition the court for a hearing on the matter.

⌨ ➙**Form Motion Points and Authorities**

CERTIFICATE OF SERVICE

This sentence appears after the attorney's signature and certifies that the attorney has served a copy of the motion on opposing counsel. It can be served in person or by mail and should specify delivery.

⌨ ➙**Certificate of Service**

AFFIDAVIT

An affidavit is a sworn statement. It is often appendixed to motions to show factual support. It will begin with a caption and an introductory paragraph; the meat of the affidavit is written in numbered paragraphs and signed by the affiant.

⌨ ➙**Form Affidavit**

ORDER

The order is the actual document you are asking the court to sign. It should specify that the judge is granting (or denying) the motion and should have a signature and date line for the judge.

⌨ ➙**Form Order**

→**More Sample Forms from the Superior Court of the District of Columbia, Civil Division**

▣ Annotated Sample Pretrial Brief 1
▣ Annotated Sample Pretrial Brief 2

Legal Documents — Client Letters

Lawyers write a variety of letters including cover letters, demand letters, and letters to opposing counsel. This section focuses on letters written to clients. Client letters are written to provide the client with a legal opinion and advice. They should answer the client's questions in clear, concise, and easy-to-understand language. Client letters are similar in purpose to the →**memorandum of law** in that they provide objective analysis of a legal issue; they differ, however, in audience, scope, and view.

Purpose: A client letter informs the client of her options under the law. It provides answers to the client's questions and explains the reasoning for those answers. A letter to a client also provides a paper trail for the lawyer — oftentimes to memorialize the lawyer's opinion and the facts of the case at the time.

Audience: The client is the primary audience for this type of letter. However, clients can vary enormously in background, education, and knowledge. Therefore, keep in mind your particular audience for each letter; a letter written to a CEO of a large business will differ greatly from one written to an incarcerated drug offender. Your audience will determine if you use legal terms, discuss cases, provide citations, and reveal all of your research.

Scope: The client letter should answer the question whether to, and provide advice on how, the client should proceed. It should also clarify the limitations of the letter for the client; for example, it should inform the client that if the facts change, the lawyer's opinion might change as well. In addition, a lawyer should keep in mind clarity and costs when writing a client letter. A long letter might be too cumbersome to read and might indicate that the lawyer has spent a lot of money in its preparation.

View: The view of a client letter can vary greatly, depending on the audience. The reasoning may be cursory or in-depth; the tone can be conversational, friendly, or formal. However, client letters should always be professional; avoid slang and flippant remarks.

▣ →**Annotated Client Letter #1**
▣ →**Annotated Client Letter #2**

Legal Documents — Formal Requirements of a Client Letter

Before writing a client letter, you should gather the facts from your client, research the legal issue, and clarify the client's question. The requirements of a letter vary greatly depending on the audience, the particular purpose, and the scope of the letter. The traditional requirements, listed below, are similar to the formal requirements of a memorandum. However, you need not provide headings labeling each requirement.

- →**Date and Salutation**
- →**Opening Paragraph**
- →**Facts Section**
- →**Analysis Section**
- →**Closing**

Legal Documents — Client Letters — Date and Salutation

The **date** on the letter memorializes when you have given your opinion. If facts or law changes after that date, your opinion may no longer be valid. The **salutation** sets the tone of the letter; therefore, determine if you want to use a first name or a title and last name. When in doubt, choose formality over informality.

Legal Documents — Client Letters — Opening Paragraph

The opening paragraph usually provides the context for the letter and restates the issue. Oftentimes, it will provide an answer, especially if the answer is one the client would like to hear right away. This paragraph serves a function similar to the ↪**question presented** and ↪**brief answer** of a memorandum of law.

Sample Opening Paragraph

On November 12, 2004, we discussed the trial tactic of requesting a jury instruction of the lesser-included offense of voluntary manslaughter in your murder trial. As I explain below, I believe the trial judge will include a voluntary manslaughter instruction; however, I am not certain whether the jury will find you guilty of murder or voluntary manslaughter.

Legal Documents — Client Letters — Facts Section

The facts section provides background information as well as legally significant facts. This section should be written objectively. The facts may be based on documents you have reviewed, client or witness interviews, or your own investigation. Consider noting the source for some of your facts in complicated cases. In addition, ask the client to review the facts and make any necessary additions or corrections. The facts you present in your client letter memorialize those facts as of that date.

Sample Facts Section

I have based my opinion on the facts below. Please read them carefully and inform me of any changes, corrections, or additions as these might alter my legal opinion.

On September 13, 2004, you were riding in a rental car in Memphis, Tennessee ...

Legal Documents — Client Letters — Analysis Section

The analysis section of a client letter is similar to the ↪**discussion** section of a memorandum of law. It should be organized around the law itself with clear topic sentences and explanations for your conclusions. This section should be written objectively, providing counterarguments where appropriate so that the client understands both sides of the issue. This section differs from a discussion section in a memo in the form of the analysis. A client wants to understand how the law applies to her problem, but she might not want to know the details, citations, or intricacies of the law itself. Here, you must determine how much detail you will provide regarding the cases, statutory definitions, and policy behind the law. If you must use detailed case descriptions or legal terms of art, consider providing an explanation for the reader.

Analysis Section

- ◆ Organized around law itself
- ◆ Provides clear topic sentences and explanations for conclusions
- ◆ Objectively written
- ◆ Provides audience-tailored analysis
- ◆ Explains how the law applies to the client's issue

Legal Documents — Client Letters — Closing

The closing of a client letter is similar to the ➥**conclusion** of a memorandum of law. It provides a conclusion and your advice. Provide enough information so that your client understands the next steps she should take. In addition, consider mentioning other issues that might be pursued in the future.

Closing Sample

I believe the judge will grant our motion to include a jury instruction on self-defense; however, I am concerned about the jury's willingness to find you guilty of voluntary manslaughter as opposed to murder. Therefore, I suggest you come in at your earliest convenience to discuss the voluntary manslaughter instruction. The sooner we discuss this lesser-included offense, the easier it will be to prepare for trial. In addition, we might consider other lesser-included offenses that might apply to your situation. When you come in to meet with me, please bring the names and phone numbers of any witnesses to this accident.

⌷ ➥**Sample Annotated Client Letter**

Legal Documents — Scholarly Writing

While the other sections of this book address writing in legal practice, this section focuses on writing to criticize the law or propose new ideas within the legal scholarly community. Scholarly writing takes on many forms. Professors usually write law review articles; students often write seminar papers, law review notes, and law review competition papers.

Purpose: All forms of scholarly writing are written to provide a particular point of view. They usually criticize a particular body of law, specific case, or traditional principles. In addition, they should propose original ideas and novel theories. The best scholarly papers have clear thesis statements and consistently focus on those thesis statements. Most students struggle with focusing on a specific purpose and proposing novel ideas.

Audience: The primary audience is other scholars — law professors and students. However, oftentimes the secondary audience is the practicing lawyer and judge focusing on a particular issue as law review articles are often cited when judges create new law. Lawyers specializing in specific areas of practice are also familiar with scholarly articles on their subjects. The biggest mistake students make is assuming that the primary audience is the professor in the seminar course. While the professor is the actual audience, the student should assume the professor is reading the paper as a scholar in the field.

Scope: The scope of any scholarly paper should be narrow. The best papers remain focused on one specific thesis. The biggest mistake students make is to address multiple issues on a superficial basis instead of providing an in-depth analysis of one issue.

View: The point of view of the author is crucial in scholarly writing; the reader is expecting to hear what the author thinks and why. Therefore, the author's voice, personal opinions, and novel ideas are expected to be heard throughout the article. Use of the first person (e.g., I will address the following ideas ...) is expected.

Legal Documents — Seminar Papers and Law Review Notes

Seminar papers and law review notes are very similar. One is written as a requirement for a class; the other is written as a requirement for law review. Often, seminar papers are published as law review notes. Therefore, this section will focus on the process of creating either a seminar paper or law review note.

- Selecting a Topic
- Performing a Preemption Check
- Researching the Issue
- Writing and Rewriting a Scholarly Piece
- Cite-Checking
- Getting Published

➥ **Sample Law Review Article**

Legal Documents — Seminar Papers — Selecting a Topic

Selecting a topic is the most critical step in the seminar paper process. Be sure you set aside enough time for this decision.

First, the topic should be relevant to the seminar or to your law review (many law reviews address particular areas of law such as international environmental law or ethics). Often, professors provide lists of possible subject matters. However, don't rely solely on these lists to decide what interests you most; instead, look at the readings, consider the discussions in class, and follow the news. Helpful sources for legal news and current trends include The United States Law Week, and the new developments sections of Westlaw and Lexis. Choose a topic that will keep you interested; writing about a boring subject makes for boring writing.

Second, the topic should be narrow; it should focus on a specific issue — not just a broad area of law. Write an issue statement to focus your topic on a particular question within your field.

Third, try to answer that issue statement. In doing so, you will create your proposed thesis for the paper. That thesis might change as you start researching and writing, but it will help you focus at this stage of the process.

Fourth, be sure your issue is novel. The purpose of a scholarly paper is not to summarize the law on a particular issue, but to create original ideas about that issue. Therefore, your paper will need to say something different from other papers. Your topic can, therefore, be on a totally new issue or it can be a different spin on an old issue.

Selecting a Topic

- Generally relevant to field of law in seminar or law review
- Narrowed to a specific issue within that field
- Proposed thesis
- Provide creative, novel ideas

Legal Documents — Seminar Papers — Performing a Preemption Check

Because your paper is expected to propose novel ideas, you must check to make sure that no one else has written on the same subject with the same issue and thesis. Therefore, you will need to do a preemption check — a search through other law reviews and journal literature to determine what has been written on your subject. As you perform your preemption check, take note of helpful articles that might help in your future research.

To perform a preemption check, search the indexes and databases of ➥**law review articles.**

Preemption Check

The search of other scholarly writing to ensure that no one has written on your particular issue and thesis.

Legal Documents — Seminar Papers — Researching the Issue

Scholarly research has two phases: background research and specific issue research. First, you want to understand the general field of law you have chosen to write about. You need to know where your topic fits into the broader picture. Therefore, consider a secondary source, such as a ➥**treatise or hornbook.** ➥**Law review articles** and ➥**looseleafs** can also prove helpful to educate yourself at this stage of the process. As you read, take notes of citations throughout the readings that you think might prove useful.

Second, you want to narrow your research to articles and primary law that focus directly on your thesis. Your starting point for this research can be your list of relevant citations you found doing your background research. It is at this point in the process that you will begin to take notes on the substance of the topic. Of course, you are bound to find more articles cited within these sources. Be sure to research current articles first; these will help you find some of the older sources as well as provide recent ideas on the topic. In addition, consider asking other scholars in the field. Often the professor of the seminar is the best research source.

Researching the Issue

Background Research
- Hornbooks and treatises
- Law review articles

Specific Research
- Take notes
- Find citations within articles
- Stay current
- Ask your professor

Legal Documents — Seminar Papers — Writing and Rewriting a Scholarly Piece

The same techniques described in ➥**Writing and Rewriting** apply for scholarly writing. Your article should be well organized, thoroughly analyzed, and concise.

When writing the scholarly article, provide the following:

An **introduction** that gives some context for the topic and specifically tells the reader where the paper will lead. Typically, roadmaps are included at the end of the introduction section and are written in the first person: I will first address …; Next, I will discuss …; Finally, I will propose new ideas ….

A section of the article that informs the reader of the **current state of the law** in that topic. Most readers need some background information before they can appreciate your new ideas on your topic.

A section where you propose **novel ideas and areas of reform**. Here is where your original thought should shine. Creativity, thoughtfulness, and logical analysis are the ingredients to good writing in this section.

Provide a **conclusion** so that the reader can understand a summary of your thesis. Make sure your thesis is consistent here with the introduction.

When rewriting the scholarly article, consider the following:

Purpose: Have you provided a clear, focused thesis? Is your thesis consistent throughout your article?

Audience: Have you addressed a particular audience for this paper? Who is that audience? Have you answered the audience's concerns? Be sure that you have not tried to address multiple audiences; this problem often leads to a paper that is not focused.

Scope: What was your particular thesis? Have you gone beyond the scope of that thesis? On the flip side, have you provided enough depth to address your issue and prove your thesis?

View: Your point of view should shine throughout your article. Your voice, opinions, and theories should stand out and be heard.

Writing and Rewriting a Scholarly Paper

Writing

- Introduction with context and roadmap
- Current state of law
- Novel ideas and theories
- Conclusion

Rewriting

- Audience
- Purpose
- Scope
- View

Legal Documents — Seminar Papers — Cite-Checking

Cite-checking is a two-part process. First, you need to check the substance of your citations. Does each article you cite really say what you purport it to say? You must find each source and read it to perform this part of the cite-check. Second, you need to make sure that the citation format is correct. If you are using Bluebook format, refer to the front inside cover of the Bluebook where you will find a quick summary of law review article citation. If you are using ALWD format, see ALWD Rule 23 and the Fast Formats section under that rule. Remember that the Bluebook rules are written primarily for law review articles; the practitioner's notes (the Bluepages in the beginning of the Bluebook) modify the rules for legal documents filed in court and legal memoranda. Be careful, though: Most first-year students are taught citation as practitioners, not as cite-checkers for law reviews. Therefore, consult the rules of the Bluebook or ALWD as you cite-check.

Cite-Checking

Substantive Cite-Checking

- Look up each citation
- Read each source
- Determine if substance is correct: Does it say what you purport it to say?

Cite-Checking for Format

- Make sure each citation is in proper Bluebook or ALWD format.
- Format should be for law review articles.
- Refer to the Bluebook's inside front cover for a quick reference guide or to ALWD's Rule 23 Fast Formats.

Legal Documents — Seminar Papers — Getting Published

Be sure your paper is in the best possible shape before you submit it to a publisher. Have other colleagues read it and discuss it with you before submission.

If you have written a seminar paper, you should consider trying to publish your paper. Although it might seem like an unnecessary "hassle" to you as a busy student, it will be well worth your time in the future. If you have written a law review note, you will submit it to your law review. The law review editors will then decide whether it is a note that is worthy of publication in the journal. If your law review decides not to publish it, consider sending it to other journals.

Here's how to publish your note or paper:

Find appropriate law journals: To publish a note or seminar paper, first create a list of appropriate law reviews — journals that publish articles on your topic. Your seminar professor will have some good ideas for appropriate journals. There are directories of law journals that you can consult as well: Directory of Law Reviews, Current Law Index, and Index to Legal Periodicals and Books.

Consider timing: General folklore suggests that you should avoid sending out articles (unless they are time sensitive) from October through February. Because most editorial boards start in March, that is usually a good month to submit articles. And because August is the month that editorial boards come back from summer break, August and early September are also good times to submit articles.

Write a cover letter: The purpose of the cover letter is to make the editor interested in your article. Therefore, provide a concise summary of the paper and show why it is novel and important in the field. A one-page cover letter should be sufficient.

Getting Published

- Find appropriate law journals
- Consider timing
- Write a cover letter

Legal Documents — Law Review Write-On Competition Papers Notes

To join a law review, all first-year students are invited to participate in a "write-on competition." The competition, which usually occurs at the end of the first year or during spring break, requires students to write a paper during a limited amount of time. The students receive (or purchase) a closed-packet of materials (no outside research is required), and the instructions in the packet lay out the rules and issues for the competition. Usually, students are required to write a "case note" for the competition.

- ➥ **Should I Participate?**
- ➥ **What Is a Case Note?**
- ➥ **Writing a Case Note**
- ➥ **Citation**

Legal Documents — Write-On Competition — Should I Participate?

When deciding whether to participate in the write-on competition, you should ask yourself:

1. Do I want to join a law review (also called a journal)?
2. Do I want to write the competition paper?

First, you should consider whether you want to join a law review. Typically, second-year students spend time on their law reviews cite-checking other author's articles and notes to make sure they are substantively correct (i.e., the source actually says what the author claims) and in the correct citation format (most schools still use the Bluebook for this task; others use ALWD). During your third year in law school, you might become an editor on your law review, editing the substance of the article as opposed to the citations. In addition, you might write your own note for publication in your law review. While the law review experience is not always glamorous, it will help you improve your writing and editing skills. In addition, many judges prefer that their clerks have law review experience.

Even if you do not want to join a journal or if you are undecided, you still might want to participate in the write-on competition. The experience of writing a scholarly paper is worthwhile. It will force you to critically analyze a particular legal subject and help improve your writing process. If you plan to take a writing seminar during your second or third year in law school, the writing competition will provide a transition from the first-year practical writing course to upper-class scholarly seminar papers. In addition, the challenge of writing a concise paper in an abbreviated amount of time, while daunting, is extremely rewarding when accomplished.

If you decide not to participate in the write-on competition, make sure you have a good reason. That reason should never be that you do not think you will qualify for a law review or that you are not a good enough writer.

Should I Participate?

◆ Do I want to join a law review?
- o Second-year students on law review edit citation
- o Third-year students on law review edit text and write notes
- o Judge's often prefer law review members for clerkships

◆ Do I want to write the paper?
- o The writing experience
- o Transitioning from practical to scholarly writing

Legal Documents — Write-On Competition — What Is a Case Note?

A case note, or case comment, is a critique of a judicial opinion. Typically, the write-on packet will contain the opinion as well as background information on the legal issue. The author of a case note will comment on the court's decision and its reasoning. The author can agree, disagree, or both (agree on one part and disagree on another). However, a good case note should not simply repeat the court's (or the dissent's) reasoning; instead, it should go beyond the opinion itself using the background materials and novel ideas to present clear, logical legal reasoning to show why the court was correct or incorrect.

A Case Note or Case Comment

- A critique of a judicial opinion
- Agrees, disagrees, or both with decision
- Uses clear, logical reasoning to show why court was correct or incorrect
- Goes beyond the text of the court's opinion and dissent

Legal Documents — Write-On Competition — Writing the Case Note

Writing a case note is similar to the process of writing any legal document. You should research the issue, take a stance on the issue, write a first draft, rewrite, and then polish.

Research: The good news is that usually in a write-on competition no outside research is permitted. Instead, all you need to do is read the materials provided in the packet. However, this reading may take some time, and you should consider reading the packet through once for an overview before you read it over and over to take notes and become familiar with the material.

Take a stance: You need to decide on your stance. Will you agree with the court or disagree (or both)? Try not to spend too much time deciding on your stance as the law review judges do not care which way you come out on the issue; instead, they are judging you on your reasoning and how you prove your stance.

Write a first draft: Write a draft as soon as possible. You want to save as much time as possible for rewriting and editing. If you have organizational problems, consider creating an outline before you begin drafting. Remember to consider audience (upper-class students on law review), purpose (to critique an opinion), scope (stick to issue and page limit), and stance (let your voice be heard).

Rewrite: You want to spend as much time as possible on rewriting. Here, you should refer to the ➥**Writing and Rewriting** section of this ebook to review ➥**Large-Scale Organization**, ➥**Analysis**, and ➥**Conciseness**.

Polish: You will also need to spend an enormous amount of time on your polishing—especially citation. While your grammar should be excellent, your citation needs to be perfect. See the next page for more information on law review citation.

Writing the Case Note

- Research by reading the packet numerous times
- Take a stance
- Write a first draft
    - Purpose (to critique)
    - Audience (upper-class student judges)
    - Scope (issue and page limit)
    - Stance (your point of view)
- Rewrite
    - Large-scale organization
    - Analysis
    - Conciseness
- Polish—especially for citation

Legal Documents—Write-On Competition—Citation

Proper citation is one of the most important pieces in the write-on competition because most law reviews require their members to "Bluebook" as their first assignments. Therefore, the judges want you to prove that you can properly cite to authority. Here are a few tips:

1. **Provide citations for scholarly writing.** In your first-year class, you most likely learned to cite in legal documents. Now, you need to shift gears and provide citations for law reviews. This shift is not very difficult; follow all the same rules but without the practitioner's notes.

2. **Use the inside front cover of the Bluebook.** The inside cover page of the Bluebook provides a quick summary for law review citation. In your first-year class, you probably referred to the back inside cover of the Bluebook, which summarizes citation style for legal documents. For law review citation style, refer to the Bluebook's inside cover page.

3. **Cite to all authority in footnotes or endnotes.** In your first-year class, you probably cited to authority right in the text. For law review articles, you need to provide the citations in the endnotes or footnotes (look at the packet rules). Remember to cite to authority whenever you write a legal proposition, quote, or paraphrase. Cite to authority often in law review articles.

4. Use basic citation as well as complicated citations. You should prove that you can follow basic citation rules perfectly. In addition, you should provide some complicated citations so that the judges will recognize your ability to succeed when Bluebooking complicated citations.

Citation

- ◆ Provide citation for scholarly writing
- ◆ Use the inside front cover of the Bluebook
- ◆ Cite to all authority in footnotes or endnotes
- ◆ Use basic citations as well as complicated citations

Legal Documents — Quick Reference — Memo Format

HEADING

A legal memo, like any other memo, should have a heading with lines for sender, recipient, date, and subject. However, the subject line should contain more than just the client name and file number; it should also include a brief description of the specific issue discussed in the memo.

QUESTION PRESENTED

The question presented is one sentence that provides the reader with a quick summary of the issue addressed by the memo. It should include three major elements:

1. *Jurisdiction:* A question presented should include a brief statement of the jurisdiction and applicable law. A statement such as "under New Jersey law" may be sufficient, but the statement can be more specific, such as "under New Jersey common law" if the author deems it necessary. Reference to a specific code provision or case name is usually too specific, unless it is well known and conveys meaning, such as "Roe v. Wade."
2. *Legal issue:* The legal issue presented defines the legal scope of the memo. For example, "Did Mr. Jones assault Mr. Smith?" or "Can Ms. Brown prove libel?"
3. *Legally significant facts:* The legally significant facts are the facts that apply to the client that will most likely affect the outcome of this particular issue. Here, the writer needs to choose only those facts that are most significant so that the sentence is readable. The writer should also be careful to include facts from both sides of the argument to present the most objective view to the reader.

The basic format of a question is as follows:

Under [jurisdiction], did/can/will [legal issue] when [legally significant facts]?

BRIEF ANSWER

The brief answer quickly answers the question presented with a simple "yes," "no," "probably," or "probably not." Next, using no more than a few sentences, the brief answer uses the terms of art from the applicable law to answer the question presented. A repetition of facts stated in the question presented is not necessary, nor are citations.

STATEMENT OF FACTS

The statement of facts presents the facts to the reader in a clear, concise, and objective manner. Only legally significant facts and background facts are necessary in a memo fact section. If a particular fact is not referred to later in the memo, it probably isn't necessary to put it in the statement of facts unless it is important background information. In this section, the writer should avoid argument and persuasive tactics.

DISCUSSION

The discussion section is the meat of the memo. Here, the writer presents the law and applies it to the client's situation. Legal analysis is required, as is citation to all authority so that the lawyer can refer to the actual law. This section should be well organized, clearly analyzed, and concisely written.

CONCLUSION

The conclusion answers the particular question, but with more detail than the brief answer. An effective conclusion usually breaks down the component parts of the law and uses specific client facts to show why that element of the law is either favorable or unfavorable for the client. A busy reader should be able to read your question presented, brief answer, and conclusion to have a complete summary of the issue, the law, and the effect on the client.

Legal Documents — Quick Reference — Brief Format

The following are the possible formal elements of an appellate brief. Not all courts require all these elements. You should always consult the rules in your jurisdiction before beginning to write an appellate brief. These rules not only require specific elements of a brief, but they also dictate page, font, and filing requirements.

TITLE PAGE

Because a brief is filed in a court, it needs identification. Therefore, the title page contains the name of the court itself, the name of the case, the docket number and judge's name (if available), the type of brief, and the names and addresses of counsel.

TABLE OF CONTENTS

This page refers the reader to page numbers for certain sections. Usually page 1 begins with the statement of the issue presented for review and the previous pages, including the table of contents, referenced as i, ii, iii, etc. Pointheadings are specifically referenced in the table of contents; if they are effectively written, they allow the reader to understand your organization from a quick glance at the table of contents. Pointheadings are essentially thesis statements for each part of the argument, using a mixture of law and facts to persuasively inform the reader of your client's point of view.

TABLE OF AUTHORITIES

This page alphabetically lists the legal authority cited within the brief with references to page numbers. The most heavily relied-on law should be cited with an * asterisk. Various types of legal authority (e.g., constitutions, cases, statutes, regulations) are often separated when listed.

JURISDICTION

Not all courts require a jurisdiction section. When one is required, this section briefly states the jurisdictional basis for appeal by providing relevant facts and a specific legal foundation.

STANDARD OF REVIEW

In appellate cases, the court must apply a certain standard of review over the trial court, which is similar to the burden of proof in trial cases. Standard of review essentially has to do with how much deference the appellate court will give to the trial court. For questions of fact, the very deferential "clearly erroneous" standard applies. For questions of law, the nondeferential "de novo" standard applies. For mixed questions of law and fact, the middle-ground "abuse of discretion" standard applies. Briefs should include a statement of the applicable standard of review.

STATEMENT OF THE ISSUE PRESENTED FOR REVIEW

This is similar to the question presented section of a memo, but it should not include a jurisdictional statement, as this is provided elsewhere. The issue statement in a brief should be written persuasively, and the answer should be implicit. A brief may include several issue statements if it deals with several issues.

STATEMENT OF FACTS

The statement of facts presents the facts to the reader in a clear, concise, and persuasive manner. Legally significant facts, background facts, and emotional facts are necessary in a brief's fact section. This section is a significant opportunity for the writer to tell the story in such a way that allows the reader to see the client's perspective. The writer should be persuasive, developing and working in a subtle theory of the case. The writer should not avoid facts that are harmful to the case, but, instead, should downplay or distinguish them.

SUMMARY OF THE ARGUMENT

The summary of the argument briefly summarizes the main legal points of the document, using key facts from the client's case. However, in a brief, this section is persuasive and designed to give a compelling overview for the very busy reader. This section may or may not include citations.

ARGUMENT

The argument section is the meat of the brief, complete with pointheadings and subheadings. Here, the writer presents the law and applies it to the client's situation in a persuasive manner, applying the theory of the case and other persuasive techniques to the writing. The theory of the case should be woven throughout the argument, and this section should be well organized, clearly analyzed, and concisely written.

CONCLUSION

The conclusion in a brief differs from that in a memo. In a brief, the conclusion simply states the relief requested, usually in one sentence. It does not summarize the argument.

   Example: For the aforementioned reasons, this Court should reverse the trial court and remand for new trial.

SIGNATURE AND CERTIFICATE OF SERVICE

The attorney's signature, name, bar number, and address are required at the end of every brief. In addition, the court requires a short statement indicating that the writer has provided a copy of the brief to opposing counsel, indicating whether service was hand-delivered or mailed. An attorney's signature is required after the certificate of service as well.

Legal Documents—Quick Reference—Client Letters vs. Memos vs. Briefs

Formal Elements:

Client Letter (Objective)	**Memo** (Objective)	**Brief** (Persuasive)
▶ *Date and Salutation:*	*Heading:*	*Title Page:*
Memorializes date on which your opinion is given and sets tone for the letter.	Includes lines for sender, recipient, date, and subject. In addition to the client name and file number, the subject line should also include a brief description of the specific issue discussed in the memo.	Serves as a means of identification; contains the name of the court, the name of the case, the docket number and judge's name (if available), the type of brief, and the names and addresses of counsel.
▶		*Table of Contents:*
		Refers the reader to page numbers for each section of the brief. Includes individual pointheadings and subheadings from argument section, forming an outline of the author's argument.
▶		*Table of Authorities:*
		Lists, in alphabetical order, each legal authority cited within the brief, with references to page numbers. Different types of legal authorities (e.g., constitutions, cases, statutes, regulations) are cited separately.
▶		*Jurisdiction:*
		When required, this section consists of a brief statement of the jurisdictional basis for appeal, including relevant facts and a specific legal foundation.

		Standard of Review:
		Dictates the level of deference given to the trial court. Questions of fact are reviewed under the deferential clearly erroneous standard, while questions of law are subjected to nondeferential de novo review.
Opening Paragraph:	**Question Presented:**	**Statement of the Issue:**
Provides context for the client, restates the legal issue presented, and often offers a brief statement summarizing the author's conclusion (similar to the brief answer in a legal memo).	Provides the reader with a brief summary of the issue addressed in the memo. It contains three elements: **1)** Jurisdiction: consists of a brief statement of the jurisdiction and applicable law (e.g., "Under New Jersey law"). **2)** Legal issue: defines the scope of the memo (e.g., "Did Mr. Jones assault Mr. Smith?"). **3)** Legally significant facts: these include those facts (and only those facts) that are most likely to affect the outcome of the legal issue presented. As a legal memo is an objective document, facts from both sides should be included.	Provides the reader with a brief summary of the issue(s) addressed in the brief. An issue statement in a brief does not contain a jurisdictional component; jurisdiction is addressed elsewhere in the document. Issue statements contained in briefs are written persuasively, implying a specific answer or conclusion.
	Brief Answer:	**Pointheadings and Subheadings:**
	Provides a short response to the question presented (e.g., yes, no, probably, probably not), followed by a short explanation, employing applicable legal terms of art to support the answer. It is unnecessary to include citations or to repeat facts included in the question presented.	The pointheadings and subheadings, when read together, provide the arguments supporting the answer to the issue statement.

▶		Summary of Argument:
		Provides a short, persuasive statement of the main legal points advanced by the argument, including any legally significant facts.

▶ Analysis Section:	Discussion:	Argument:
Should be organized around the law itself and provide the client with an understanding of how the law applies to the facts of her particular case. Citations, statutory definitions, and substantial analyses of prior case law are usually unnecessary for this audience. Should be written objectively.	The meat of the memo; here the author presents the law and applies it to the facts of her client's case in an objective manner. Citation to legal authorities is required. Large-scale organization (e.g., roadmaps, subheadings, topic sentences, and mini-conclusions), conciseness, and clear legal analysis are particularly important in this section.	Here the author presents the law and applies it to the facts of her client's case in a persuasive manner, providing legal support for the theory of the case established in the statement of the facts. Pointheadings and subheadings should be included to structure the presentation of significant legal points. As with the discussion section of a legal memo, large-scale organization, conciseness, and clear legal analysis are important.

▶ Closing:	Conclusion:	Conclusion:
	Provides a more detailed response to the question presented than the brief answer; breaks the law into separate elements and uses specific facts to illustrate why each element of the law either favors or does not favor the client.	Does not summarize the argument. Unlike a conclusion in a legal memo, a conclusion contained in a brief simply states the relief requested, usually in one sentence.

▶		Signature and Certificate of Service:
		Required at the end of every brief; includes the attorney's name, bar number, address, signature, and a short statement indicating that the document has been served on opposing counsel.

Functional aspects:

▶	**_Client Letter_** (objective)	**_Memo_** (objective)	**_Brief_** (persuasive)
Purpose	Should inform the client of what the law is and how it applies to the facts of her particular case; provides a paper trail for the lawyer.	Should inform the supervising attorney of what the law is and *objectively* analyze how it applies to the client's case.	Should inform and *persuade*, showing both sides of an issue while subtly framing both the issue and the analysis in the way that most benefits the client.
Audience	The client; letters should be tailored to the background, education, and knowledge of each client.	Supervising attorney. Proper Bluebook format is necessary, contractions are inappropriate, and legalese should be avoided.	The appellate judge (or panel of judges). Secondary audience includes opposing counsel, your client, and the public.
Scope	Should advise the client on how to proceed; limitations should be clarified, as changes in facts can alter legal conclusions.	Should focus on the particular issue the attorney is asked to address. Stick to the issue!	Should focus on errors committed by the trial court; appellate courts review only issues raised at the trial level. Brief must conform to court-imposed page limit.
View	Varies according to audience; letters should always be professional and avoid flippant remarks.	Tone is generally very formal; the author should avoid accusatory or condescending language.	Tone is generally very formal; author should persuade by incorporating theory of the case throughout the document.

Legal Documents — Quick Reference — Oral Argument

What Is Oral Argument? An oral argument is more of a conversation with the court than a speech. It is an opportunity for the judges to ask questions of each side to clarify the significant points of law, and it is an opportunity for counsel to stress the important aspects of the case and persuade the court. A judge may often use her questions as a way to convince the other judges of her position, or she may ask antagonistic and challenging questions to draw out the weaknesses in the attorney's case. Successful attorneys at oral argument are good listeners, respond well to questions, and can convince judges to change their original positions to side with them.

Preparation for Oral Argument: Novices should prepare an outline of their arguments. The law should also be handy for reference during the argument. The outline and law should provide you with a general guideline for what to discuss, but be prepared to be flexible. "Mooting" your argument in front of other attorneys beforehand is a helpful way to prepare for the unexpected and to get more comfortable with your presentation. Also work on the level, tone, and speed of your voice. Arguments that are strong on substance can be weakened by poor delivery.

Conventions of Oral Argument: Typically, before beginning to speak, you should ask permission from the court to do so by saying "May it please the court" and introduce yourself. It is often helpful to give a brief introduction to your argument that lays out your major points for the court. After this introduction, you will spend the rest of your time arguing your case and answering the judge's questions. At the end of the argument, you should conclude with a brief summary of the points you made and a request for relief. In most cases, however, you will run out of time. If you are in the middle of answering a question when time runs out, ask the court for permission to briefly answer the question and wrap up.

When Opposing Counsel Is Speaking: When opposing counsel stands up to give his or her presentation, you should be paying attention and taking notes. The best arguments respond directly to points raised by opposing counsel.

Rebuttal: Rebuttal should not be a rehashing of your arguments. Instead, plan to address one or two compelling points, usually counterpoints to opposing counsel's best arguments. If opposing counsel brings up a case that seems compelling, make sure to distinguish it in your rebuttal.

DO'S AND DON'TS DURING ORAL ARGUMENT

Do's	Don'ts
Answer the judges' questions	Put off the judges' questions
Have a flexible outline	Strictly adhere to your outline
Have a conversation with the judges	Make a speech
Rely on authority	Pretend to know a case you have not read
Listen carefully and ask for clarification of questions	Think ahead to your next point while the judge is asking a question
Keep constant respect for the court	Get frustrated or angry with the judges
Keep a positive and professional tone	Become defensive or attack the other attorney personally
Dress and act professionally	Fidget, slouch, chew gum, or otherwise act unprofessionally

Legal Documents — Quick Reference — Complaints Format

WHAT IS A COMPLAINT?

The complaint is the document that commences the legal action. It also provides notice to the defendants and stops the running of the statute of limitations on the action. It is written to and served on the defendant, but it is basically written for the legal audience as it is also filed with the court and read by the eventual counsel for the defense. The complaint actually sets the scope of the lawsuit by alleging particular legal claims against the defense. This is a very formal document and is usually written with numbered allegations.

HOW DO YOU WRITE A COMPLAINT?

Before drafting a complaint, a lawyer must (1) research the rules for filing in the particular jurisdiction, (2) research the substantive law of the case to determine the legal causes of action to assert and their elements, and (3) research the facts of the case to determine if it meets the cause of action.

Each jurisdiction will have rules governing the content of a complaint and the procedures for filing them. You should check the civil procedure rules for your jurisdiction as well as the local rules. These rules will set out the appearance, content, and filing requirements for the complaint.

A complaint usually contains the following elements:

- *Caption,* which contains the name of the court, jurisdiction, and the names of the parties.
- *Commencement,* which introduces the complaint.

  Example: Now comes David Brink by his attorney, Diana Donahoe, and herein alleges ...
- *Body, or charging part,* which is the meat of the complaint and is comprised of numbered paragraphs. Initial paragraphs often state the parties' names and addresses. The following paragraphs give notice of the legal causes of action and allege each element of those actions. If you are requesting a jury trial, some jurisdictions require that the jury demand be made in the charging portion of the complaint or in a separate section labeled "jury demand." The last paragraphs of a complaint usually describe the plaintiff's injuries and damages.
- *Prayer or demand for judgment,* which lists the relief requested, such as specific performance, special damages, punitive damages, and equitable relief. The demand for judgment is not numbered, usually begins with "WHEREFORE," and usually ends with a catchall phrase requesting all other relief appropriate.
- *Signature and verification,* which includes the attorney's name, bar number, signature, and address and appears at the end of the complaint. In the verification clause, the party swears under oath that the allegations are believed to be true.

Legal Documents — Quick Reference — Answers Format

WHAT IS AN ANSWER?

The answer responds to each allegation in the complaint by indicating whether the defendant admits, denies, or is unable to answer. The scope of the answer is related to the scope of the complaint, as the answer must admit or deny each of the plaintiff's allegations.

A complaint can contain the following elements:

- **Caption and introductory sentence:** The caption is identical to the one in the complaint, except that it is labeled "Answer." Introductory sentences are used before the answer.
- **Admissions in answers:** Some rules require defendants to admit portions of the complaint that are true so that attorneys are acting "in good faith." In addition, by admitting portions of the complaint, the defendants help to narrow the issues. You can admit specific paragraphs individually, group admissions together, or admit only parts of paragraphs.
- **Denials in answers:** The defendant may make a general denial, which denies the whole complaint, or a special denial, which denies only certain paragraphs or parts of paragraphs. In addition, the defendant may state that there is insufficient evidence to deny or admit certain parts of a complaint, which, in effect, acts as a denial.
- *Example general denial:* "The Defendant denies each allegation in the Plaintiff's complaint."
- *Example specific denial:* "The defendant denies the allegations in paragraphs 11, 12, 14-21, and 23."
- **Affirmative defenses:** Some jurisdictions require certain affirmative defenses to be raised in an answer or they are waived. When writing affirmative defenses, you can separate them by headings or by count.
- **Affirmative claims and demand for judgment:** Counterclaims, cross-claims, and third-party claims are made in the same form as the complaint, using numbered paragraphs with separate headings to label each claim. If a defendant alleges a claim, he should also include a demand for judgment.
- **Signature and verification:** Similar to the complaint, an answer typically requires a signature and verification.

Legal Documents — Quick Reference — Briefs — Self-Evaluation

When evaluating your writing, do not try to comment on everything at once. Instead, focus your attention on one aspect of the brief at a time. Start with the rewriting issues before moving on to revising issues. Answer each question as fully as possible, writing on both this form and your document, before moving on to the next question.

Brief in General

A. **General Format:** Do you provide a title page, a table of contents with clear pointheadings and page numbers, and table of authorities?

B. **Statement of the Issue(s) Presented:** Does the issue statement provide the reader with the specific legal question, written in a persuasive manner? Why or why not? Can you read the whole issue statement aloud in one breath?

C. **Statement of the Case:** Does the statement of the case tell a clear and concise story? Does it provide the legally significant facts from the case? Is it written persuasively?

C1. What is the theory of the case?

C2. What specific word choices do you use that make the statement of the case persuasive?

I. Argument Section

1. **LARGE-SCALE ORGANIZATION**

    A. Do you start the argument section with a statement of the law that applies to the client's problem? Where is that "roadmap"? (Either circle on the brief or state where it is located.)

    B. Create a "reader-based outline" by reading only the topic sentences and writing a one- or two-word description of the point of each topic sentence. (You can make the outline on the margins to the brief or on this form.)

    B1. Does the reader-based outline parallel the structure of the roadmap? Why or why not? Do you use the same legal terms in the topic sentences as in the roadmap?

    C. Read the substance of each paragraph. Either here or in the margin of the paper, give a one- or two-word issue or sub-issue discussed in each paragraph. Does the paragraph actually discuss the issue and only the issue that the topic sentence addresses? Why or why not?

    D. Do you provide a mini-conclusion at the end of each element (1) to let the reader know that you have completed the discussion of that element, and (2) to reiterate your position on that element? Which mini-conclusions are effective?

2. **LEGAL ANALYSIS**

    A. Do you use legal authority to back up your arguments? Where?

    B. Look at the case analogies. For each analogy, do you use the facts, reasoning, and holding from the prior case and compare them to the specific facts of your case to prove your point? Do you use more complicated comparisons by referencing more than one case at a time? Be specific in your answer.

    C. Which is the best case comparison? The worst? Why?

    D. What other techniques do you use to make your arguments? Which are effective and which are not?

3. PERSUASIVE TECHNIQUES

    A. Can you tell what the theory of the case is in the argument section? If yes, what it is? Is it consistent with the theory of the case in the statement of the case?

    B. Is the roadmap written persuasively? Are the topic sentences written persuasively? Be specific.

    C. What specific word choices do you use that help with the persuasion?

    D. What other techniques do you use to make the document persuasive?

Editing and Polishing

1. Do you find any patterns of grammar problems? Where?
2. Are there any citation problems in this brief? Where?

Legal Documents — Quick Reference — Briefs — Peer Evaluation

One of the goals of this book is to help you become your own editor. This Quick Reference is designed to help you continue developing your evaluation process. By evaluating a peer's brief, you become another set of eyes for that peer and begin reevaluating your own brief.

When evaluating your peer's writing, do not comment on everything at once. Instead, focus your attention on one aspect of the brief at a time. Start with the rewriting issues before moving on to revising issues. While it is important to give positive feedback, focus on places where the writer needs improvement so that every writer gets ample opportunity for helpful criticism. Answer each question as fully as possible, writing on both this form and your peer's paper, before moving on to the next question.

After evaluating the brief, you should meet with your peer to discuss your evaluation.

Brief in General

A. **General Format:** Does the writer provide a title page, table of contents with clear pointheadings and page numbers, and a table of authorities?

B. **Statement of the Issue(s) Presented:** Does the issue statement provide the reader with the specific legal question, written in a persuasive manner? Why or why not? Can you read the whole issue statement aloud in one breath?

    B1. How does this writer's issue statement(s) differ from your own?

C. **Statement of the Case**: Does the statement of the case tell a clear and concise story, providing the legally significant facts from the case? Is it written persuasively?

    C1. What is the theory of the case?

    C2. What specific word choices does the writer use that make the statement of the case persuasive? Where could it be more persuasive?

    C3. How does this statement of the case differ from your own?

I. Argument Section

1. **LARGE-SCALE ORGANIZATION**

   A. Has the writer started the argument section with a statement of the law that applies to the client's problem? Where is that "roadmap"? (Either circle on the brief or state where it is located.)

      A1. How is that roadmap different from your own?

   B. Create a "reader-based outline" by reading only the topic sentences and writing a one- or two-word description of the point of each topic sentence. (You can make the outline on the margins to the brief or on this form.)

      B1. Does the reader-based outline parallel the structure of the roadmap? Why or why not? Does the writer use the same legal terms in the topic sentences as in the roadmap?

      B2. How does the writer's organizational scheme differ from your own?

   C. Read the substance of each paragraph. Either here or in the margin of the paper, give a one- or two-word issue or sub-issue discussed in each paragraph. Does the paragraph actually discuss the issue and only the issue that the topic sentence addresses? Why or why not?

   D. Does the writer provide a mini-conclusion at the end of each element (1) to let the reader know that she has completed the discussion of that element, and (2) to reiterate her position on that element? Which mini-conclusions are effective?

2. **LEGAL ANALYSIS**

   A. Does the writer use legal authority to back up his arguments? Where? Where can the writer cite to more authority?

   B. Look at the case analogies. For each analogy, does the writer use the facts, reasoning, and holding from the prior case and compare them to the specific facts of your case to prove his point? Does the writer use more complicated comparisons by referencing more than one case at a time? Be specific in your answer.

   C. Which is the best case comparison? The worst? Why?

   D. What other techniques does the writer use to make the brief's arguments? Which are effective and which are not?

3. **PERSUASIVE TECHNIQUES**

   A. Can you tell what the theory of the case is in the argument section of the brief? If yes, what is it? Is it consistent with the theory of the case in the statement of the case?

   B. Is the roadmap written persuasively? Are the topic sentences written persuasively? Be specific.

   C. What specific word choices does the writer use that help with the persuasion?

   D. What other techniques does the writer use to make the document persuasive?

Editing and Polishing

1. Do you find any patterns of grammar problems? Where?
2. Do you find any of your own grammar problems in this brief? Where?
3. Are there any citation problems in this brief? Where?

More Ebook Interactivity

 Legal Documents — Quick References and Checklists

QUICK REFERENCES

- Memo Format
- Brief Format
- Client Letters vs. Memos vs. Briefs
- Oral Argument
- Complaints Format
- Answers Format
- Briefs - Self-Evaluation
- Briefs - Peer Evaluation
- Memos - Self-Evaluation
- Memos - Peer Evaluation

CHECKLISTS

- Memos
- Briefs
- Client Letters
- Complaints
- Answers
- Interrogatories
- Motions
- Scholarly Writing
- Law Review Competition

 Legal Documents — Class Exercises

- Memos - Facts
- Memos - Question Presented
- Memos - Brief Answer
- Memos - Conclusion
- Briefs - Issue Statement #1
- Briefs - Issue Statement #2
- Briefs - Pointheadings
- Briefs - Summary of Argument
- Oral Argument

Legal Documents — Quizzes

⚇? Memos
⚇? Briefs
⚇? Client Letter
⚇? Pleadings and Motions
⚇? Scholarly Writing
⚇? Write-On Competition
⚇? Persuasive Techniques
⚇? Oral Argument
⚇? Rewriting Briefs - Self-Assessment

Legal Analysis

Legal analysis is the use of law to create reasoned, logical arguments. In this section, you will learn how to gather and analyze the facts as well as how to interpret rules before you begin to analyze the law. In addition, you will learn basic jurisprudence and the classical rhetorical devices of deductive and inductive reasoning and then employ both types of reasoning to create logical, legal analysis through statutory interpretation, case analysis, and policy arguments.

Legal Analysis — Introduction

Legal analysis is the art of creating reasoned, logical, legal arguments and applying those arguments to a particular set of facts. To create sound legal analysis, you must find and analyze the **facts** as well as the **law**.

Collecting the Facts

As a law student, you will probably be given a set of hypothetical facts to begin your analysis. However, as a lawyer, you will never receive such a "fact pattern." Instead, you will work for a client, and the facts will unfold in anything but a timely or thorough manner. Typical sources for collecting facts will be the client, other witnesses, documentation and tangible evidence, experts, and often a site visit (such as a crime scene). Be sure to prepare questions before you investigate, interview, or depose. The questions you ask should not only center around understanding the background, history, or client's story, but they also should help you to find relevant law. Questions organized by editor's categories are often helpful:

West Categories	Lawyers Cooperative Categories
Parties	Persons
Places, Objects, Things	Places
Basis or Issue	Acts
Defense	Things
Relief Sought	

Keep in mind that facts will often change as you collect more information. In addition, you will need to retrace many of your steps in the fact-finding process, so do not assume that you will visit a crime scene or interview a client only once.

Analyzing the Law

Once you have a general sense of the facts of the case, you will need to begin to apply the law to those facts. Remember to be flexible; as the facts change, your analysis of the law might change as well. Applying the law to the facts requires a number of steps. You need to identify legal issues, find controlling law, understand the relationship among the various legal branches, and then apply a variety of legal reasoning techniques to create sound, logical, legal arguments.

Identifying Legal Issues: As a law student, you will often be told the exact legal issue for the hypothetical. However, as a lawyer, you will need to identify the legal issues by analyzing the client's facts. Keep in mind that there are usually many issues in every case. The plaintiff's lawyer or prosecutor often defines the issues. The defense lawyer can also help define issues by providing counterclaims and defenses.

Finding Controlling Law: Once you have identified the issues, you need to find the law that controls on each issue. This section does not discuss ↪**research strategies**; instead, it discusses whether a particular provision you found actually controls. Basically, you will be looking for a "rule of law," either from statutes, cases, or regulations. You will need to determine whether this particular law controls the issue. For example, if you find a applies to "only property owned" and your client leases the property, then that particular statute does not control. Often, the terms are ambiguous, and part of your legal argument will focus on what law controls. For example, if a statute applies to "all employees," you might need to argue that your client, who contracts with this employer, is actually an employee.

Understanding the Relationship Among the Legal Branches: Statutes are usually the starting point in the law. A statute binds the courts of that jurisdiction (a Maryland statute binds Maryland courts), but courts have two roles in interpreting a statute. First, a court may find a statute to be unconstitutional; such a finding makes the statute invalid unless the legislature amends the statute to cure the problem. Second, assuming the statute is constitutional, a court interprets the meaning of a statute. Once a court has written a decision interpreting the statute, other courts in that jurisdiction are bound by that interpretation under the doctrine of ↪**stare decisis**. However, if the legislature disagrees with the courts' interpretation, the legislature can amend the statute to clarify its intent.

In addition, sometimes the law starts as common law. A legislature might codify the common law. Thus, when finding law in the jurisdiction, you might find common law that predates the statute; these cases can still be applicable and binding as long as they are consistent with the way the law was codified.

Therefore, when finding controlling law, it is important to pay attention to any history of the law and look for dates of enforcement and amendments.

Applying a Variety of Techniques to Create Logical Legal Arguments: Lawyers use a variety of techniques to produce sound legal arguments. The most pervasive techniques are reasoning based on (1) rules, (2) analogies, and (3) policies.

1. **Rule-Based Reasoning:** The starting point for most legal analysis is rule-based reasoning. Here, a statute or case law dictates the rule to be applied. A lawyer's job is to break down the rule into its component elements. Oftentimes, a rule will clearly enumerate these elements; other times, a rule can be structured in many different ways. Once the elements of a rule are enumerated, the lawyer analyzes each element separately, applying the general rule to the particular client's facts to come to a conclusion. This type of analysis is similar to ↪**deductive reasoning** in that the lawyer starts with a premise and then applies his client's facts to that premise. Rule-based reasoning is addressed in ↪**statutory interpretation** and ↪**case synthesis**.
2. **Analogies:** To analyze the elements of the law, lawyers use analogies. Here, the lawyer compares his client's case to cases that have already been decided. A lawyer will argue that his client's facts are similar to the facts of a prior case to show that the outcome should be the same. This technique is called an analogy. When a lawyer argues that his client's facts are different from the prior case, he is distinguishing that case. A good lawyer will use the facts and the reasoning of the prior case to show why the client's case should have a similar or different holding. Analogies use ↪**inductive reasoning** and are addressed in ↪**case analysis**.

3. **Policies:** Lawyers make policy arguments when there is no applicable rule on the subject (this is called a case of first impression), when existing rules are ambiguous, and to bolster other legal arguments. A policy argument will show why an interpretation of the law is consistent or inconsistent with the goals of the rule (if there is one) or of society in general. Policy arguments use both <u>deductive and inductive reasoning</u> and are addressed in <u>policy arguments</u>.

Legal Analysis — Understanding Legal Rules

The rule of law is the starting point for most legal analysis. Rules can come from statutes, regulations, or cases and they come in a variety of forms. As a lawyer, you need to determine what type of rule you are applying, understand which terms of the rule are in contention, and break down the rule into its component parts and important terms so that you can apply your client's facts in a cohesive argument.

TYPES OF RULES

The first step in rule application is determining the type of rule that applies. Rules come in many forms, including (but not limited to) an elements test, a balancing of factors test, a test with exceptions, and a combination of these tests.

The Elements Test: An elements test may be very simple and have only one element that must be met or it may be more complicated. Some rules have two-part tests, three-part tests, or even more. Sometimes the elements are clearly enumerated (1,2,3 or a,b,c). Oftentimes a rule will have only one sentence but will have multiple parts; you will need to break down that rule into sub-elements.

➥ **One-Part Test**

➥ **Multiple-Part Test**

➥ **One-Sentence Test That Breaks Down into Multiple Elements**

The Balancing of Factors Test: A balancing of factors test sets out two or more considerations that must be weighed against each other. Here, factors may be used to add weight to each side of the argument. This test truly conjures up images of the scales of justice.

➥ **Balancing of Factors Test**

The Totality Test: A "totality test" sets out a number of factors but they need not all be met; instead they are all considered and added up together into a totality. In this type of test, some of the factors may be more important than other factors, and not all factors need be met.

➥ **Totality Test**

The Exceptions Test: Here, a rule is set out with one or more exceptions. Therefore, to argue that the rule does not apply, you must argue that the exception applies. To argue that the rule applies, you will need to argue that one or more of the exceptions do not apply.

At times, rules combine a number of these tests. So, in a factors test, one factor might include some sort of balancing or an exception. In a balancing test, many factors might apply to one (or both) sides. The trick is to understand what type of test (or tests) your rule uses to begin to decipher the rule itself.

TERMS WITHIN RULES

Once you have an understanding of the type of rule you are applying, you must look closely at its terms and phrases. First, you should be familiar with terms that always carry a specific meaning.

***And* vs. *Or*:** The term *and* has a conjunctive meaning. For example, when *and* appears within a factors test, both or all parts of the factors must be met. *Or* has the opposite effect. When *or* appears in a factors test, only one of the factors need be proven.

⌨ ↪**And vs. Or**

***Shall* vs. *May*:** *Shall* and *may* also have very different meanings. *Shall* is mandatory — it leaves no discretion to the judge or the subject of the rule. *May* is discretionary — a judge or the actor has some discretion to decide whether to take some action. (Oftentimes factors or some sort of balancing will help the judge decide.)

⌨ ↪**Shall vs. May**

Second, you need to determine the terms of the rule that are in dispute. While *and*, *or*, *shall*, and *may* will never be in dispute, many of the other terms will be. Therefore, you need to parse out the rule by looking at each word or term individually and asking yourself whether each side has an argument regarding that particular term. Terms may be a combination of words (*clear mandate of public policy*) or they can be a single word (*causation*).

ORGANIZING AROUND THE RULE OF LAW

Once you have determined the type of rule you are analyzing and made an initial determination of the terms in dispute, you will be better able to organize the rule into its elements or subcategories. This process is important because legal documents are organized around the legal rule. To organize the rule, you should first break it down into its component parts and then analyze the terms in dispute.

Breaking the rule down into its component parts should be easy if you have identified the rule's test. If it is an elements test, list the elements. If it is a balancing of factors test, write down the two conflicting considerations that must be balanced. Next, determine how those factors relate to each other. Is there an *or* or an *and* in the test? Is it a mandatory test or a discretionary test? Third, within each factor or consideration, highlight the terms of art that will come into play. One factor might have three terms in dispute; another factor may have no terms in dispute.

To analyze the terms of art, you will need to look at each term separately. Here, you will determine the meaning of each term. In persuasive writing, you will argue that it means one thing while your opponent will likely argue that it means another. In objective writing, you will predict what the term means. Here, you might use ↪**statutory interpretation**, ↪**case analogy and distinction**, and ↪**policy** arguments to interpret the meaning. Words and their meanings become especially important to lawyers because of this process. By analyzing each term within a rule, one word can change the outcome for your client. The best lawyers are able to spot ambiguities within terms and argue their meanings.

While this process of organizing a rule of law may seem simple, it can become quite complicated. For example, some statutes are relatively simple and confined to a few lines. However, others can be quite elaborate and cover pages and pages of the code. These complicated rules will require you to parse through all the different pieces of the rule, pull out the applicable sections, and piece them together in a coherent organizational scheme. In addition, even if concise, rules are not always enunciated clearly. For example, when a rule comes from common law, all the judges writing opinions on the same issue may not articulate the rule in exactly the same way. Some may add language to an already existing rule, and others might actually slightly change the interpretation of the rule. In this situation, you will need to either ➥**synthesize** the cases into one coherent rule or articulate a few possible readings of the rule and analyze them separately.

Legal Analysis — Jurisprudence

Before you begin making legal arguments, it is helpful to have a basic understanding of legal philosophy — or jurisprudence. If you understand where legal arguments come from, how they have been applied, and when they have changed, you will be able to craft more creative and reasoned arguments in your own writing. American jurisprudence has developed over time. Below you will read about some major legal trends in our history: natural law, formalism (or positivism), realism, and a variety of critical legal studies.

Natural Law

When the Declaration of Independence was signed, American jurisprudence centered around natural law, a philosophy inherited from English law. Natural law intertwines morality with the law. Naturalists argue that our beliefs in what is right are grounded in nature (and sometimes God), and the law should be built around these natural moralities. Our "inalienable rights," "due process," and "equal protection" come from natural law theory. When making a natural law argument, lawyers rely on arguments based on reasonableness, equity, and fairness.

Formalism or Positivism

During the nineteenth century, natural law was replaced by the theory of formalism (also known as positivism). Under this theory, law is not created by natural forces but by those rules formulated by the government. These rules can be categorized and then easily followed uniformly and objectively. The ➥**key number system** and the ➥**Langdell method of teaching** were developed during this time of jurisprudence and reflect the categorization of legal rules. When making a formalism argument, lawyers enumerate the applicable rules and then apply those rules with legal precedent.

Realism

Realism grew out of a reaction to formalism. Realists believe that law cannot be applied uniformly and objectively as in the formalist approach; instead, they believe that law is interpreted subjectively. Rules vary based on the judges making the decisions, not on the law itself. When making an argument based on realism, lawyers will make creative ➥**policy arguments** and try to play to the judge's emotions to influence the decision.

Critical Legal Studies (CLS)

Critical legal studies (CLS) comes directly from realism. The theory behind CLS is that law is not only subjective, it is political. CLS theorists believe that laws are not neutral; instead, they are created to perpetuate political agendas — specifically the agenda of the white, male majority. As a result, there are a number of CLS movements, including critical race theory and feminist legal theory. A lawyer making a CLS argument will rely less on existing law and more on policies based on helping the underprivileged or marginalized members of society.

Law and Economics Theory

Law and economics theory is based on the principles of economics and wealth. These theorists believe that law should be based less on government interference and more on market controls. Lawyers making law and economics arguments often rely on economic policy, pointing to economic growth and wealth maximization as reasons for the judge to rule in their favor.

Legal Analysis — Classical Rhetoric — Deduction vs. Induction

The classical rhetorical devices of deduction and induction are both used in legal reasoning. Lawyers should have some basic understanding of these types of reasoning to create logical arguments and to find weaknesses in opponents' reasoning.

DEDUCTION

Deduction is a type of logic that leads to conclusive results. The syllogism is the basic form of this reasoning. A syllogism is a statement that contains each of the following:

1. A first premise: $A = B$
2. A second premise: $B = C$
3. A conclusion: $A = C$

If the first and second premises are true, then the conclusion is valid through deductive reasoning. For example:

First premise	All humans are mammals.	$A = B$
Second premise	Mammals breathe air.	$B = C$
Conclusion	All humans breathe air.	$A = C$

However, if one of the premises is invalid, then the conclusion is invalid. For example:

First premise	All fish are mammals.	A does not equal B
Second premise	Mammals breathe air.	$B = C$
Conclusion	Fish breathe air.	$A = C$

Here, because the first premise is wrong, the conclusion is not valid.

Syllogisms can also be invalid if the premises are not logical. For example,

First premise	All mammals breathe air.	$A = B$
Second premise	Reptiles breathe air.	$C = B$
Conclusion	Reptiles are mammals.	$C = A$

Here, because there is nothing to indicate that breathing air makes mammals equivalent to reptiles, the logic is flawed.

SYLLOGISMS IN THE LAW

Syllogisms are used frequently in legal arguments. For example, here is a valid syllogism:

First premise	A conviction for solicitation is a minor offense.	A = B
Second premise	If convicted of a minor offense, a defendant will receive no jail time.	B = C
Conclusion	If convicted of solicitation, a defendant will receive no jail time.	A = C

This syllogism correctly follows the formula and contains valid premises. Therefore, the conclusion shows valid deductive reasoning.

However, the syllogism is invalid if one of the premises is invalid. For example:

First premise	A conviction for murder is a minor offense.	A does not equal B
Second premise	If convicted of a minor offense, a defendant will receive no jail time.	B = C
Conclusion	If convicted of murder, a defendant will receive no jail time.	A = C

Because the first premise is invalid, the conclusion is invalid.

The syllogism is also invalid if the premises are not logically ordered. For example:

First premise	A conviction for solicitation is a minor offense.	A = B
Second premise	A conviction for shoplifting is a minor offense.	C = B
Conclusion	A conviction for shoplifting is a conviction for solicitation.	C = A

Because the second premise does not use the B = C formula, the conclusion is invalid.

A good lawyer will be able to create valid syllogisms and find the faults with invalid syllogisms. The simple A = B, B = C, A = C equation will help you to write and dissect syllogisms to create arguments and to poke holes in your oppositions' arguments. Oftentimes, rule-based reasoning such as ⇒**statutory interpretation** and case synthesis takes the form of deductive reasoning.

INDUCTION

While deductive reasoning creates absolute conclusions, inductive reasoning creates probable conclusions. In induction, the writer shows why a conclusion is more likely than another conclusion. An analogy is a typical form of inductive reasoning. For example:

- A mammal breathes air and births its young live.
- A human breathes air and births its young live.

- A snake breathes air and lays eggs.
- A human is more likely a mammal than a snake because while both breathe air, a human also births its young live and a snake lays eggs.

Here, through inductive reasoning, the writer shows why one conclusion is more likely than another. The trick with the analogy is deciding which characteristics are more important in the comparison.

INDUCTIVE REASONING IN THE LAW

In law, the analogy is often used to show why a case is more likely to be decided one way instead of another. Usually, prior cases are the basis for the comparison. For example, in a case involving the solicitation of a minor, note the different analogies:

A defense lawyer's argument:

"My client should not go to jail for his first offense of solicitation because in most prior cases that involved first offenses, similar defendants received only fines."

Here, the lawyer is using an analogy, comparing a number of offenses to make a conclusion.

The prosecutor's argument:

"The defendant should get jail time because in other cases in which the person solicited was a minor, jail time was the usual sentence."

Here, the lawyer bases his inductive reasoning on a different characteristic—age.

In both analogies, the lawyers use inductive reasoning to create sound logic. However, the different characteristic used in the comparisons makes a difference in the conclusions. In this example, the judge needs to decide which characteristic (or which prior case) is more compelling to decide the outcome. A lawyer's job in using inductive reasoning, then, is to provide enough reasoning of the prior case to show why one characteristic is more compelling than another. As you read through ➥**case analysis**, you will see analogies in the law and learn techniques to show how a prior case can be effectively analogized.

Legal Analysis — Statutory Language

Statutory interpretation is **rule-based reasoning**. The lawyer starts with a rule, the statute, and then uses ➥**deductive reasoning** to apply the general rule to the particular facts of her case to come to a conclusion. However, because legislative bodies rarely write a statute to apply to one particular case, the language and purpose become ambiguous when the client's facts are applied. A lawyer's job, therefore, is to analyze the language of the statute to determine the intent of the legislature that wrote the particular statute – what did the lawmakers mean for the law to do when they wrote it? A good lawyer applies a number of steps in statutory interpretation.

1. **Finding an applicable statute:** The first step in statutory interpretation is finding a statute that applies to your client. At times, there may be more than one statute that applies. Other times, only common law may be available. Also, there may be a dispute as to whether a statute even applies. (For example, does an employment statute apply to independent contractors?)
2. **Reading the whole statute:** Many law students who find a relevant statutory section online never realize there are a number of related statutory provisions that exist on the screen prior to and immediately after their particular provision. Therefore, many good lawyers prefer to read a

statute in its printed format so they can look at a statute in the context of the entire act. Whether you read a statutory provision online or in the books, be aware that most statutes have many provisions or fall within a specific act. You should at least skim the whole act and look for some of the most important provisions for your particular statute, such as the following:

- The title of the act and the title of specific provisions
- The date of enactment (of the act or specific provisions)
- The date of any amendments
- A preamble or purpose section
- A definition section
- The language of the specific provisions that apply to your issue
- The language of provisions that appear in close proximity to your issue
- The remedy or relief provision of the act

3. **Breaking down your specific provision into its elements:** Once you begin to focus on the particular statutory provision you will apply, you need to break it down into its component parts. At times, the language will clearly lay out the structure for you (e.g., the plaintiff must prove a, b, and c). However, often you will need to analyze and break down the structure yourself. One trick to do this is to draw brackets around different language so that each bracketed section becomes one element that needs to be proven. Opposing lawyers will often break down the elements differently. Judges, in their case decisions, often will try to clarify the structure of a statute.

4. **Reading signaling words carefully:** Particular words and punctuation can change the meaning of a statute. Therefore, you need to dissect specific statutory provisions very carefully. Here are some key words and their meanings:

- *And* = must prove all items in the list to meet statutory provision
- *Or* = must prove only one in the list to meet statutory provision
- *Including* = implies an exclusive list
- *Including but not limited to* = implies list is not exclusive
- *And any other factors* = states that previous list is not exclusive
- *Must* = required
- *Shall* = required
- *May* = not required

Legal Analysis — Statutory Interpretation Techniques

Once you have dissected a statute and broken it down into its component parts, you can begin to interpret the meaning within each element. However, the language of the statute is usually ambiguous, and the lawyer uses a variety of techniques to interpret the statute. The main goal of statutory interpretation is to determine the legislature's intent when creating the law.

A good example to illustrate statutory interpretation techniques is ➥**Smith v. United States**, 508 U.S. 223 (1993), where the Supreme Court examined language in 18 U.S.C. § 924(c)(1), "uses or carries a firearm," to determine if Congress intended that language to include using a firearm as barter for drugs. Both Justice O'Connor's opinion and Justice Scalia's dissent use statutory interpretation techniques to determine the intent of Congress. Those typical techniques include the following (click on each ⌕ to view O'Connor's and Scalia's arguments from the Supreme Court case):

1. **The plain language** of a statute means how a term of a statute is usually used in the English language. A court starts interpreting a statute by looking at the plain meaning of the text. If the court can determine a statute's meaning using the plain language of the statute, it should not need to look to other forms of statutory interpretation.

   🔍 ↪**Plain Language**

2. **Definitions** for particular terms of a statute. Often lawmakers provide a definition section, which usually appears in the beginning of the code section. You should always look for a definition section in a statute because it provides key definitions to certain provisions. If no definitions exist, lawyers often look to other sources, such as definitions from other statutes, definitions from Black's Law Dictionary or other dictionaries, or definitions from scholars or judges.

   🔍 ↪**Definitions**

3. **Context** of the language. Lawyers look at: **where** the terms of art appear in the statute; **what** words appear near those terms; and what terms appear **nowhere** in the statute to access the meanings of the terms.

   🔍 ↪**Context**

4. **Case law** to determine the way in which other courts have interpreted the meaning of the statute. Employing ↪**case analysis** techniques, lawyers use cases as binding precedent in statutory interpretation. ↪**Annotated statutes** provide references to cases that have interpreted the statutes. You should research these cases because judge's opinions will provide interpretations, definitions, and important policy arguments that may apply to your case. If a court interprets a statute incorrectly, the legislature can rewrite the statute.

   🔍 ↪**Case law**

5. **Legislative history** to discover what the lawmakers said when they wrote, debated, and discussed the statute. To find ↪**legislative history**, a lawyer would research committee reports, floor debates, and speeches. Legislative history is also useful to determine congressional intent if the statute has been amended. Some judges (Justice Scalia, for example) do not believe legislative history is helpful when interpreting statutory language.

   🔍 ↪**Legislative history**

6. **Policy** arguments that could have determined the legislature's intent. Oftentimes a statute contains a policy or purpose section. Therefore, you should always check your statute for such a section. If there is no policy section, lawyers often employ various policy arguments to interpret the statute such as determining particular policy issues at the time the statute was enacted. See the section on ↪**policy arguments** and ↪**jurisprudence** for specific ideas.

   🔍 ↪**Policy**

7. **Canons of construction** are commonly accepted ways to interpret particular provisions or phrases. Examples of canons of construction, some of which use Latin names, include the following:

Read the statute as a whole;

When no exception exists, none should be applied;

Different statutes on the same issue should be interpreted consistently;

A later provision takes precedent over an earlier one;

In pari materia ("upon the same matter") = statutes on similar subjects are to be construed similarly

Ejusdem generis ("of the same genus") = when a statute contains a list followed by a catchall phrase, the catchall phrase includes only items similar to the ones on the list

Expression unius ("expression of one excludes another") = if a statute expressly includes something, then it excludes what is not mentioned

Be careful when using canons. Some of the canons contradict each other, and many courts do not rely on them.

🔍 ➥ **Canons of construction**

📖 ➥ **Read <u>Smith v. United States</u> in its entirety.**

Legal Analysis — Understanding Common Law

Common law is the body of law that develops through case precedent. Before you begin using cases in your analysis, it is important to understand the organization and function of the courts as well as the precedential weight of each case.

Function and Organization of the Courts

The American court system actually has two different kinds of courts: federal and state. The federal courts generally have jurisdiction over cases where the U.S. Constitution or federal law applies or where there is diversity of citizenship. Most of the other cases are heard in state courts.

🔍 ➥ **Federalism**

The Federal Court System: The federal courts are broken down geographically by "circuits." There are thirteen circuits, the First through the Eleventh Circuits, as well as the D.C. Circuit (which hears D.C. federal cases) and the Federal Circuit (which hears specialized federal cases such as patent cases). To find the circuit in your geographic area, see the ➥ **Federal Circuit Court Map**. Each circuit has a court of appeals; when you speak of a "circuit court," you are referring to the court of appeals in that circuit (so, for example, the First Circuit would be the U.S. Court of Appeals for the First Circuit). Each circuit is further subdivided into districts. Each state has at least one federal district, and many have more. The courts sitting in the district are the federal trial courts (so, for instance, the District Court of Maine is a federal trial court within the First Circuit). To find the district court in your geographic area, click on your circuit within the ➥ **Federal District Court Map**.

If you bring a case in the federal system, it will start in the district court in the appropriate circuit. If it is appealed, it will go to the court of appeals in that circuit. If appealed further, it might be heard in the U.S. Supreme Court.

U.S. Supreme Court

↑

U.S. Court of Appeals for the District of Columbia

↑

U.S. District Court for the District of Columbia

The State Court System: Each state has its own system, and many of those mirror the federal system with a trial court, an intermediate appellate court, and an appellate court. Some jurisdictions do not have an intermediate court, while other states have intermediate courts with multiple divisions. Each state has different names for the various courts (for example, in New York, the Supreme Court is the trial court and the Court of Appeals is the highest court). You can access each state's court system through links on the ➥**state map.**

New York Court of Appeals

↑

New York Appellate Division

↑

New York Supreme Court

The Function of the Courts: The trial courts and appellate courts have different functions. The trial court consists of a judge who sits on the bench listening to both legal arguments and evidence. Therefore, the trial judge has an opportunity to observe witnesses and judge credibility. During the process at the trial level, the judge decides both questions of law and questions of fact (if it is a jury trial, most factual questions are decided by the jury). The appellate court serves a much different function; it does not simply sit in the trial court's shoes. An appellate panel usually consists of three judges who listen to arguments from lawyers about the specific errors of the court below. Therefore, the appellate court reviews limited decisions of the trial court, using different levels of deference, or ➥**standards of review.** Usually, when you read judicial opinions, you are reading appellate cases — either from the highest court of appeal or the intermediate court of appeal in your jurisdiction.

Precedential Weight of Cases

You have already been introduced to stare decisis, the concept that courts treat current cases consistently with past precedent. However, this concept becomes more nuanced when deciding which cases to apply to your issue. When deciding how much precedential value to give to a case, it is important to consider both the organization and function of the courts. Although an appellate case will have more authority than a trial court case, other distinctions also come into play.

Primary Law vs. Secondary Sources: You have already been introduced to this concept in ➥**Research Strategies.** All case law is primary law. (Articles written about cases are considered to be secondary sources.)

Binding vs. Persuasive Authority: You have already been introduced to this concept in ➥**Research Strategies.** However, it becomes more complicated when dealing with case law. Mandatory cases are those cases that must be followed. These include cases from a higher court within the same jurisdiction. On the other hand, persuasive cases need not be followed. A persuasive case is one from the same level court or a lower court within a jurisdiction or from a different jurisdiction altogether. Therefore, if you look at the court systems above, the New York Court of Appeals is binding on the New York Appellate Division. If you are writing a brief to be filed in the New York Appellate Division, you would rely heavily on New York Court of Appeals cases. However, New York Appellate Division cases (even from that specific division) would be only persuasive. In addition, a case from the federal court, even the Court of Appeals from the Second Circuit, would be only persuasive in the New York Appellate Division because the case is from a different jurisdiction.

Most students are surprised to discover that federal courts usually do not bind state courts. In fact, the decisions of the state's highest court (the New York Court of Appeals above) are binding not only on the rest of that state's courts, but also on federal courts applying that state's law. (So, the Second Circuit must follow the New York Court of Appeals decisions on matters of state law.) The U.S. Supreme Court does bind all state courts on matters of federal constitutional law, but states may still impose more rights under their own constitutions or laws.

Holding vs. Dicta: When relying on judicial opinions, it is important to realize that only the case holding is binding—not the dicta. The holding is that part of the case that resolves the issue in dispute. Other statements the court makes in explaining its holding is called dicta. Only the holding is binding on other courts.

Majority Opinions vs. Dissents: The majority opinion is the decision of the court that binds other courts. The dissent is not binding. Concurring decisions are also only persuasive.

Other Traits Affecting the Weight of Cases: There are a number of other traits that affect the weight of cases. Whether a decision is binding or persuasive, it will carry more weight depending on these factors:

> **Date:** A recent decision carries a lot of weight. Trial judges do not like being reversed. Therefore, when they write their opinions, trial judges are often wondering what the appellate court is thinking. A recent case will answer that question. On the flip side, a case that has been around for a while and has been followed consistently also carries a lot of weight.

> **Number and Names of Judges:** Most appellate courts use three-judge panels. However, at times, the full appellate court will hear a case in an *en banc* hearing. *En banc* decisions carry more weight because they are issued from the whole bench, not just a three-judge panel. Also, look for the name of the judge writing the decision. Oftentimes cases from well-known judges (such as Judge Posner) carry more weight.

> **The Court Itself:** Certain courts carry more weight than others, even when they are only persuasive authority. The U.S. Supreme Court is the most prestigious court, but other courts, such as the Second Circuit, also carry a lot of weight. Also, state courts often look to the decisions of their federal circuits for guidance (so, for example, the New York state courts might look to the Second Circuit). Also, state courts often look to neighboring states for guidance (The District of Columbia, for instance, might look to Maryland courts.) In addition, some courts have reputations based on their past rulings. For example, the Ninth Circuit is considered to be a liberal court, whereas the Fourth Circuit is considered to be conservative.

> **The Treatment of the Case:** A case will carry more precedential value if other courts have followed its ruling. ➥**Updating** the case is very important to discover not only how often a case has been

cited but also by which courts. If other jurisdictions have followed suit, the case gains even more precedential value.

Now that you understand the organization and function of the courts as well as the relative weight of authorities, you are ready to use the concept of stare decisis to begin using case analysis in your legal reasoning.

Legal Analysis — Case Analysis

Case analysis is the use of cases to make legal arguments. The American legal system relies on common law through the concept of ↪**stare decisis**, which dictates that similar cases are treated in a similar manner. Therefore, courts look to past decisions when making law so that citizens are treated fairly, predictably, and consistently. Case analysis is one of the hardest concepts for students to master, but one of the techniques most often used by lawyers to make arguments in the United States.

Case analysis is used in multiple situations:

1. **Interpreting statutes using cases:** When a statute or regulation exists on point, lawyers and courts look to past decisions to determine how a term or phrase or policy of a statute has been applied in the past. This technique uses deductive, rule-based reasoning and is discussed in ↪**statutory interpretation.**

2. **Case synthesis:** When there is no statute on point, common law is used to determine the rule of law. Oftentimes, a body of cases will clearly enunciate a rule of law. However, when there is no clear rule, the lawyer needs to create the rule using a number of cases pieced together to form a coherent rule. Case synthesis, discussed in detail below, is used to articulate both general rules of law as well as specific rules and definitions within those rules.

3. **Case comparisons:** Third, once the rule of law is established, cases are used as comparison to apply the same law to different situations using case analogies and distinctions. Case comparisons are discussed in detail below.

Case Synthesis

Case synthesis is the weaving together of cases to create a clearly enunciated rule. Lawyers use case synthesis to create a rule when there is no statute or regulation on point (for example, to articulate the elements of intentional infliction of emotional distress) or to create a specific rule or definition for a particular element in an already enunciated rule (for example, to define the outrageous element within intentional infliction of emotional distress).

Case synthesis can be tricky. While courts make decisions on similar points of law, each case is based on a specific set of facts, so no two decisions are exactly alike. A court can base its holding on specific facts or certain reasoning or policies. As a result, when a lawyer tries to synthesize a whole body of case law on a specific point, there might not be a lucid rule. If there is a clear rule, it is usually readily apparent as a court will state a rule and follow it; this rule then will often be cited in most subsequent cases on point. However, when no clear rule exists, a lawyer will need to synthesize the rule by combining the rulings from the prior cases. This task is usually difficult as the lawyer needs to determine if the court's rulings were based on reasoning, facts, or policies.

Many law students incorrectly believe they have "synthesized" a rule by simply describing a list of cases in a book report fashion. However, a synthesis involves pulling together similar threads from cases and weaving them into a coherent picture — not merely listing them in chronological order. Good lawyers can synthesize the law from cases into a number of viable rules and then choose the one that works best for the client's issue.

While there is no one way to synthesize a rule from a group of cases, there are some guidelines:

1. **Compile all the cases on point.** You will need to thoroughly research your issue in order to find the relevant cases on point. Focus first on binding cases within your jurisdiction. If you need to rely on persuasive cases, you may do so, but keep in mind that they might not fit in consistently with the synthesis nor will a court be bound by persuasive decisions.

2. **Read all the relevant cases carefully.** Here, you are not just trying to pick out relevant quotations for the reader. A typical novice writer will mistakenly rely on language taken out of context and mislead the reader. Instead, be sure that you understand the whole case before you rely on one specific piece of it.

3. **Group cases according to explicit rules.** When a case sets out an explicit rule, try to find another case with a similar explicit rule. Sometimes the language will be exactly the same; other times the language will differ. In either instance, pull out the important rule that the court applied and group the cases according to that rule.

4. **Group cases according to implicit rules.** Oftentimes courts will make rulings without explicitly identifying the reasoning. However, you can imply the reasoning from the facts or from policy arguments within the opinion.

5. **Fit the pieces together.** Combine the explicit rules cases with the implicit rules cases to create a cohesive and consistent rule on the issue. By definition, this synthesized rule will not be articulated by any one case. However, the rule should be consistent with all the relevant cases on point. If a binding case in your jurisdiction contradicts the rule, then your synthesized rule will not be an accurate reflection of the law.

Avoid these typical mistakes when synthesizing cases:

1. **Synthesizing in chronological order.** At times, it might make sense to create a synthesis based on the historical, chronological development of the law in your jurisdiction because cases often build on each other as the law develops. However, the law often develops in fits and starts so that one part of the rule may be enunciated and not revisited again for 10 or 20 years. Therefore, create your synthesis based on different facets of the law as opposed to a chronological arrangement.

2. **Confusing different terms of art that apply to the same part of the rule.** Some courts might create the same rule but use different terms of art to do so. Here, a novice writer might mistakenly use the different terms of art to articulate two different parts of a rule when, in fact, they are identifying the same part of the rule. Here, you will need to be flexible and craft a piece of the rule that incorporates both terms.

3. **Using quotations out of context.** Do not rely on quotations taken out of context to mislead the reader. Instead, you need to understand the case holistically to ensure that the piece you have isolated is still consistent with the holding and reasoning of the case.

4. **Ignoring rules articulated only by one court.** In synthesizing rules, you will be looking at an array of rules that come from various courts. While one part of the rule might come from multiple decisions, another part might come from just one court's ruling. Therefore, if a binding court in your jurisdiction adds another element to an already-existing rule, you cannot ignore that case (there is an exception to this rule — if the case has been ignored by subsequent cases in your jurisdiction).

⌨ ➙Case Synthesis Sample

Once you have synthesized a rule, you apply the rule to the client's facts. Here, you can use rule-based reasoning (➙**deductive reasoning** whereby you move from the general rule, apply your particular client's facts, and reach a conclusion), analogical reasoning (see case comparisons below), or ➙**policy arguments**.

Case Comparisons

When a rule is clearly delineated, whether through statute or case synthesis, previous cases are used to compare and distinguish the current case. This method of analogical reasoning is based on the doctrine of ➙*stare decisis*—that like cases should be treated similarly. If a prior court (hopefully in the same jurisdiction) has struggled with a similar issue and come to a conclusion, then this court should follow that decision. Here, the lawyer uses ➙**inductive reasoning** to create case comparisons.

When searching for cases effective for comparisons, a lawyer should look for cases addressing similar issues. So, if you are in a custody battle, look for cases involving custody disputes. Second, look for cases where the facts of the prior case are similar to your client's facts or where the reasoning of the prior case can be used in your case. Third, determine if the holding of the prior case is similar to the predicted or preferred outcome in your case. If the outcome is the same, you will be creating case analogies. If the outcome is different, you will be distinguishing cases.

ANALOGIZING CASES

Analogizing a case is usually the strongest kind of case comparison because it allows a lawyer to argue that a prior case with a favorable holding is similar to his or her case, so that it should be followed. However, a prior case need not be exactly the same as your case for it to be analogous. In fact, it will be rare if you ever find a case during your career that is exactly on point. Therefore, you will need to determine if the similarities between your case and the prior case are legally significant to make it analogous.

DISTINGUISHING CASES

On the other hand, at times you will find only cases where the holdings run contrary to your preferred outcome. In these situations, you will distinguish the unfavorable case by arguing that the rule doesn't apply at all or that it should be applied differently. While distinguishing cases can make you feel as if you are on the defensive, this technique can help you produce very effective legal arguments. However, do not feel as if you have to distinguish a case merely because it is different. All cases are different from one another. The question is whether the differences are legally significant.

CRAFTING EFFECTIVE CASE COMPARISONS

The creative aspect of crafting effective case comparisons is deciding what is important to compare. It might be the facts or the reasoning. You might argue that one particular fact is most important while your opposing counsel will focus on a different fact. You will have to show why your focus is more compelling.

While there is no formula for creating a case comparison, there are some helpful ingredients to consider:

Holding: Be sure to include the holding of the prior case. The judge needs to know which way the other court decided. Remember that a holding is very specific to the particular case. A holding does not include dicta or policy arguments.

Facts: You should also explain the important, relevant facts of the prior case. Because you are comparing the prior case to your case, be sure to show what facts from your case are applicable. In addition, you need to illustrate how your case is similar or different from the prior case. Be specific for the reader so that he understands how the two are tied together.

Reasoning: You should also explain the reasoning the prior court used to justify the holding. Because you are comparing the prior case to your case, you should show what reasoning is applicable to your case and why. Be specific so that the reader understands how the reasoning from the prior case relates to your case.

While most effective case comparisons include a comparison of the facts, reasoning, and holding of the prior case to your case, there is no magic formula. Do not try to fit the same ingredients into every comparison, and do not attempt to do so in the same order every time. Instead, be creative and remember that your goal is to compare the two cases to show why the result should be the same or different.

COMPARING ONE CASE

Most law students start with using just one prior case for comparison. In these situations, it is helpful if you provide the reader with the legal context, such as a rule or definition, before launching into a case comparison that applies the rule. To begin the actual comparison, consider starting with the prior case so that the reader understands the legal precedent first. Explain the relevant facts, reasoning, and holding, but be careful to provide only the information that is necessary to make your point clear. There is no need to provide all the facts from the prior case; you will only overload the reader with irrelevant information. Next, compare the prior case to your case and explicitly tie the relevant facts or reasoning together. Show why the cases are similar or different. Do not force the reader to flip back to your fact section to understand your case comparison. Consider counterarguments as well when appropriate. Be sure to provide a conclusion on the legal element so that the reader understands the outcome of the comparison.

🗔 ↬**Sample of Effective Case Analogy and Distinction**
🔍 ↬**Constructing Legal Analysis**

COMPARING MULTIPLE CASES

While comparing one case to your case can be effective, it is often too simplistic and might not thoroughly and accurately reflect the law. Usually, multiple cases exist for each rule of law. Therefore, the judge will need to determine which prior cases are more on point and which are closer to the facts and issues presented by your client's case. By providing multiple cases for comparison, you present a broad view of the law and explain where your client's situation fits into that law.

Comparing multiple cases is similar but a bit more complicated than comparing just one case. While you still want to provide a rule up front for context when one is available, the comparison can take many forms. For example, you might start by explaining the facts, reasoning, and holding of the prior cases and explain the similar thread of these cases before applying them to your case. In fact, the thread might be the rule you provide up front for context. Or you might explain one case, compare it to your case, and then move on to a comparison of the second and third case. Yet another formulation would be to present two cases and then explain why one case is similar to your case and the other is different. No one formula is correct, and you should determine how to craft comparisons so that they are both clear and ↪concise.

💾 ↪Sample of Effective Multiple-Case Comparison

USING MULTIPLE CASES TO SET OUT LEGAL PARAMETERS OR A SLIDING SCALE ARGUMENT

At times, you will find multiple cases that, when combined together, set out a legal parameter or a sliding scale of the law. Your job will be to use these cases to first set out the sliding scale for the judge and then to argue where your case falls on that scale.

For example, assume you are analyzing the reliability of a witness identification in a criminal case where you represent the defendant. One of the factors determining reliability of the witness identification is the time between the crime and the identification by the witness. You find a case that holds that the identification was reliable because there was only one day between the crime and the identification. You find another case that holds that a six-month delay was unreliable. In your case, there was a three-month delay between the crime and the identification of your client. To argue this particular factor, you would use these cases to set out the sliding scale for the judge, such as "one day is reliable, but six months is unreliable." Next, you would need to compare your case to these cases and argue where your case falls on the sliding scale: "Three months is closer to the six months that was found unreliable." You would need to look at the reasoning or policy from the prior cases to argue the appropriate outcome.

Sliding Scale:

↪One Day_____Six Months

       ? ← ← Three Months (your case) →→ ?

Or consider adding even more cases to the scenario:

↪One Day   One Week   Four Months   Six Months

       ? ← ← Three Months (your case) →→ ?

Here, you could incorporate all four of the cases into your analysis to determine whether three months would be too much delay between the crime and a reliable identification.

💾 ↪Sample of Sliding Scale Argument

Legal Analysis — Typical Problems with Case Comparisons

Typical problems with case comparisons include the following:

1. **Using quotations from cases instead of analysis.** Oftentimes new lawyers rely on quotations, assuming that the author of the opinion will carry more weight and articulate the analogy better. This assumption is often wrong in case analogies. By definition, analogies compare a prior case to the present one. If a lawyer simply relies on language from the prior case, then the comparison itself is lost. While quotations are often useful, especially when enunciating a rule of law, do not overrely on them for analogies. Block quotations are especially cumbersome, and readers often skip over them.

2. **Using only facts of your case and omitting case precedent.** Grounding your arguments in the law is the key to case comparisons. A typical mistake of new lawyers is to provide a rule and then use only facts from the client's situation to show why the rule applies or doesn't apply. Instead, a lawyer should try to use prior cases to show how that rule has been applied (or not) in the past and then show why the facts of the case are similar (or not) to case precedent.

3. **Omitting the holding of the precedent.** A case is not going to be useful for analogies if the reader does not know which way the court held. Be sure to include the court's ruling in your analogy.

4. **Using too much of the prior case.** Use only the relevant facts and the reasoning of the prior case to make your point. Do not inundate the reader with extraneous parts of the case because these will only cause confusion with the current case.

5. **Omitting the facts of the current case.** Relying solely on case precedent is not enough for a comparison. You should also supply enough of the facts of your case to show why the prior case is similar or not.

6. **Omitting the tie between the prior case and the current case.** Don't forget to show why the prior case is similar or different from your case. Here, facts, reasoning, and policy are often used for support.

7. **Ignoring the other side's argument.** Case analogies are stronger if they anticipate the other side's argument and show why that argument will fail.

⟼Determining the Problems Within Your Case Comparisons

Legal Analysis — Policy Arguments

When lawyers make policy arguments, they focus on broad social goals that will be affected by the outcome of the case. Policy arguments are made in a number of contexts. First, as discussed in ⟼**statutory interpretation**, lawyers make policy arguments when they interpret the legislature's purpose in writing the statute. Second, lawyers also make policy arguments when no clear rule exists; the lawyers will then argue what the rule should be based on a particular policy. This type of situation is called a case of first impression. Third, lawyers make policy arguments in addition to other legal arguments in ⟼**constructing their legal analysis**. In all of these instances, the lawyers will argue why the interpretation or creation of a particular law is consistent or inconsistent with the policy of the jurisdiction or society in general.

As a lawyer, you can be very creative with policy arguments. You can weave your policy arguments throughout your document or delineate a separate section for them. Think of as many different policy reasons as you can for your desired outcome and then choose the one or two that are most compelling. You should also refer to the section on ⟼**jurisprudence** for some policy background. Some possible policy arguments include the following:

- **Moral values.** Policy arguments based on moral values argue that a particular law will offend or perpetuate a moral value. For example, "Teenagers should be required to get parental approval for an abortion." Here, the moral issue is teen abortion and the argument would focus on the moral implications of killing a fetus or the protection of a teenager's right to choose. Oftentimes, these arguments are viewed as political, and it can be helpful to know your audience before you advance these arguments.

- **Social justice.** Policy arguments based on social justice are similar to those based on moral values except that the focus is on society in general instead of on a personal basis. For example, "The death penalty should not exist for minors." Here, arguments would be made by looking at the way society currently views the death penalty. Again, these arguments are often viewed as political, so it is helpful to know your audience.

- **Fairness.** Fairness arguments are based on fairness of the justice system specifically. For example, "Minors should not be held accountable as adults." Here, the arguments would revolve around the implications on the criminal justice system.

- **Economics.** Economic arguments focus on the effect the law will have on economic principles, such as allocation of sources or efficiency arguments. Here, lawyers argue how much rulings will cost society or particular organizations. For example, "Corporations should not be required to reduce greenhouse gases." Here, the focus would be on the cost benefit analysis of such a requirement.

- **Institutional roles and the administration of justice.** Here, the arguments are based on the role the court should play in society as well as whether the court can or should administer a particular rule. For example, a lawyer may argue that the court's role is not to legislate this particular issue or that the rule will lead to a "slippery slope" in the law or a plethora of unwanted litigation that would clog the court system.

As a lawyer, you can be very creative with these policy arguments. Brainstorm many different policy reasons for your desired outcome and then choose the one or two that are most compelling. Consider whether other courts have used the same policy arguments to support their reasoning. If you can cite to other opinions, your policy arguments will be stronger.

Lawyers sometimes weave policy arguments throughout their documents in a fashion similar to a ➥**theory of the case.** Amicus briefs filed in the U.S. Supreme Court often use policy arguments and reflect the beliefs of the organization filing the brief. (For example, the N.R.A. would file a brief in support of gun rights.)

Some lawyers will argue the law first and then delineate a separate section in a document to craft policy arguments. In these situations, lawyers either argue in the alternative or use the policy arguments to show why their interpretation of the legal rule is correct.

🔍 ➥**Jurisprudence**

Legal Analysis—Constructing Legal Analysis

Once you have a basic understanding of the various basic tools of legal analysis (➥**statutory interpretation,** ➥**case synthesis,** ➥**case analogies,** ➥**policy arguments**), you need to use them all to create a cohesive, legal argument. This skill is usually the most challenging to learn and to teach. Students often complain that they receive no guidance until after they have written and submitted a document, and then they are "only told what they have done wrong." Students wish they could have been told "exactly what to do before writing." On the other hand, professors resist providing a "perfect" example or a formula for writing analysis because there are truly an infinite number of ways to write each document, and professors want the students to think about their choices instead of simply following one model or formula.

The following section provides a number of different "formulas" to use as guides when you first begin writing legal analysis. First, however, a warning: Do not follow the formulas blindly; instead, treat them as guides to begin the thinking process. Consider the formulas as myths; do not take them literally, but let them serve as legal compasses to focus you in the right direction and force you to ask the right questions. You need to understand the purpose of each part of the formula so that you can consider varying the formula or choose to ignore it altogether when your creativity allows for better choices.

The Formulas

IRAC (pronounced "eye-rack"): This is the formula that most professors use to teach legal analysis.
I — Issue. Present the issue in the beginning of your analysis.
R — Rule. Explain the legal rule. (This rule might come from a statute, a case, or a regulation.)
A — Application. Apply the legal rule to the facts of your case.
C — Conclusion. Conclude on the issue.

CRAC: This formula is a variation of IRAC; it basically replaces the "issue" with "conclusion" so that the conclusion appears both in the beginning and the end of the analysis.
C — Conclusion. Present your issue in a conclusive manner.
R — Rule. Explain the legal rule. (This rule might come from a statute, a case, a regulation.)
A — Application. Apply the legal rule to the facts of your case.
C — Conclusion. Conclude on the issue.

CRuPAC: This is simply a variation of CRAC, but with a bit more detail.
C — Conclusion. Present your issue in a conclusive manner.
Ru — Rule. Explain the legal rule.
P — Proof of rule. Citation to the authority to prove the rule exists.
A — Application. Apply the legal rule to the facts of your case.
C — Conclusion. Conclude on the issue.

These formulas are often very helpful when writing law school exams, essays on the bar exam, and simple legal writing. For example, when writing a paragraph on the term *outrageous* in an intentional infliction of emotional distress exam question or on a first-year memo assignment, a student might do the following within the formulaic structures:

1. **Issue:** Start with a topic sentence that tells the reader that the plaintiff must prove that the conduct was outrageous. (Or, if using CRAC, state that the conduct was or was not outrageous.)
2. **Rule and Proof:** Provide a definition of outrageous and provide a citation.
3. **Application:** Use a case to compare its reasoning, holding, and facts to the client's facts.
4. **Conclusion:** Conclude on the issue (the conduct was or was not outrageous).

This formula works fine for such a simple analysis. However, what if the analysis is more complicated? What if the rule comes from many sources? What if the rule is not clear? What exactly does application mean? Where should a counterargument go? How does a policy argument fit into these formulas? Students who don't ask these questions and rely on the formulas alone often write legal analysis that is too simple for the existing law. In addition, many students incorrectly assume these formulas must always fit within one paragraph, whereby the topic sentence provides the issue or conclusion, the final sentence of the paragraph is the conclusion, and everything in between is the rule and the application. These paragraphs often span pages and pages of a memo, creating too much information within one paragraph for the reader to digest.

Unraveling the Myth of the Formulas

So what should you do when writing complicated legal analysis? First, if you choose to use a formula, understand why each part of the formula exists. Understand how legal readers think and what they expect. Second, you should rely on your own creativity in legal analysis. Do not assume that there is only one way to interpret, analyze, or apply the law.

Understanding Your Audience and the Formulas: If you choose to follow a formula, you should understand its purpose and its limitations.

Issue or Conclusion: The issue, as used in this context, is not the issue statement or the whole issue for the underlying case. Instead, issue here is used to describe a specific issue or element within the law (such as the meaning of outrageous within intentional infliction of emotional distress). Keep in mind that legal readers want to understand the issue, but they are almost always in a rush. Therefore, the issue should be easy to find. Most busy readers skim documents by reading topic sentences. Thus, by placing your issues in topic sentences, they will be prominent for the skimming reader.

The Rule: The legal reader usually wants to understand the law before it is applied. Therefore, it makes sense to provide the legal context, or rule, before the application. However, this context can be a policy argument, a term of art, a definition, a rule from a case, or from many other sources. Many students mistakenly place a long quote from a case to explain the rule. While quotations are sometimes helpful, they are often too complicated when trying to explain a simple rule. Oftentimes, the term of art from the quotation is enough or a synthesis from a number of cases is necessary. Another mistake here is that students often forget to cite to the source of the rule. A legal reader wants to be assured that the writer did not simply make up the rule. It must come from some authority. Therefore, the authority needs to be cited. If the rule comes from multiple authorities, cite to all of them in a string cite.

Application: Application of the law can be accomplished through ➟**case comparisons,** ➟**case synthesis,** ➟**statutory interpretation techniques,** ➟**policy arguments,** or any combination of these sources, and more. As a legal writer, you need to understand the purpose of legal application. The legal reader will want to know not only **if** the law applies to your client but **why and how** the law does or does not apply. Because your reader will be a doubting audience, you need to prove all your points. You will use the law and your facts in doing so. The trick here is to give the reader enough information so that she does not have to look elsewhere for information. So, you should have enough of your facts in the analysis so she does not have to flip back to your facts section. You should have enough law so that she does not have to read a case or look to the statute separately to make sure you are correct. Do not make your reader do your work for you. Provide all the information she needs within the analysis itself. On the other hand, do not provide information the reader does not need. For example, if you are analyzing the element of outrageous conduct in an intentional infliction of emotional distress memo, you do not need to discuss facts or law that discuss the intentional requirement. Wait for the analysis of that issue.

Counterarguments: When reading your application, a legal reader should mentally ask questions and then find your answers to those questions within the analysis. For this reason, you should also address counterarguments in your application. Deciding which counterarguments to put in and where to place them will require some thinking on your part, and your decisions will often depend on the purpose of your document. For example, in briefs, you should address only those counterarguments that you think the other side will address; otherwise, you run the risk of creating arguments that your opposing counsel did not consider. In memos, you will include more counterarguments, but do not address counterarguments that don't pass the laugh test. In addition, in briefs, counterarguments are usually best placed after your own argument. Downplay them by arranging them within a paragraph instead of at the beginning or end of a paragraph. They should not get more "air time" in your document than your own arguments. In addition, they are usually most effective when they do not begin with "the other side will argue" or "the defense has claimed." These opening clauses only highlight the other side's argument and create a defensive tone in the brief. In memos, however, you might want to emphasize the strength of the counterargument by placing those arguments in the beginning of your application section, giving them priority in your writing, or using a defensive tone.

Conclusion: Finally, the reader wants a conclusion on your particular issue. Here, you should provide not only the ultimate conclusion but also the main reason for your conclusion. That way, the skimming reader will have an answer to the issue as well as a legal reason.

Creativity in Legal Analysis: If you simply follow the same formula over and over within your document, your writing will be very simple, boring, and not very effective. In addition, the formula might not make sense in every situation. Here are some other options and questions to consider:

Persuasive Facts: In persuasive writing, you might want to present your client's facts before you provide the rule, especially if the facts are compelling and the law is not very beneficial.

Policy: What if the policy behind the rule helps your client more than the rule itself? You might want to start with an application of the policy before you present the rule.

Counterarguments: Sometimes it makes sense to address them within your analysis of the issue; other times, it might make more sense to address them separately as their own issues in a point-counterpoint organization.

Parties: At times, you might abandon starting with an issue altogether; you might start with the party and analyze the law around each party's main arguments.

Various Rules: When the law is very complicated or a rule is not clear, you might address multiple scenarios or various possible rule structures before you begin to apply each one separately.

Various Issues: When you have separate issues, you may decide to combine issues instead of applying each one separately within the formula.

Themes: You might organize persuasive analysis by themes instead of by issues.

Once you understand the reasoning behind the formulas, you can choose to abandon the formulas and apply the law creatively and effectively. Remember to think about your various choices and make your decisions according to your specific purpose and audience.

📋 ➥ **Quick Reference**

Legal Analysis — Quick Reference — Statutory Interpretation

Statutory Interpretation Note-Taking Chart

Use this note-taking chart to organize your arguments for your statute.

Code § Elements *(breakdown of law)*	Plain Language and Definitions	Purpose / Policy	Legislative History	Case Law	Context
	Pro: Con:	Pro: Con:	Pro: Con:	Pro: Con:	Pro: Con:
	P: C:	P: C:	P: C:	P: C:	P: C:
	P: C:	P: C:	P: C:	P: C:	P: C:
	P: C:	P: C:	P: C:	P: C:	P: C:

Quick Reference — *Legal Analysis — Case Comparisons*

Case Comparisons Note-Taking Chart

Use this note-taking chart to organize your cases and arguments within each element of the law.

Relevant Issue	Case Name (citation)	Facts	Reasoning	Holding	Tie to Our Case

Quick Reference — Legal Analysis — Statutory Interpretation

The following statutory interpretation techniques are used to help determine the legislature's intent when writing a particular statute:

1. **Plain language:** How a word or phrase is usually used in the English language.
2. **Definitions:** Often lawmakers provide a definition section, which usually appears in the beginning of the code section. If no definitions exist, lawyers look to other sources, such as definitions from other statutes, definitions from Black's Law Dictionary or other dictionaries, or definitions from judges or scholars.
3. **Context of the language:** Lawyers look to see where the terms of art appear in the statute, what words appear near those terms, and what terms appear nowhere in the statute to assess the meaning of the terms.
4. **Case law:** Judges write opinions that interpret the meaning of the statute. These cases then act as binding precedent in statutory interpretation.
5. **Legislative history:** When writing a statute, lawmakers discuss, debate, and write about the proposed statute. These pieces of legislative history can provide insight into the legislature's purpose in passing the statute. To find legislative history, a lawyer would research committee reports, floor debates, and speeches. Legislative history is also useful to determine congressional intent if the statute has been amended.
6. **Policy arguments:** Lawyers often make policy arguments to show why a particular statute was passed. Oftentimes the statute itself contains a policy or purpose section.

Quick Reference — Legal Analysis — Case Comparisons

DO'S OF CASE COMPARISONS

1. **Do include enough of both your case and the prior case.** You must provide enough information on both your case and the prior case for the reader to understand the analogy.
2. **Do make the tie between your case and the prior case clear.** You cannot assume that the reader will be able to see the connection herself; make the tie clear with specific language.
3. **Do be creative.** Case comparisons do not always need to follow the same format. In fact, you may lose the reader's attention if yours do. The typical IRAC (issue, rule, analysis, conclusion) format does not work for every piece of analysis and can become boring and redundant even when effective.
4. **Do use complicated case analysis.** Using more than one prior case in a case comparison can often be a powerful form of analysis, particularly if the synthesized rule from the prior cases is applicable to your case.
5. **Do remember that your argument should be based on case comparisons, not simply long quotes or abstract rules.** Simply stating the law or quoting a prior case is not helpful to your case analysis if the reader cannot see how it applies to your case. While quotations and rules are often necessary, be sure to take your analysis one step further and show the reader how the quote or rule applies to your particular facts.

DON'TS OF CASE COMPARISONS

1. **Don't use quotations from cases instead of analysis.** Analogies are, by definition, comparing a prior case to the present one. If a lawyer simply relies on language from the prior case, then the comparison itself is lost. While quotations are often useful, especially when enunciating a rule,

do not overrely on them for analogies. Block quotes are especially cumbersome, and readers often skip over them.

2. **Don't use only the facts from your case and omit case precedent.** Grounding your arguments in the law is the key to case comparisons. A typical mistake is to provide a rule and then use only facts from the client's situation to show why the rule applies or doesn't apply. Instead, when available, use prior cases to show how that rule has been applied (or not) in the past, and show why the facts of the case are similar (or not) to case precedent.

3. **Don't omit the holding of the precedent.** A case is not useful for analogies if the reader does not know the court's holding.

4. **Don't use too much of the prior case.** Use only enough facts and reasoning from the prior case to make your point. Do not inundate the reader with extraneous parts of the case as it only confuses the reader.

5. **Don't omit the facts of the current case.** Relying solely on case precedent is not enough for a comparison. You should also supply enough of the facts of your case to show why the prior case is similar or not.

6. **Don't omit the tie between the prior case and the current case.** Don't forget to show *why* the prior case is similar or different from your case. Here, facts, reasoning, and policy are often used for support.

More Ebook Interactivity

 Legal Analysis — Quick References and Checklists

QUICK REFERENCES

- Statutory Interpretation - Note-Taking Chart
- Case Comparisons - Note-Taking Chart
- Statutory Interpretation
- Case Comparisons

CHECKLISTS

- Legal Analysis Generally
- Statutory Interpretation
- Case Analysis
- Policy Arguments
- Jurisprudence and Rhetoric
- Constructing Legal Analysis

 Legal Analysis — Class Exercises

- Case Synthesis (Tank)
- Case Comparisons (Tank)

↤ Statutory Interpretation (Tank)
↤ Statutory Interpretation
↤ Case Synthesis #1
↤ Case Synthesis #2
↤ Case Synthesis #3
↤ Policy Arguments

 Legal Analysis — Quizzes

⚇? Legal Analysis

Writing and Rewriting

In this section, you will learn legal writing techniques to help the reader follow and understand your analysis. This writing section will focus on the writing process rather than particular →**legal documents**. The rewriting section will provide techniques that will help you in both writing and rewriting your documents. The section on persuasive writing provides techniques specific to briefs and motions.

Writing and Rewriting — The Writing Process

Legal writing is different from any other writing you have done before. Whether you have been an undergraduate student, a business executive, or a paralegal, you are still a novice legal writer. As a novice, you will need to adjust your writing to meet your new audience, the legal reader, and to reach the goals of your writing in the legal community.

The Legal Reader

The legal reader has many traits specific to the legal discourse community. As you enter this new community, you will need to understand these nuances and adjust your writing to meet your audience. Below are common traits of the legal reader as well as suggested tips to assist the reader in understanding your writing.

Trait #1: The legal reader is a doubting audience. As he reads your writing, he will expect you to prove everything you say with legal authority and analysis.

Tip #1: To help the doubting reader, you need to cite to legal authority and use concrete legal analysis to prove your arguments. Thus, whenever you write a proposition, back it up with a citation to a legal authority. (Most of these citations will appear within the text, not as footnotes.)

Trait #2: The legal reader talks to himself. As he reads your document, he will ask questions and expect answers immediately within your writing.

Tip #2: Answer all possible relevant questions when writing. This does not mean that you should write questions within your document and then answer them. Instead, it means that you should show both sides of the legal issue and respond to all possible issues presented by the facts and the law.

Trait #3: The legal reader is reading for an answer to a specific question. Whether it is a supervising attorney who has asked you to write about a legal issue or a judge who is going to decide a case, he is looking for the answer to a particular issue or set of issues.

Tip #3: Answer the question up front. Do not make the reader wait for the answer. Use the rest of your document to prove the answer.

Trait #4: The legal reader is in a rush. He often skims documents and wants a solid understanding of the law through a quick read. Assume his attention span is weakest mid-paragraph and mid-document.

Tip #4: Use roadmaps and strong topic sentences. The reader should be able to skim the document reading only the roadmaps and topic sentences and be able to understand the basic structure of the law. The roadmap should present the law in an organized fashion, and the topic sentences should use the terms of the specific elements of the law.

Trait #5: The legal reader does not want to be bothered with too much detail or tangential information. The reader is looking for a specific answer to a specific question. However, when you research the issue, you might stumble across other issues as well that might affect the outcome of the case. Oftentimes, the supervising attorney has already considered these issues or has asked someone else to research them.

Tip #5: Be sure to focus on the issue assigned. Ask the reader ahead of time, when possible, about other avenues or legal theories before you go on and on about them for wasted pages. On the other hand, it is a good idea to bring important issues to the reader's attention, whether in the particular document or in some other form of communication such as a conversation or an email.

Trait #6: You, as the writer, know more than the reader. You have spent the time researching, studying, and analyzing the issue. The reader has asked you to do so, so that you can teach him about the law and its application.

Tip #6: Be specific. Do not assume the reader understands either the law or the facts. You know the issues, the facts, and the law better than the reader, so you need to spell out your analysis. Avoid holes in your arguments, and do not assume that the reader knows what you mean without making your point explicit.

The Goals of Legal Writing

Although the purpose of each legal document will be different, there are common goals and expectations within the legal writing community that differ from other writing communities. Below are some common goals in legal writing and some tips for reaching them.

1. **Legal documents rely on legal precedent, not on your personal opinions.** In your undergraduate studies, you might have written papers to show your new ideas or perspectives on a certain subject. In legal writing, however, your opinions do not have the same value. Legal precedent is valued, not your personal opinions or beliefs. This does not mean that you cannot be creative or use your ideas to craft legal arguments—you can. However, the law will be your starting point, you will rely on and cite to legal authority, and you should omit "I believe" and "I think" from your vocabulary.

2. **Legal writing has an effect on others.** If you are representing a client, your writing may help win or lose the case. If you are a judge (or a clerk), your writing not only will decide the particular case, but it also will affect cases in the future. If you are writing a contract, your writing will bind the parties for years to come. Your writing will also have an effect on yourself. Your reputation as a lawyer often rests on your writing abilities. A good legal writer usually makes a very marketable lawyer.

3. **Legal writing comes with responsibility.** When you write to a client, you must be accurate and thorough. If you are wrong, you could be liable for malpractice. When you write to the court, you must also be accurate and ➥**ethical.** Failure to do so can lead to disbarment.

4. **Legal writing should be concise.** In undergraduate studies, long papers were often rewarded. In legal writing, long documents are frowned on. Instead, clear and concise writing is rewarded and appreciated.

5. **Legal writing should be well organized.** Because the law is often complex, legal writing needs to be well organized so that the reader can follow the legal arguments and analysis. A strong organizational scheme helps lead the legal reader through the complicated arguments.

6. **Legal writing should follow assigned formats.** Courts (and often law offices) have stringent rules for filing legal documents. If you fail to follow a simple formatting rule, courts often reject the document. Therefore, it is important to research your local court rules and follow them word for word.

Although legal documents share similar general audiences and overall goals, each document is written for a specific audience and has specific goals. A memo written to a partner in a law firm differs from one written to a different partner in the same firm. A brief to an appellate judge differs from a motion to a trial court. Before you begin to write any ➥**legal document**, first consider purpose, audience, scope, and view. Each of these appears in this ebook at the introduction to each new document.

Read the following sections if you are having trouble with any one of the topics listed:

1. ➥**Creating Your Own Effective Writing Process**
2. ➥**Managing Your Time**
3. ➥**Overcoming Writer's Block**
4. ➥**Writing Creatively**
5. ➥**Organizing Before You Write**

Writing and Rewriting — Creating Your Own Effective Writing Process

Writing is a personal matter. For some it comes naturally; for others it is a chore. Many writers, especially in the undergraduate setting, do not think about their process; they simply sit down to write. While this method might have been successful for you in the past, it will not be an efficient or effective process for legal writing.

As a legal writer, you will need to develop a writing process that works for you. Consciously developing an efficient and effective process now will save you time and money later. When thinking about your process, consider breaking it down into these manageable categories:

1. **Prewriting** — Researching, reading, and organizing the law before you begin your draft. Outlining may or may not be a part of your prewriting strategy. In this book, most of the prewriting areas are addressed in ➥**Research Sources** and ➥**Research Strategies.**

   🔍 ➥**Prewriting**

2. **Writing** — Writing the first draft of the legal document. In this book, writing is addressed in this section.

   🔍 ➥**Writing**

3. **Rewriting** — Reworking the draft, time and again, focusing on large-scale issues such as content, large-scale organization, analysis, and conciseness. A well-written legal document is often rewritten over ten times. In this book, rewriting is addressed in the next part of this section.

    🔍 ➥**Rewriting**

4. **Editing and Citation** — Editing for syntax, sentence structure, and grammar; polishing for typos and citation. In this book, these areas are addressed in ➥**Editing and Citation.**

    🔍 ➥**Editing and Citation**

When creating your own process, determine which category is your weakest and allot more time for it. Keep in mind that the process is not linear. Once you begin writing, you will often need to revisit the prewriting category for more research.

Writing and Rewriting — Managing Your Time

Lawyers typically encounter rigid deadlines, either court-imposed or specified by a supervisor. Often, as a deadline approaches, another project implodes or a client is arrested and needs immediate attention. Therefore, time management, especially of written products, is important for lawyers to master. The best lawyers are often those that remain on schedule.

Here are a few tricks for effectively managing your time:

1. **Create a false deadline.** Instead of writing the supervisor's due date on your calendar, mark the due date a few days earlier.
2. **Self-impose a schedule.** Create dates for each step of the writing process. Come up with dates, for example, for finishing the first draft, the large-scale organization of the first draft, and the rewritten analysis of the revised draft. Make these dates realistic so you can stick to your schedule.
3. **Create incentives.** Give yourself a reward when you have finished a particular section.
4. **Set aside time to walk away from your document.** You will need time away from your document to begin to hear the reader's voice instead of your writer's voice. Allot time to spend on other projects before you come back to your document.
5. **Set aside time for unpredictable disasters.** Your computer will always crash hours before an assignment is due. Therefore, make sure your assignment is complete in enough time to deal with the computer or other problems that are bound to occur. An extra day on the calendar relieves a lot of anxiety, which may then contribute to writer's block.

The timeline below animates the adjustment many students need to make from an "all-nighter" writing process, where the draft is written and rewritten in one sitting, to a paced writing process, where the first draft is written with plenty of time for rewriting subsequent drafts and taking time away from the document. The key is adjusting your "draft" due date from the end of the timeline to the middle.

➥**Timeline Animation**

Writing and Rewriting — Overcoming Writer's Block

Lawyers typically encounter writer's block either when (1) their task seems too daunting, or (2) they expect to write a perfect draft at the first sitting.

If your task seems daunting: If a project seems too complicated or large, break it up into small manageable chunks. Set small goals and realistic deadlines for each chunk. Envision the project as a group of smaller projects and then set out to accomplish one small project at a time.

If you expect to write a perfect draft: For some, writer's block stems from a seemingly incurable need to write the document perfectly the first time. For these legal writers, the draft is the final product. A writer with such a conviction will surely suffer as the law is such a malleable mess. Typically, the legal writer learns more about the law as she writes about it than she learned as she researched it. Therefore, the lawyer who assumes she can write about the law once and have a complete document will become frustrated. Instead, a legal writer should assume that writing is a learning process and that multiple drafts will be necessary to massage the law into a form that will be logical and readable. A legal writer should embrace the idea that the first draft is a starting point. Once that mindset is established, writer's block will fade as the writer begins her learning process in her draft.

Writing and Rewriting — Writing Creatively

Creativity is the key to effective legal writing. As a legal writer you must first develop creative arguments and then present them in a manner most likely to inform and sometimes persuade your audience. Legal writing should not feel or sound formulaic or staid. Use legal writing conventions as a method of understanding your audience, not as a way to stifle your creativity.

Here are some ways to write creatively:

1. Develop a unique ➥**theory** for your case.
2. Use the facts of your case to tell a compelling story.
3. Create a novel argument.
4. Use ➥**case law** creatively in a traditional argument.
5. Anticipate the other side's arguments and distinguish them.
6. Reorganize your document in a nontraditional manner.
7. Look at the judge's opinions not only for what is there, but also what is not.
8. Create ➥**policy** arguments.
9. Vary your ➥**sentence structure**.
10. Do not be trapped into the IRAC (issue, rule, analysis, and conclusion) box.
11. In general, think outside the box.

Writing and Rewriting — Organizing Before You Write

Before you begin writing, it is a good idea to get organized. For some, this simply means getting all the research materials together in a coherent fashion. For others, it also means creating an outline of the document before writing the draft.

Getting Research Materials Together

Once you have researched the law, you will most likely have a pile of materials ready to include in your document. However, first, you need to organize these materials. Second, you must decide which materials are relevant — do not assume they will all be included in your document simply because you found them when doing your legal research.

Organizing the materials can be done in a variety of ways, depending on your comfort level and needs. Some writers prefer to print out all research (even if found online) and then organize it into piles. These piles are usually based on legal elements or issues. For those who are more comfortable on the computer, research can be organized by folders and files without the need for printing. Keep in mind that some materials can be copied and pasted (or physically piled) into numerous folders. So, a case on one issue might also discuss another issue; therefore, it would be placed in both folders, but for different reasons. For example, a case on intentional infliction of emotional distress might be placed in a folder for the element of "intentional;" if it also discusses damages, it would be placed in the damages folder as well. (This is where using the computer is especially helpful.)

Determining what materials are relevant is a bit trickier. At times, it will take outlining the document to make this determination. Other times, it will take the actual drafting of the document to determine relevancy. And, even further along in the process, you might decide on relevancy during the rewriting stage of your process. Therefore, it makes the most sense to be overinclusive in your outline as it is usually easier to delete material than it is to add it later.

Outlining Your Document

Some writers prefer to begin writing right away without creating an outline. This process is fine if it works for you. However, just because this process worked for you in undergraduate school, do not assume it will work for you in law school or your future legal writing career. It might, but it might not. Because organization is so important in legal writing, try creating a writer's outline before writing at least one legal document in law school. That way, you can determine if the process works for you before you begin representing real clients.

Creating an outline is a very personal process and can be done in a variety of ways. The following section provides some tips for writing an outline for a typical legal document where you apply a particular rule of law to a set of facts. However, do not assume this is the only way to create an outline; there are an infinite number of ways to write effective outlines, and there are an infinite number of documents you might write. Tailor your outline to the needs of the document. The overall goal is to create organization out of chaos.

As with your legal document, your outline should revolve around the rule of law. Therefore, your starting point and the foundation of your outline should be the actual legal rule you are going to apply. Rules come in many forms (see ➥**Understanding Legal Rules**), and you should begin your outline by writing out the legal rule.

Once you have written the rule, you should separate it out into its component parts or sub-elements. That way, you will have space to begin adding your research within each part.

Now, pour through your research, file by file or pile by pile, and start filling in information under each element. Is there a definition? Where does it come from (it might come from multiple sources)? Are there cases that analyze that element? If so, what are the holdings, reasoning, and facts from each case? List each case separately under each issue. One case might appear under one element as well as under a different element (although you might include different facts and reasoning). This process will take some time as you are both rereading the law and deciding where each source fits within the analysis.

Now that your outline contains the rule of law and some of the definitions and applicable cases under each element, you can begin to add your facts from your own case. It is at this stage that you will begin to make some clear-cut relevancy determinations as your facts might differ substantially from other cases. If another case is factually very different from your own, it might not be useful for a case comparison (although it might have a useful definition or policy argument). As you fill in your facts, you can start writing notes about how the remaining cases might be compared to your facts.

By the end of this process, you might have produced a very long document. Some outlines are thinner than others, but some can be longer than the final document itself. The process is very personal, so you need to determine what works best for you. Keep in mind that the outline is to help you get started and to serve as a guide for writing. Do not let it confine you or stifle your creative thinking. Oftentimes, your outline will not be the best organizational scheme as it is your first attempt to organize the analysis. Feel free to keep reworking the organization and the law as you write, or consider writing multiple outlines before you even begin writing.

Typical Questions About Outlines

1. **What if there is more than one issue?** Oftentimes, there is more than one issue. You might create separate outlines for each issue or create one outline with multiple issues. It is up to you, and it will depend on how you decide to write the document as a whole.

2. **How do I know what kind of test I am applying?** There are numerous types of tests in the law. For typical breakdowns, see ➥**Understanding Legal Rules**. The test itself will be found in a statute, in a regulation, or within cases. Oftentimes, the same rule is repeated by various legal sources.

3. **What if one element of the test is easily met (or not met)?** In objective writing, you should still analyze the element in case your determination is wrong (unless it is absolutely certain: for example, "The victim is deceased."). In persuasive writing, you will make determinations based on different ➥**persuasive tactics**.

4. **How do I show the relationship between elements?** Remember to include connectors such as *and*, *or*, *may*, and *shall* in your outline so that the relationship is clear in your organization.

5. **Do I need roman numerals?** Labeling or numbering your outline is a personal choice. It works for some people and not for others. Be careful if you do use numbers to be flexible. You might determine that your first argument is not your best once you fill in the outline.

6. **Can I use the outlining feature in my word processing software?** Yes, but you don't have to. It works well for some people, but not for others. Also consider using a table or a spread sheet for your outlining.

7. **Do I need to address elements in the same order as they appear in the rule?** For persuasive writing, you should address elements in the most persuasive order, which is often not the same order as the rule itself. At times, it might make sense to address the elements that are easily met first and then the others afterwards. The best advice is to start with the order as it appears in the rule, but digress from that order if you have good reasons to do so and if the writer can still follow the rule clearly and logically.

8. **Do I start an outline by following the formal requirements of the document, such as the question presented in the memo?** You can do that, but the best starting point for an outline is with the law, which basically begins in the discussion section of a memo or the argument section of a brief. It often makes more sense to start here, with the analysis, and then fill in the question presented, facts, and so on later, once you understand the law better.

Although there is no one set way to compile your research materials or to outline your document, you should find some way to organize the law before you begin writing. The process of culling, organizing, and writing an outline often helps you understand the basics and some of the intricacies of the law before you begin writing the document. Oftentimes, writing an outline saves a lot of time later in the writing and rewriting process.

Writing and Rewriting — Rewriting

Rewriting, for the legal writer, is the process of reworking the large-scale facets of the document. Do not confuse this section with ➥**editing** for grammar.

It is important in the rewriting process to remember that you — the writer — have lived with this law for an extended period of time and have learned the nuances and intricacies of the analysis. The reader, however, is about to experience the law for the first time through your document. Therefore, one of the tricks to rewriting is to step into your reader's shoes by assuming you know nothing about the law or the client's situation.

TIPS FOR STEPPING INTO THE READER'S SHOES:

Take time away from your document. Take a week, a day, an hour. The longer you are away from your document, the easier it will be to hear your reader's voice instead of your writer's voice.

Read your document out loud. A "read aloud"— either done by yourself or a colleague or friend — allows you to hear the words that have floated inside your brain for a while. The difference between what you hear orally and what you "hear" in your mind is striking.

Create a reader-based outline. Outline your first draft by reading only the topic sentences. The outline you create will simulate the busy reader's impression of your major points as she skims your document. If your reader-based outline mirrors the writer-based outline you may have created in the prewriting process, then your arguments will be clearly organized.

Use a focused rewriting process. Develop a rewriting process where you focus on one aspect of the writing at a time. If you try to rewrite everything at once, you will become overwhelmed and will not rewrite very effectively. Instead, focus on each of the following categories separately, spending days or hours on each one:

1. ➥**Content**
2. ➥**Large-Scale Organization**
3. ➥**Paragraph Organization and Legal Analysis**
4. ➥**Small-Scale Organization — Sentence Structure**
5. ➥**Conciseness**

Writing and Rewriting — Content

When rewriting, make sure that your content is accurate. To do this, reread the actual law relied on in the document. Reread the whole case or statute. Oftentimes, writers take notes when reading the law and then transfer those notes into the document. However, it is important to go back to the law — especially when it is case law — to ensure that you are accurately referencing the law. Oftentimes, you will find nuances within a case that further bolster your argument, or that you are misrepresenting a case or taking it out of context, which will hurt your credibility with your reader.

TIPS:

1. Reread in its entirety the law you have cited to make sure your characterizations are accurate.
2. Read a ➥**secondary source** on your issue to make sure you have not omitted any important concepts and to ensure that you have accurately reflected the law.

3. Reread each piece of the law separately and compare it to the way you use it in your document.

4. Find any quotation and be sure you are using it properly and within context to ensure your credibility.

5. Be sure you are ➥**citing** the law accurately, including pinpoint cites, so your reader can easily find your authorities.

Writing and Rewriting — Large-Scale Organization

Because the law is often complicated and dense, good organization is critical for the legal reader. To help the reader navigate your document, you should not only clearly identify the issues and outline the breakdown of the law, but you should also provide hand-holding techniques to help your reader understand those issues and legal elements.

Identifying Issues and Breaking Down the Law

One of the first things you will do in writing and rewriting is focus on your document's large-scale organization — the organization of the document as a whole. You need to decide how to break down the issues and how to present them in a manageable package for the reader. Although you will have a lot of discretion and room for creativity in your documents, your large-scale organization usually will be dictated by the issues and the legal rule.

First, you need to decide the issues you will address. As a law student, often you will address just one issue, usually dictated by your professor (e.g., you will write a memo on the issue of intentional infliction of emotional distress). However, as a lawyer, you will need to decide the relevant issues and the order in which to address them. You should address each issue separately and, to help your reader, identify those issues up front.

Think of your document as an inverted triangle. The top part of the triangle should be a broad identification of the issues for your reader. As you work your way down the triangle, your writing becomes more and more focused.

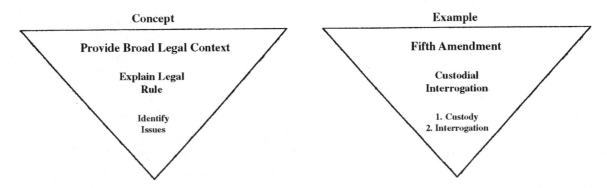

Second, organize each issue around the relevant legal rule. Whether they come from statutes, cases, regulations, or a combination, most legal rules are easily identified. Typical types of legal rules include a balancing test, a totality test, a multi-factored test, and a test with multiple exceptions. See ➥**Understanding Legal Rules**. Regardless of the type of rule, break down the law into its sub-elements. Similar to the issues themselves, address each sub-element separately and, to help your reader, identify those sub-elements at the beginning of each issue section.

Think of each issue as an inverted triangle. Start off your discussion of that issue broadly by providing the context for the reader as well as the breakdown of the sub-elements. Then, as your triangle becomes more narrow, your document focuses on the specific issues.

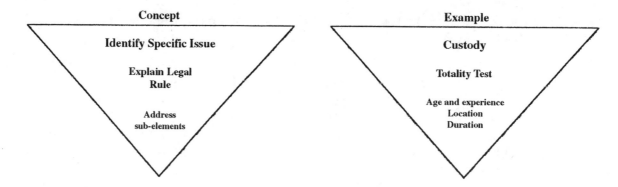

Third, each sub-element should be clearly organized by identifying the sub-element, providing the legal context for the reader, and applying the law to the facts. The organization of the ➤**legal application** is complex. Here, many legal writers provide the legal definition for the sub-element before they start applying the facts to that rule in a formula often called ➤**IRAC**. While this organizational scheme often makes sense, don't be tempted to fit your analysis into it all the time. First, the formula is too simplistic. Rules are sometimes much more complicated than the IRAC system allows for and cannot be easily defined. Second, the facts may provide a better starting point for context, especially in persuasive writing. Third, formulaic writing leads to boring writing. As a legal writer, you want to keep your reader's attention to inform or persuade. Don't get caught up in a formula when addressing each issue. Instead, follow the general principle of the inverted triangle: Begin broadly with context and focus your analysis more specifically as you work your way through the issue.

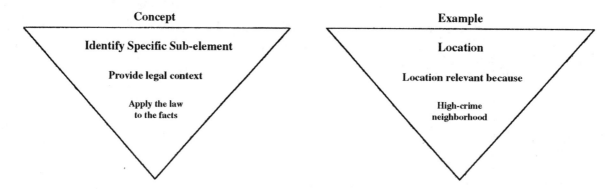

Keep in mind that there are a number of different, effective ways to organize your document. The above example shows an organizational scheme that revolves around legal elements. However, you can create any organizational scheme within the law that works for the purpose of your document. For example, in persuasive writing, you might choose to organize around a particular theory. When writing a memo to a partner or a letter to a client, you might decide to arrange the document around each party's arguments (we say/they say). You may choose to argue policy instead of the law, especially if you are arguing a case of first impression or you ever get a chance to argue in front of the Supreme Court. In addition, when multiple issues need to be addressed, you will have to determine which issues to discuss first and how the issues relate to each other.

Techniques to Help Guide the Legal Reader Through Your Document

Once you have decided on your issues, found the relevant law, and broken down the law into its sub-elements, you should use techniques to help guide the legal reader through the document. Legal readers are busy. They like to read documents quickly, often hoping to skim them for meaning. Therefore, you should craft documents that are easy to understand when skimmed. Two techniques — roadmaps and topic sentences — help guide the legal reader through the organization of the document.

Roadmaps: Law students are desperate to understand the black-letter law of a problem as quickly as possible. The legal reader is no different. Therefore, a document that references the law at the front of the document is beneficial. "Fronting the law" or providing a "roadmap" usually helps the reader understand the writer's organization and the layout of the law. A roadmap is a signal to the reader that the document is organized around the law provided up front. The better legal documents provide a clear roadmap, which is dictated by the organization of the law, and then follow that organization throughout the document, using consistent legal terms. A roadmap may be one sentence, one paragraph, or longer, depending on the complexity of the law. A roadmap can identify issues or the law that defines each issue.

➥**Roadmap**

Mini Roadmaps are another technique to help guide the reader through a complicated piece of the law. Just as a roadmap fronts the law of the whole document, a mini roadmap provides a guide to a subsection of the document or one part of the analysis already laid out in the major roadmap. You may need a mini roadmap to each subsection of the law or none at all.

➥**Mini Roadmap**

Topic Sentences: Once a roadmap is provided, the document should use clear topic sentences that mirror the language and structure of the roadmap. Do not vary terms of art; words, after all, are what make up the law. In addition, transitional words such as *first, second,* and *finally* help hold the reader's hand and move him from one element of the roadmap to the next. (Note: *firstly, secondly,* and *lastly* are not grammatically correct.)

➥**Topic Sentences**

Reader-Based Outlines: To ensure that your reader understands your large-scale organization, you should step into the reader's shoes by creating a "reader-based outline." A reader-based outline is not the same as the outline you might use in ➥**prewriting** to ➥**organize your document** before you write (a writer-based outline). Instead, a reader-based outline is created after you have written a full draft.

To create your reader-based outline, you should start at the analysis section of your document (the discussion section of a memo or the argument section of a brief). First, find and label your roadmap. Next, read only the topic sentences and try to create an outline — either in the margin or on a separate paper — using one or two words that describe the legal element or point made.

Here are additional tips:

- If you cannot label the topic sentences with a one- or two-word description of the legal element, your reader will not be able to understand your organization.

- If your labels resemble case names, your reader will not have a sense of the organization of the law itself because case names mean very little to a reader who is unfamiliar with the law.
- If your labels mirror your writer-based outline, then you have successfully conveyed your ideas to the skimming reader. If your reader-based outline does not mirror your writer-based outline, you still may want to keep your organization since it may have improved on your original design.

⌨ ➥**Reader-Based Outline**

Writing and Rewriting — Paragraph Organization and Legal Analysis

Once you have addressed large-scale organization, you need to focus on the organization within each paragraph as well as ➥**legal analysis**.

Paragraph Organization: A paragraph usually discusses one idea, thesis, or element of the law. Each paragraph should be a discreet unit; it should contain only enough information to analyze that particular idea or element. An effective paragraph usually starts with a clear topic sentence, identifying the issue, idea, or theme to be discussed. The paragraph should then focus on that idea without digressing into other issues or tangential matters.

Paragraphs that focus on legal application are often problematic for novice legal writers to organize. Beginning writers mistakenly spend unnecessary space in their paragraphs quoting the law, discussing irrelevant ideas, or complicating legal issues. The internal consistency of a legal paragraph is especially important in complicated legal analysis. Better writers simplify the law for the reader by synthesizing it into a clear, concise package. An effective legal analysis paragraph sets forth a rule and applies it to the facts at hand.

Sometimes it takes more than one paragraph to accomplish a complete analysis of an issue, especially when the analysis uses a combination of legal authority such as cases, statutes, and policy arguments. As a general rule, a paragraph that is one double-spaced page is too long for your reader to digest; break it down into multiple paragraphs for the reader.

While each paragraph should stand adequately on its own, all your paragraphs should work together to create a cohesive, logical argument. If you believe your reader may become lost either within one paragraph or when moving from one paragraph to the next, reconsider the organization and the content of your paragraphs. In addition, use transitions to help the reader move from one paragraph to the next and to understand your ordering of the paragraphs.

⌨ ➥**Sample Transitions**

The Analysis Within the Paragraph: When organizing analysis within each paragraph, start with the broad context of the law and work your way to the more specific application. Generally, you will present a rule and apply it to the facts of the case.

> **Presenting the Rules:** When presenting the rule, you might use a definition from a statute or case, a policy statement, or a proposition you have created using case synthesis. Simplify the rule for the reader. Long quotations are usually not very helpful. While most lawyers try to present the rule in the beginning of the paragraph to provide a legal context for the reader, there will be times, especially in ➥**persuasive writing**, when a lawyer might start with compelling facts or policy arguments instead of the legal rule.

Rule Application: When applying the rule to your facts, you will use case comparisons, policy arguments, statutory interpretation techniques, and other arguments discussed in legal analysis. As you apply the law to the facts, show how the rule has been applied in the past and how it should therefore be applied in this case. Rule application is extremely complicated. Therefore, various methods of rule application are discussed in-depth in the following sections:

🔍 ↪**Statutory Interpretation**

🔍 ↪**Case Analysis**

🔍 ↪**Policy Arguments**

🔍 ↪**Constructing Legal Analysis**

The application of the law to the facts is often complex and difficult to explain to the reader. Remember that you have read and organized the law before you drafted the document; therefore, you are intimately involved with its nuances. Assume the reader has no such knowledge of the law. To provide clear analysis for your reader, scrutinize your document for holes in logic, omissions in the presentation of the prior law, and mistaken assumptions that the reader understands the facts of your case as well as you do.

Penny-Franc Analogy: An analogy is helpful when rewriting your case comparisons. First, try to draw a penny — both sides — from memory. Go ahead. It will only take a minute and it will illustrate an important point.

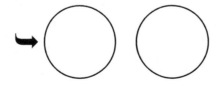

Now that you have drawn the penny, move your mouse over the ↪**circles** to see all the details of the penny.

How many of the details did you miss? If you are like most people, you have missed many of the fine details of the penny, an item you live with every day. Now, look at your drawing (not the real penny) and try to compare your penny to a French two-franc piece. Your reaction should be confusion. This will be the reaction of your reader if you are not explicit with the prior law and the facts of your case.

Here is the analogy. The penny is similar to the facts of your case. Do not assume that your reader is familiar with them just because you have placed them in your statement of the facts. Instead, you need to keep taking them out of your pocket as you analyze the law and compare it to your facts. Be specific with those facts.

The franc is the prior law. Assume your reader has not gone to France or read the prior cases. If she has gone to France, it was a while ago (perhaps before the euro), and she probably does not remember all the details of her visit. Similarly, if she has read the prior case to which you are referring, she probably does not remember it with any detail. Therefore, you need to provide specifics. When referring to the prior case, it is often helpful to provide the facts, reasoning, and holding to help the reader understand its significance.

In addition, you should tie the penny to the franc. For example, under the analogy, the penny presents a stoic bust of Lincoln; the franc piece has a flowing picture of Marianne flitting across the sand under a burning sun. The penny writes out the number "one," whereas the franc piece uses the numeral "2." These "ties" are helpful to compare the two coins. Similarly, you should compare the prior case to your facts to illustrate the logical connection for the reader. Be explicit.

Typical Analysis Mistakes: Legal writers make typical mistakes when performing case comparisons. First, when synthesizing the law, the novice legal writer often tries to explain all the case law up front before applying it to the case at hand. This is different from fronting the law or providing a ➥**roadmap** as mentioned earlier. Instead, the novice often spends pages laying out all the law she has read; then, pages later, she attempts to apply the client's facts to the law. The result is that the reader is required to constantly flip back to the prior pages to understand the prior law as it is being applied. This approach also leads to lengthy documents. Instead, provide a quick statement of the law and then address each element of that law with a layout of that element and simultaneous application of the facts to that element before moving on to the next facet of law. That way, the legal reader understands the law and its application to the facts at the same time. Each issue or element is addressed in full before moving on to the next.

Second, when performing case comparisons and actually showing how the prior case is similar or different from your case (see penny/franc analogy above), novice writers typically omit either the penny or the franc. There are four typical problems with annotated samples:

1. **The Lazy Analogy:** Here, the writer takes the easy way out and provides block quotes or parentheticals instead of full analysis. Block quotes are usually difficult for the reader to digest and make the document painful to read. Oftentimes, the writer can rewrite the quote, utilizing only the most relevant language. Parentheticals are useful for secondary information but should not be used to make the actual case comparison. The writer should take the information out of the parenthetical and place it directly in the text with an explicit tie to the present case.

   ➥**Lazy Analogy**

2. **The Case Study Method:** Here, the writer provides brief descriptions of one case and continues with descriptions of other cases without actually applying these cases to the facts at hand. While this method might be appropriate for case briefs for a law class or case summaries if requested by a lawyer, they do not perform the function of analyzing the law and how it applies to the facts.

   ➥**Case Study Method**

3. **The One-Sided Approach:** Some legal novices, especially when writing memos to supervising attorneys, forget to provide a full, objective analysis in an attempt to please the partner and the client. However, if cases exist that are not very helpful to the client's position, the writer should address and explain them. Even in a persuasive document, the writer should use the opportunity to distinguish these cases for the reader instead of ignoring them.

   ➥**The One-Sided Approach**

Effective Use of Signals in Your Analysis: ➥**Citation signals** (such as *see, cf., but see*) can add depth to your analysis without distracting the reader. A signal is typically used in legal writing for two different reasons: (1) to inform the reader of the authority for the point made; and (2) to provide additional information to the reader. The latter is useful in adding depth to your analysis. For instance, if you have provided a case comparison to illustrate a point of law and another case illustrates the same point, you can provide a signal (see also) with a parenthetical to that case to show the reader that there is even more case law to back up the proposition without providing redundant analysis. In addition, at times a full case comparison is not necessary, and a signal will make your point concisely.

Appropriate Use of Signals: A four-hour interrogation is enough for a suspect to be in custody. See, e.g., Smith v. United States, 542 U.S. 366 (1982) (4 hours, 20 minutes, enough for custody); United States v. Jones, 252 U.S. 543 (1975) (3 hours, 30 minutes, enough for finding of custody).

The key to using signals to add depth to analysis is to remember that signals provide additional or secondary information; they should not provide the actual analysis. If you are using signals and parentheticals to provide the actual analysis, you are making the Lazy Analogy mistake discussed above.

➥Using Signals in Your Analysis

Writing and Rewriting — Small-Scale Organization — Sentence Structure

Small-scale organization refers to the way in which you organize each sentence. Legalese and lengthy sentences, though often used in judicial opinions, are not very helpful to the busy legal reader. Instead, strive for simple, concise, clear sentences.

Here are some general rules to help with sentence structure in legal writing:

Use Strong Subject-Verb Combinations and Avoid Annoying Clauses

English readers like to know the subject and verb as quickly as possible, so create strong subject-verb combinations and place them in the beginning of the sentence. Because readers often get lost when you separate the subject from the verb, place modifying clauses and qualifiers after the subject and verb or in a separate sentence. As a result, you will avoid long sentences with annoying clauses.

Poor sentence structure: The victim of the assault, who was only sixteen at the time of the assault and photo array but now eighteen sitting in the courtroom, testified that she recognized the defendant from a photo array.

Better sentence structure: The eighteen-year-old victim testified she recognized the defendant from a photo array. She was only sixteen when assaulted.

Avoid beginning sentences with phrases such as There was, It is, and There were. Instead, start with a strong subject-verb combination.

Poor sentence structure: There were multiple defendants entering the courtroom when the judge took the bench.

Better sentence structure: Multiple defendants entered the courtroom when the judge took the bench.

DO NOT VARY TERMS OF ART

In legal writing, the words create the law. Varying words or phrases can change the whole meaning of the law. Therefore, do not vary terms of art as you may have in undergraduate studies.

AVOID LONG QUOTATIONS

Readers' eyes often skip over long quotations, especially block quotes. Consider writing part of the language in your own words and quoting only the necessary phrases.

USE PARALLEL STRUCTURE

When writing sentences that have lists or multiple rules, use consistent grammatical form. Parallel structure makes it easier for the reader to understand your ideas.

> *Poor sentence structure*: The jury considered the evidence, the testimony, and what the judge had to say during jury instructions.

> *Better sentence structure*: The jury considered the evidence, the testimony, and the judge's instructions.

BE CONSISTENT IN THE USE OF TITLES

When referring to a person by name, be consistent so as not to confuse the reader. In addition, when referring to multiple people in a document, be consistent in how you refer to them. For example, if you use "Mr. Jones," do not use "Edith Jones" to refer to his wife; refer to her as "Mrs. Jones" or "Ms. Jones." Unless you have a specific reason, use *Ms.* instead of *Mrs.*

Use a parenthetical to explain a name only when it is necessary to clarify for the reader.

> *Poor use of parenthetical*: The defendant, Mr. John Jones (Jones), ...

> *Better use of parenthetical*: The employer, American Foundation for Better Learning (AFBL), ...

WRITE SHORT, SIMPLE SENTENCES

Do not assume that you need to write long, complicated sentences to sound lawyerly. Instead, short, simple sentences will help you write clearly and apply the law logically. In persuasive writing, short sentences pack the most punch.

For more information, see ➥**Conciseness** and ➥**Grammar and Usage Rules.**

Writing and Rewriting — Conciseness

Legal readers are in a rush. They do not want to be bothered with long documents or excessive words. Short documents are often most effective and hold the readers' attention. Clear ➥**large-scale organization** and ➥**analysis** should help cure some wordiness issues. In addition, when rewriting, you can make your document more concise by editing for relevancy and redundancy, and remembering some word choice tricks.

Here are three tricks to eliminate wordiness:

1. **Relevancy:** What makes a fact relevant enough to place in your fact section? If you use a fact in your analysis, it is relevant and should appear in your fact section. What makes legal application relevant? If you use law to advance your argument, it is relevant. If it does not advance a point or help illuminate a breadth of case load supporting your point, omit it. You should not include law just to show you have completed a lot of research.

2. **Redundancy:** Some redundancy is helpful for clarity. For example, topic sentences might seem redundant with headings and roadmaps, but they help guide the reader. In addition, consistent terms of art are conducive to good legal writing because the terms of art are constantly being interpreted. Therefore, do not vary terms of art. However, if certain words reappear within the same sentence or two, consider combining sentences to avoid redundancy. Never, though, sacrifice clarity for conciseness.

   ⊬ ⇥ Tutorial on Redundant Words

3. **Word Choice Tricks:** Word choice is the art of legal writing. It gives the document meaning and voice. Concise word choice is preferred in most legal writing. By using the following word choice tricks, you can omit many extraneous words.

   1. **Omit "glue words":** One author, Richard Wydick, distinguishes words into two categories in each sentence: working words and glue words. The goal is to eliminate as many glue words as possible to make the documents less sticky.

      ⊬ ⇥ Tutorial on Glue Words

   2. **Avoid passive voice if unnecessary:** Active voice, when the subject of your sentence is the actor, is usually preferred language because it is more concise. However, if you want to downplay the actor, passive voice might be the better option.

      ⊬ ⇥ Tutorial on Passive Voice

   3. **Avoid legalese:** Words that sound lawyerly are often long-winded and unnecessary. Avoid words such as *wherein*, *whereon*, *inasmuch*, *insofar*, *herein*, and *aforementioned* whenever possible.

   4. **Avoid unnecessary phrases:** Lawyers often use twice the amount of necessary words in order to seem lawyerly. Avoid this temptation. Aim for conciseness. Instead of the following phrases, use simple words that are more concise:

      By means of ⇥ by
      For the purpose of ⇥ for
      In order to ⇥ to
      Begin to develop ⇥ develop
      Void and unenforceable ⇥ unenforceable
      Period of five years ⇥ five years
      Distance of 100 miles ⇥ 100 miles
      Due to the fact that ⇥ because
      In the event that ⇥ if
      At this point in time ⇥ currently or now
      Be able to ⇥ can
      Was aware of the fact ⇥ knew
      Despite the fact ⇥ although
      As a consequence of ⇥ because

Employ ➥ use

Endeavor ➥ try

5. **Create strong subject-verb combinations:** Shorter sentences usually begin with a subject-verb combination. Sentences that begin with *There is*, *There was*, *It is*, or *It was* place their subjects and verbs midsentence, making it harder for readers to immediately grasp the meaning. To make these sentences more concise, omit *There is* or *It was* and begin with a subject-verb combination.

   ⬌ ➥**Tutorial on Strong Subject-Verb Combinations**

6. **Avoid unnecessary commentary:** Lawyers sometimes like to extend their personal thoughts into their persuasive writing. Avoid making this mistake as such commentaries are likely to distract from the merits of the case or provide unprofessional personal attacks against the other side's counsel.

7. **Avoid nominalizations:** A nominalization makes a verb into a noun. Leave the word as a verb. Some examples:

   Give consideration to ➥ consider

   Make a contribution to ➥ contribute

   Have an understanding of ➥ understand

   Gain knowledge from ➥ learn

Writing and Rewriting — Persuasive Writing

Persuasive writing is the art of convincing another that you are right. In most legal writing, whenever you are writing a persuasive document, someone on the other side is trying to persuade the reader that you are wrong. As a result, when learning to write persuasively, you need to consider the techniques for legal writing in general as well as additional techniques to make your argument more compelling than that of your opposing counsel.

This section introduces you to the following techniques used in persuasive writing to highlight your side while downplaying the other:

- Moving from Objective to Persuasive Writing
- Designing the Theory of the Case
- Crafting the Fact Section
- Drafting the Argument Section
- Using Effective Sentence Structure and Word Choice
- Taking Advantage of Technology

Specific forms of persuasion, such as ➥**oral argument**, ➥**briefs**, and ➥**motions**, are discussed in the ➥**legal documents** section.

Writing and Rewriting — Persuasive Writing — Moving from Objective to Persuasive Writing

Some legal documents are written to show both sides of the argument and therefore present the information and analysis objectively. Memos, client letters, and other work product usually present information in an objective manner so that the attorney and client can make informed decisions.

Other documents are written persuasively—to win. Although the writer discusses the other side's argument, she does so in a light most favorable to her client. By distinguishing cases used by opposing counsel or illuminating gaps in reasoning, the legal writer can present persuasive documents that subtly persuade while informing about law on both sides. Trial briefs, motions, pleadings, and appellate briefs include typical persuasive documents; the opposing side is privy to these documents, and service is often required.

This section illustrates some of the differences between objective and persuasive writing. However, keep in mind that most legal documents combine objective and persuasive writing. For example, briefs are considered to be persuasive, but they usually persuade the reader more effectively if they sound objective. On the other hand, legal memos are considered objective because they illustrate both sides of the argument; however, the writer usually tries to find every possible creative and viable argument for his client, so there are some persuasive undertones.

Objective Writing: In objective writing, such as ➥**legal memoranda**, the writer's goal is to inform the reader of both sides of the argument so that the reader can make an informed decision. Thorough analysis of the arguments and counterarguments are required, and the writer should make a prediction as to the legal outcome.

Oftentimes, an objective document suggests that the client refrain from engaging in a particular activity or inform the client that she has performed some illegal act. The basic goal of an objective document is to thoroughly inform the reader, for better or worse. A typical mistake made in objective writing is to tell the reader what she wants to hear instead of presenting the facts and the law objectively.

Persuasive Writing: In persuasive writing, such as ➥**briefs**, the writer's goal is to inform and persuade. Persuasion does not mean informing the reader of just one side of the argument. The best persuasive documents address the other side's arguments, but downplay or distinguish them. One of the biggest mistakes in persuasive writing is to hit the reader over the head with persuasion so that the arguments sound hyperbolic or become personal attacks against the other side. Therefore, subtle persuasion is the trick in persuasive writing.

Many students enjoy writing persuasively. Not only is there a degree of competition involved, but the writer need not decide how the law should come out, as is the case with most objective writing. Instead, your position is dictated by the side you represent, and your goal is to choose the best strategy to win. As a lawyer, there may be times when you do not like the side you represent. However, your goal is to zealously represent your client and to do your best to win regardless of your distaste for the client or the position you are forced to argue.

Writing and Rewriting—Persuasive Writing—Designing the Theory of the Case

What Is the Theory of Your Case?

Each persuasive document should contain a subtle theory. This is not a legal theory; instead, it is a simple, factual theory that will help your reader empathize with your client. For example, in a bus accident case, a legal theory might be negligence, but the theory of your case might be "the bus driver was in a rush." Such a simple theory is easy to understand and goes hand in hand with the legal theory. Thus, as you develop the law of negligence in your persuasive document, you can also use facts to enhance your theory of the case, such as the speed of the bus or the bus driver not paying careful attention. By using a subtle theory that is simple and easy to understand, the reader can sympathize with your client before she even understands the law. The theory of the case should be evident throughout your document, from the fact section to the argument section.

→ **Sample Theory of the Case from Supreme Court Briefs in <u>Clinton v. Jones</u>**

How to Develop a Theory of the Case

When you first begin to research and prewrite your document, you should brainstorm a number of potential theories for your case. Do not settle on one theory until you have had time to really think about the advantages and disadvantages of each one. Consider your audience: Which theory will best influence your particular judge? Look at the facts and the law: Which theory will be easier to prove? Consider the large-scale organization: Which theory will help your organizational scheme become stronger and more persuasive? Think about the other side: What will the other side choose for a theory? (You may already know your opponent's theory if, for example, you are writing an appellee's brief or opposition to a motion.)

Checklist for an Effective Theory

1. **Is the theory simple?** If you can't explain your theory in one or two sentences, it is too complex. In addition, be sure to stick to one theory. While you may argue the legal arguments in the alternative, you should have one overarching theory for your whole case.

2. **Is the theory subtle?** If you have to explain your theory over and over, it is not subtle. In fact, in persuasive writing, the best theories are those that are not written; instead, when the judge puts down the document after reading it, he should state your theory out loud. For example, if your theory is that the defendant, a grandmother and breast-cancer survivor, is lying, you probably should not write out in your brief that she is lying. Instead, you should lay out the facts in a persuasive manner so that when the judge is finished reading, he claims, "That grandmother is lying!"

3. **Does your theory take the high ground?** Make your client "the good guy" so that the judge wants to find for your side. You might provide a theory that makes the other side seem like the "bad guy," motivating the judge to punish her.

4. **Does your theory make sense within your factual framework?** Your theory must work not only within your own factual background, but also within all the facts that are not in dispute. If your theory also works within the other side's facts, it will be even more effective.

5. **Does your theory make sense within your legal framework?** Although your theory of the case is different from your legal argument, it still must fit within the legal framework. For example, arguing that your client is a wonderful teacher of new doctors in a hospital might not be a good enough theory to defend him against a medical malpractice case.

6. **Does your theory explain the "why" of the case?** Your facts will explain what happened. Your law will explain the legal implications of what happened. The theory should explain why it happened.

7. **Does your theory pull at the reader's heart strings?** While not all theories are emotional, some of the best theories force the judge to rule in your favor because of the emotional pull of the theory.

Writing and Rewriting — Persuasive Writing — Crafting the Fact Section

The fact section of a persuasive document is your first opportunity to tell the story from your client's perspective. A chronological presentation is usually most effective because it is easily followed. A number of techniques help make fact sections more persuasive:

Theory: Although the theory of the case is woven throughout your whole brief, the fact section is the first opportunity to tell the full story from your client's perspective. The theory should be subtly embedded throughout the fact section so the reader feels for your client as the story unfolds.

Starting Point: Choosing a starting point for your facts is crucial as it provides a focal point for your theory of the case. For example, while a prosecutor might begin a fact section with the gruesome crime, the defense brief might start with the defendant's arrest. Whatever your starting point, it should be an opportunity for the judge to crawl into your client's perspective.

Word Choice: Word choice throughout the fact section is also important. The prosecutor might use the term defendant to highlight the fact that the other side stands accused. On the other hand, the defendant's brief would use the client's full, formal name: for example, Mr. Anthony Jones or Dr. Smith (first names alone, however, are usually too informal for a brief to a court). By personalizing your client, you increase the chances that the judge will become familiar and comfortable with him.

The Facts: The fact section of a brief should be thorough and honest. Do not avoid harmful facts. If you do, the judge will read about them in the other side's brief and assume you are attempting to hide them. As a result, not only do you look distrustful, but also you lose an opportunity to distinguish and downplay the harmful facts. You can downplay them by discussing them in a light most favorable to your client. Some techniques to downplay facts are to explain them away or to place them in between more favorable facts for a less dramatic impact on the reader's impression of the client.

➥**Sample Statement of Facts from Supreme Court Briefs in <u>Rhode Island v. Innis</u>**

Writing and Rewriting — Persuasive Writing — Drafting the Argument Section

The argument section uses ➥**legal analysis** — the application of the law to the facts — to show why you should win. You should make informed decisions about the order in which you place the issues, the way in which you formulate the rule, and the way in which you handle adverse authority. In addition, avoid sounding defensive or attacking the other side personally.

Ordering of Issues

General legal wisdom is to present your best arguments first, initially using your strongest cases and other law to prove your point. The reasoning here is that you hold your reader's attention most carefully in the beginning of your document and at the beginning of each paragraph. Sometimes, however, ordering your arguments chronologically or in another order that best introduces your theory of the case makes more sense. A typical legal writer will order and reorder a persuasive document many times before filing. However, do not let the other side's brief dictate your ordering of issues. One of the biggest mistakes in writing oppositions is to follow the organizational scheme set out by the opposing side. Instead, you should choose the scheme that works best for your side and theory. In addition, keep in mind how much "air time" you give your arguments compared to the time you take addressing the other side's arguments. Your arguments should have the highest priority and so should take up the most space on the paper. While a complex counterargument may need a number of pages to cover the nuances, be wary of the subtle message that you send by spending too much time on a particular issue.

→**Pointheadings** and →**subheadings** are also useful tools in persuasive writing. Sometimes they serve as a scoreboard: The more subheadings for your side, the more good arguments you have. However, do not just write as many subheadings as you can to have the most in your brief. Instead, craft your pointheadings and subheadings carefully. Choose terms of art and facts that are favorable for your side. Do not create subheadings or pointheadings for unfavorable issues or using unfavorable facts. Instead, address these adverse issues and facts within other subheadings.

The Legal Rules

Oftentimes, the rule of law that applies can be interpreted in multiple ways. The trick it to choose the interpretation that best fits within your theory of the case and is most persuasive for your side. Do not assume that the other side's interpretation is correct, especially when writing an opposition to a strong brief. To formulate the rule in a light most favorable to your client, look for key terms of art that are easy to prove (or disprove) and strong cases within your interpretation.

Adverse Authority

You will often find cases in your research that do not help your client. You will need to decide what to do with them. →**(See ethics.)** If you decide to leave them out of your persuasive writing, you run the risk that the other side will rely on them, and you will then have lost an opportunity to distinguish them. Instead, consider addressing them head on and distinguishing them yourself.

You can use a number of strategies in dealing with adverse cases:

1. **Distinguish the facts:** Show the court that the facts of the case are so different from your facts that the case does not apply.
2. **Distinguish the reasoning or the policy:** Show the court that the reasoning or the policy of the case is so different from the reasoning or policy in your situation that the case does not apply.
3. **Find a better case:** Show how a more recent case or a case with more binding authority applies in a different fashion than the adverse case. Then rely on the better case.
4. **Downplay the case:** Address the case within a discussion of other cases so that the other cases seem more important (even if they are not).
5. **Overrule authority:** As a last resort (but not recommended), ask the court to overrule previous authority. Be aware, however, that judges, especially trial judges, rarely do so as they run the risk of being overruled by an appellate court.

🔍 →**Case Comparisons**

Do Not Sound Defensive

Many poor persuasive documents sound defensive. As mentioned above, an opposition to a motion might use the opponent's motion as a model for organization and counter each argument in the same order. This technique is not effective for two reasons: (1) The writer loses the opportunity to make organizational decisions to help prove his argument. Instead, he accepts the carefully designed organizational decisions of his opponent. (2) The document consistently argues the negative, and the tone of the document is "did not"—a very whiny approach to legal writing. Therefore, watch for topic sentences that begin with "The opposing side argues" or "The defendant incorrectly states." There is no need to present the other side's argument again for him as repetition helps the reader remember. Instead, present your arguments affirmatively and in the order in which you decide is best for your theory of the case.

➥ Samples of Defensive Writing

Do Not Personally Attack the Other Side

Oftentimes, lawyers let arguments become personal. Avoid this urge. Instead, make sure that your document addresses issues and does not attack the other side personally. Judges do not appreciate personal gripes between lawyers, and usually your credibility suffers when you use such tactics.

➥ Samples of Personal Attacks

Do Not Overstate Your Case

Your credibility is your best tool in persuasive writing. Do not lose it. If you overstate your case or a particular fact, you lose credibility with the court. If you misstate a rule of law or present reasoning from a case out of context, you lose credibility. On the other hand, if you always sound reasoned and rational and admit any weaknesses in your case (preferably those that do not matter), your arguments will have more credibility and therefore will be more persuasive.

Writing and Rewriting—Persuasive Writing—Using Effective Sentence Structure and Word Choice

If persuasive writing is the art of convincing another that you are right, then the sentences and words are the tools of the art form. The following rules can help make your sentences and words more persuasive:

1. **Short sentences have more of a punch.** Novice writers often try to pack their sentences with as much information as possible in hopes of providing the reader with all the necessary information. However, a reader who cannot understand a sentence or who does not have time to decipher all the clauses will not be persuaded. Shorter sentences are usually more persuasive and more easily digested by the reader.
2. **Affirmative language is more effective than negative language.** Here, tone comes into play as well as sentence structure. It is simply easier to understand an affirmative sentence, and a negative tone may come off as defensive or whiny.
3. **Vary the sentence structure.** Formulaic writing is boring. When you vary the sentence structure, the reader stays engaged longer.
4. **Avoid passive voice.** Sentences are easier to read and more persuasive when the actor is doing the acting. Therefore, you should generally avoid the passive voice. However, if you want to downplay an actor's involvement, use the passive voice. ("The victim was allegedly shot by my client" is better than "My client allegedly shot the victim.")
5. **Avoid unnecessary dependent clauses.** Dependent clauses often get in the reader's way. Use them for facts or law that you want to downplay. Highlight helpful facts and law within the main clause of a sentence.

6. **Put key points in the beginnings of sentences and paragraphs.** Because a reader's attention wanes easily, put the important information up front — at the beginning of sentences and at the beginning of paragraphs.

7. **Avoid *clearly* and *really*.** Language that overstates your case is not helpful. Empty words such as *really*, *clearly*, and *obviously* add nothing to your argument and make you sound as if you are stretching to make your points.

8. **Use plain English.** Do not use flowery language or try to impress your reader with obscure words. Instead, use plain English so that the reader can easily follow your arguments and rule in your favor.

Writing and Rewriting — Persuasive Writing — Taking Advantage of Technology

People retain more information and remember it for a longer time if it is provided visually. As readers, we take the words we read and make mental images. Including images within a brief, then, can help to persuade your reader. As the number of courts requiring e-filing increases, so does the number of multimedia tools available that integrate images into your briefs. The trick with using such visuals, however, is to learn how to use them to help persuade, not just to provide a "wow" factor. As a writer, you should use technology within your briefs to create a simulated environment where the reader actually steps into the client's shoes.

Here are some ideas for embedding multimedia within briefs:

1. **Pictures.** If a picture paints a thousand words, then pictures can make our briefs a lot shorter. Consider embedding a picture in a brief if it will show the crime scene, bring the victim or her injuries to life, or personalize your client.

2. **Animations.** An animation can help to show how something works — especially in patent cases — or to show how a part of the body functions (such as blood running through a vessel).

3. **Simulations.** A simulation can be very effective to show your side of the facts. A simulation can make your reader feel as if he is a part of the action. He can then hold the visual image in his mind when reading the law.

4. **Video.** Videos can help show a day in the life of your client or can show a crime scene in a three-dimensional fashion such as a walk-through of a house.

5. **Diagrams and maps.** Diagrams often use very little technology and are already used as visuals within briefs. Maps can be downloaded from the Web and embedded within briefs to give the reader a sense of direction and distance.

6. **Scanned documents.** Documents that would have been attachments to briefs can now be embedded within the brief in an appropriate place within the writing so that the reader does not need to flip back and forth to understand the text about the scanned document.

7. **Links.** Ebriefs can link directly to the law and other sources for the reader to easily locate and read referenced sources.

Make careful choices when using technology within your briefs. Develop a strategy for using multimedia that persuades the reader, for instance, by inviting her into your client's home or life. Do not simply throw technology into your brief without thinking about why and where. If you do, chances are you will not only miss the opportunity to persuade and inform, but you also might confuse and distract your reader.

Writing and Rewriting — Plagiarism and Ethics

Plagiarism

Plagiarism is the act of using someone else's words or ideas without giving credit to the author. To avoid plagiarizing, use quotation marks and citations and try to avoid the frequent use of the cut and paste feature on your computer.

Most schools have plagiarism statements to help students avoid plagiarizing and to provide them with notice of the possible penalties. If caught plagiarizing in law school, penalties are usually stiff; you might be expelled or your transcript might reflect the plagiarism. Oftentimes, plagiarism occurs as students write notes for their journals or papers for seminar classes. Here, they often lift ideas verbatim from other law review articles. Avoid this urge. Instead, quote the author and then create your own novel ideas for your issue.

It is harder to plagiarize in practice as lawyers within a firm often exchange work product so as not to reinvent the wheel. In addition, when drafting briefs, lawyers often use arguments that have been successful in prior similar cases without giving credit to the lawyers who made the earlier arguments. While this method is accepted in practice — especially with lawyers working within the same firm — it is not acceptable while in law school.

Ethics

As a lawyer admitted to the bar, you will be an officer of the court. Therefore, you will be bound to certain ethical rules, a few of which follow. Become familiar with your specific jurisdictional rules and pay close attention in your personal responsibility course.

1. You cannot knowingly make a false statement to the court. Therefore, when writing your briefs or motions, be sure that your information — both about the law and the facts — is accurate.

2. If there is authority within your jurisdiction that is directly adverse to your argument, you must bring it to the judge's attention. This means that you might be ethically compelled to include an adverse opinion within your brief.

3. You may not bring a frivolous suit or make an argument that is considered to be frivolous under existing law. Therefore, when writing your briefs, do not make an argument that is unwinnable under any scenario.

4. You may not make an ex parte communication to the judge unless permitted by law. An ex parte communication is one where you communicate with the judge without the other party being present and without notifying the other party.

Quick Reference — Memos — Self-Evaluation

When evaluating your writing, do not try to "fix" everything at once. Instead, focus your attention on one aspect of the memo at a time. Start with the rewriting issues before moving on to editing issues. For example, looking for grammar problems in a paragraph that might be substantively irrelevant would be a waste of time. Answer each question as fully as possible, writing on both this checklist and your memo.

1. **LARGE-SCALE ORGANIZATION**

   A. Have you started your discussion section with a statement of the law that applies to your client's problem? Where is that "roadmap"? (Either circle on your memo or state where it is located.)

   B. Create a "reader-based outline" by reading only your topic sentences and writing a one- or two-word description of the point of each topic sentence. (You can make the outline on the margins to your memo or on this Quick Reference.)

      1. Does your reader-based outline parallel the structure of your roadmap? Why or why not? Do you use the same legal terms in your topic sentences as you use in your roadmap?

      2. Does your reader-based outline convey the major legal points you thought you made in your memo? Why or why not? (If you write an outline before you begin writing, how does your reader-based outline differ from your writer-based outline?)

   C. Read the substance of each paragraph. Either here or in the margin of your paper, give a one- or two-word issue or sub-issue discussed in each paragraph. Does the paragraph actually discuss the issue and only the issue that your topic sentence addresses? Why or why not?

   D. Do you provide a conclusion at the end of each element (1) to let the reader know that you have completed the discussion of that element, and (2) to tell the reader your reasons for the outcome of that element?

2. **LEGAL ANALYSIS**

   A. Is there an applicable statute for your memo? If so, what statutory interpretation techniques did you use in this paper, and what statutory techniques did you choose not to address? (Explain in detail the techniques you used, e.g., plain meaning, context, purpose, definitions, cases, legislative history. Explain where you used or did not use them.)

B. Do you support your legal conclusions with specific facts and/or legal authority? Point out a conclusion and your specific facts and legal authority that support that conclusion. Point out a conclusion that is not supported by facts or authority.

3. PURPOSE

A. Do you present arguments for both sides of each element you address? Where could you have been more objective?

B. Do you answer the question for the lawyer? Where in the memo did you put the answer? Is your final answer consistent with an answer you might have placed earlier in the memo?

4. CITATION

A. Did you cite the statute correctly? What Bluebook rules did you consult to cite the statute?

5. STRENGTHS AND WEAKNESSES

List three strengths and three weaknesses in this memo.

1. _____   1. _____

2. _____   2. _____

3. _____   3. _____

Quick Reference — Memos — Peer Evaluation

One of the goals of this book is to help you become your own editor. This Quick Reference is designed to help you continue developing your evaluation process. By evaluating a peer's memo, you become another set of eyes for that peer and begin reevaluating your own memo.

When evaluating your peer's writing, do not comment on everything at once. Instead, focus your attention on one aspect of the memo at a time. Start with the rewriting issues before moving on to revising issues. While it is important to give positive feedback, focus on places where the writer needs improvement so that every writer gets ample opportunity for helpful criticism. Answer each question as fully as possible, writing on both this form and your peer's paper, before moving on to the next question.

After evaluating the memo, meet with your peer to discuss your evaluation.

I. FORMAL FORMAT

A. **Question Presented:** Does the QP provide the reader with the jurisdiction, the specific legal question, and the most legally significant facts in a coherent and objective manner? Why or why not? Can you read the whole QP aloud in one breath?

A1. How does this writer's QP differ from your own?

B. Brief Answer: Does the BA provide an answer to the QP? In addition, does the BA use the legal buzz words from the law to provide the main reasons for the conclusion?

B1. How does this writer's BA differ from your own?

C. Conclusion: Does the conclusion fill in the main facts and reasons from the Brief Answer?

C1. How does this conclusion differ from your own?

D. Statement of Facts: Does the statement of facts tell a clear and concise story, providing the legally significant facts from your case? Put square brackets around those facts that you believe are not legally significant.

D1. How does this statement of facts differ from your own?

II. LARGE-SCALE ORGANIZATION

A. Has the writer started the discussion section with a statement of the law that applies to the client's problem? Where is that "roadmap"? (Either circle on the memo or state where it is located.)

A1. How is that roadmap different from your own?

B. Create a "reader-based outline" by reading only the topic sentences and writing a one- or two-word description of the point of each topic sentence. (You can make the outline on the margins to the memo or on this form.)

B1. Does the reader-based outline parallel the structure of the roadmap? Why or why not? Does the writer use the same legal terms in the topic sentences as in the roadmap?

B2. How does the writer's organizational scheme differ from your own?

C. Read the substance of each paragraph. Either here or in the margin of the paper, give a one- or two-word issue or sub-issue discussed in each paragraph. Does the paragraph actually discuss the issue and only the issue that the topic sentence addresses? Why or why not?

D. Does the writer provide a conclusion at the end of each element (1) to let the reader know that she has completed the discussion of that element, and (2) to tell the reader the prediction for the outcome of that element? Which mini-conclusions are effective?

D1. Do you come out differently from the writer on each element? If so, where and why?

III. LEGAL ANALYSIS

A. What statutory interpretation techniques did the writer use in this paper?

B. Did the writer effectively use cases to support the legal arguments? Where? Which cases are different from the ones you chose?

C. Look at the case analogies. For each analogy, does the writer use the facts, reasoning, and holding from the prior case and compare them to the specific facts of your case to predict an outcome for the client? Be specific in your answer.

C1. Which is the best case comparison? The worst? Why?

C2. How might you now change your own case analysis techniques to make the comparisons clear and specific?

IV. PURPOSE

A. Does the writer present arguments for both sides of each element addressed? Where could the writer have been more objective?

B. Compare the writer's objectivity to that in your paper. What arguments might you make that you did not previously consider?

V. EDITING

1. Did you find any patterns of grammar problems? Where?

2. Did you find any of your own grammar problems in this memo? Where?

Quick Reference — Briefs — Self-Evaluation

When evaluating your writing, do not try to comment on everything at once. Instead, focus your attention on one aspect of the brief at a time. Start with the rewriting issues before moving on to revising issues. Answer each question as fully as possible, writing on both this form and your document, before moving on to the next question.

Brief in General

A. **General Format:** Do you provide a title page, a table of contents with clear pointheadings and page numbers, and a table of authorities?

B. **Statement of the Issue(s) Presented:** Does the issue statement provide the reader with the specific legal question, written in a persuasive manner? Why or why not? Can you read the whole issue statement aloud in one breath?

C. **Statement of the Case:** Does the statement of the case tell a clear and concise story? Does it provide the legally significant facts from the case? Is it written persuasively?

C1. What is the theory of the case?

C2. What specific word choices do you use that make the statement of the case persuasive?

I. Argument Section

1. **LARGE-SCALE ORGANIZATION**
   A. Do you start the argument section with a statement of the law that applies to the client's problem? Where is that "roadmap"? (Either circle on the brief or state where it is located.)

   B. Create a "reader-based outline" by reading only the topic sentences and writing a one- or two-word description of the point of each topic sentence. (You can make the outline on the margins to the brief or on this form.)

      B1. Does the reader-based outline parallel the structure of the roadmap? Why or why not? Do you use the same legal terms in the topic sentences as in the roadmap?

   C. Read the substance of each paragraph. Either here or in the margin of the paper, give a one- or two-word issue or sub-issue discussed in each paragraph. Does the paragraph actually discuss the issue and only the issue that the topic sentence addresses? Why or why not?

D. Do you provide a mini-conclusion at the end of each element (1) to let the reader know that you have completed the discussion of that element, and (2) to reiterate your position on that element? Which mini-conclusions are effective?

2. LEGAL ANALYSIS

A. Do you use legal authority to back up your arguments? Where?

B. Look at the case analogies. For each analogy, do you use the facts, reasoning, and holding from the prior case and compare them to the specific facts of your case to prove your point? Do you use more complicated comparisons by referencing more than one case at a time? Be specific in your answer.

C. Which is the best case comparison? The worst? Why?

D. What other techniques do you use to make your arguments? Which are effective and which are not?

3. PERSUASIVE TECHNIQUES

A. Can you tell what the theory of the case is in the argument section? If yes, what is it? Is it consistent with the theory of the case in the statement of the case?

B. Is the roadmap written persuasively? Are the topic sentences written persuasively? Be specific.

C. What specific word choices do you use that help with the persuasion?

D. What other techniques do you use to make the document persuasive?

Editing and Polishing

1. Do you find any patterns of grammar problems? Where?

2. Are there any citation problems in this brief? Where?

Quick Reference — Briefs — Peer Evaluation

One of the goals of this book is to help you become your own editor. This Quick Reference is designed to help you continue developing your evaluation process. By evaluating a peer's brief, you become another set of eyes for that peer and begin reevaluating your own brief.

When evaluating your peer's writing, do not comment on everything at once. Instead, focus your attention on one aspect of the brief at a time. Start with the rewriting issues before moving on to revising issues. While it is important to give positive feedback, focus on places where the writer needs improvement so that every writer gets ample opportunity for helpful criticism. Answer each question as fully as possible, writing on both this form and your peer's paper, before moving on to the next question.

After evaluating the brief, you should meet with your peer to discuss your evaluation.

Brief in General

A. General Format: Does the writer provide a title page, table of contents with clear pointheadings and page numbers, and a table of authorities?

B. Statement of the Issue(s) Presented: Does the issue statement provide the reader with the specific legal question, written in a persuasive manner? Why or why not? Can you read the whole issue statement aloud in one breath?

B1. How does this writer's issue statement(s) differ from your own?

C. Statement of the Case: Does the statement of the case tell a clear and concise story, providing the legally significant facts from the case? Is it written persuasively?

C1. What is the theory of the case?

C2. What specific word choices does the writer use that make the statement of the case persuasive? Where could it be more persuasive?

C3. How does this statement of the case differ from your own?

I. Argument Section

1. LARGE-SCALE ORGANIZATION

A. Has the writer started the argument section with a statement of the law that applies to the client's problem? Where is that "roadmap"? (Either circle on the brief or state where it is located.)

A1. How is that roadmap different from your own?

B.   Create a "reader-based outline" by reading only the topic sentences and writing a one- or two-word description of the point of each topic sentence. (You can make the outline on the margins to the brief or on this form.)

B1. Does the reader-based outline parallel the structure of the roadmap? Why or why not? Does the writer use the same legal terms in the topic sentences as in the roadmap?

B2. How does the writer's organizational scheme differ from your own?

C.   Read the substance of each paragraph. Either here or in the margin of the paper, give a one- or two-word issue or sub-issue discussed in each paragraph. Does the paragraph actually discuss the issue and only the issue that the topic sentence addresses? Why or why not?

D.   Does the writer provide a mini-conclusion at the end of each element (1) to let the reader know that she has completed the discussion of that element, and (2) to reiterate her position on that element? Which mini-conclusions are effective?

2.   LEGAL ANALYSIS
A.   Does the writer use legal authority to back up his arguments? Where? Where can the writer cite to more authority?

B.   Look at the case analogies. For each analogy, does the writer use the facts, reasoning, and holding from the prior case and compare them to the specific facts of your case to prove his point? Does the writer use more complicated comparisons by referencing more than one case at a time? Be specific in your answer.

C.   Which is the best case comparison? The worst? Why?

D.   What other techniques does the writer use to make the brief's arguments? Which are effective and which are not?

3.   PERSUASIVE TECHNIQUES
A.   Can you tell what the theory of the case is in the argument section of the brief? If yes, what is it? Is it consistent with the theory of the case in the statement of the case?

B. Is the roadmap written persuasively? Are the topic sentences written persuasively? Be specific.

C. What specific word choices does the writer use that help with the persuasion?

D. What other techniques does the writer use to make the document persuasive?

Editing and Polishing

1. Do you find any patterns of grammar problems? Where?
2. Do you find any of your own grammar problems in this brief? Where?
3. Are there any citation problems in this brief? Where?

Quick Reference — Persuasive Techniques

Develop a subtle theory of your case. This is not a legal theory; instead, it is a simple, factual theory that will help your reader empathize with your client. The theory of the case should be woven throughout your document, from the fact section to the argument section.

Write a persuasive fact section. The fact section is an opportunity to tell the story from your client's perspective. Choosing a starting point is important, as it provides a focal point for your theory of the case. Word choice is also crucial: the prosecutor might use the term *defendant*, while the defendant's brief would use the client's name. The fact section should not avoid harmful facts; instead, it should downplay them by discussing them in a light most favorable to the client.

Write a persuasive argument section. The argument section includes facts and law to persuade the judge that you should win. Here, you should make informed decisions about the order you place your issues, legal points, and primary authority. General legal wisdom is to present your best arguments first, using strongest cases to prove your point. The reasoning here is that you hold your reader's attention most carefully in the beginning of your document and at the beginning of each paragraph. Sometimes, however, ordering your arguments chronologically or in another order that best introduces your theory of the case makes more sense.

Avoid sounding defensive. Don't use your opponent's motion or brief as a model for your organization. This strategy is ineffective because you lose the opportunity to make organizational decisions to help prove your own argument and because you will be consistently arguing the negative. Watch out for topic sentences that begin with, "The opposing side argues . . ." Don't present the other side's argument again, as the repetition will help your reader remember. Instead, present your arguments affirmatively and in the order in which you decide is best for your theory of the case.

Don't personally attack the other side. Don't let the argument become personal. Instead, make sure that your document addresses issues and does not attack the other side personally.

More Ebook Interactivity

 Writing and Rewriting — Quick References and Checklists

QUICK REFERENCES

- Memos — Self-Evaluation
- Memos — Peer Evaluation
- Briefs — Self-Evaluation
- Briefs — Peer Evaluation
- Persuasive Techniques

CHECKLISTS

- Writing in General
- Writing
- Rewriting
- Persuasive Writing

 Writing and Rewriting — Quick References and Checklists

- Conciseness
- Conciseness #2
- Reader-Based Outline
- Sentence Structure
- Creating Objective Writing

 Writing and Rewriting — Quizzes

- Writing and Rewriting

Editing and Citation

Editing — Strategies for Editing Grammar and Legal Usage

This section is designed to help you edit at the sentence and word choice levels. You should not attempt to edit in this room until you have ➥**rewritten** your document for content, large-scale organization, analysis, and conciseness. Editing a sentence is a waste of time if you later decide to delete the whole paragraph or argument.

There are many strategies for editing your sentence structure, syntax, and word choice:

1. **Read the whole document out loud.** A "read aloud" helps you hear the words and understand how they might affect the reader. If you are breathless in your reading, your sentences are too long. If you sound choppy in your reading, your sentences are too short. Mix them up.

2. **Determine your grammar and usage weaknesses and look for them in your document one at a time.** To determine your weaknesses, you can take the ➥**editing self-assessment**. Next, focus on one weakness at a time in your document. For example, if you know you have a problem with your modifiers, read all your sentences, find the clauses, and make sure that your modifiers are correctly positioned. You will actually save time using this method as your focus will make you more efficient.

3. **Read one paragraph at a time** and look for all grammar and usage problems paragraph by paragraph. Take a break after a couple of paragraphs to ensure you remain focused.

4. **Read your document backwards**, either word by word to make sure there are no typos or starting with the last sentence or last paragraph first. The purpose of reading backwards is to distance yourself from the substance of the document. If you are reading in the correct order, from start to finish, you will tend to read for content instead of usage. If you read the last paragraph first, you will be more able to concentrate on the words and sentence structure. In addition, you tend to lose steam at the end of your editing process, and, as a result, the end of the document is usually not as well polished as the beginning. If one of your strategies is to edit from end to start, your whole document should be well polished.

Editing — Grammar and Legal Usage Rules

- ➥**Active vs. Passive Voice**
- ➥**Affect vs. Effect**
- ➥**Although vs. While**
- ➥**Apostrophes**
- ➥**Because vs. Since**
- ➥**Capitalization**
- ➥**Clearly or Obviously** (avoid using)
- ➥**Colons and Semicolons**
- ➥**Commas**
- ➥**Comparisons**
- ➥**Conciseness**
- ➥**Contractions**

- ↪**Dangling Modifiers** (avoid using) *see Misplaced and Dangling Modifiers*
- ↪**Due to**
- ↪**Effect vs. Affect** *see Affect vs. Effect*
- ↪**Farther vs. Further**
- ↪**Hyphens**
- ↪**Italics**
- ↪**Legalese** (avoid using)
- ↪**Modifiers** (avoid using when dangling or misplaced) *see Misplaced and Dangling Modifiers*
- ↪**Nominalizations**
- ↪**Numbers and Quantities**
- ↪**Obviously or Clearly** (avoid using) *see Clearly or Obviously*
- ↪**Parallel Structure**
- ↪**Passive vs. Active Voice** *see Active vs. Passive Voice*
- ↪**Pronouns**
- ↪**Quantities and Numbers** *see Numbers and Quantities*
- ↪**Quotation Marks – Placement**
- ↪**Redundancy** (avoid using)
- ↪**Semicolons and Colons** *see Colons and Semicolons*
- ↪**Sentence Fragments** (avoid using)
- ↪**Sexist Language** (avoid using)
- ↪**Short Sentences**
- ↪**Since vs. Because** *see Because vs. Since*
- ↪**Split Infinitives** (avoid using)
- ↪**Strong Subject-Verb Combinations**
- ↪**Subject-Verb Agreement**
- ↪**That vs. Which**
- ↪**Terms of Art** (avoid variation in)
- ↪**Verb Tense**
- ↪**Which vs. That** *see That vs. Which*
- ↪**While vs. Although** *see Although vs. While*
- ↪**Who, Whom, and Whose**

Editing — Active vs. Passive Voice

In active voice, the subject is doing the acting:

> The judge ruled.

In passive voice, the subject of the sentence is not the actor; instead, the subject is being acted on:

> The ruling was made by the judge.

Usually in legal writing, active voice is preferred because it makes for more concise writing. However, passive voice is sometimes appropriate, especially when the writer wants to downplay the actor:

> The gun was possessed by my client.

⚇? ↪**Quiz: Active vs. Passive Voice**

Editing — Affect vs. Effect

Generally, *effect* is a noun and *affect* is a verb:

> The effect of the medication was severe: It affected Plaintiff's ability to stay awake while driving.

The exception is *effect* when it is used to mean "to cause to come into being" or "to effectuate":

> Defendant effected the transaction only after Plaintiff's consent.

⚇? ↪**Quiz: Affect vs. Effect**

Editing — Although vs. While

Although should be used to introduce a counterargument or for a causal relationship:

> Although Defendant opened the door to his apartment, he did not consent to the search.

While should be used for temporal circumstances:

> While the police were in the apartment, they seized the contraband in plain view.

⚇? ↪**Quiz: Although vs. While**

Editing — Apostrophes

- Because legal writers avoid ↪**contractions**, apostrophes are generally used for the possessive.
- Do not use an apostrophe for possessive pronouns such as *hers, its, theirs, ours, yours,* and *whose.*
- *Its* is the possessive. *It's* means "it is."
- Because legal writing is generally formal writing, avoid using contractions such as *he's, we're,* or *didn't.*

⚇? ↪**Quiz: Apostrophes**

Editing — Because vs. Since

Because should be used for causation:

> I am going to study because my exam is going to be difficult.

Since should be used for temporal circumstances:

> I have been studying since 9:00 a.m.

⚇? ↪**Quiz: Because vs. Since**

Editing — Capitalization

The Bluebook and ALWD use the following capitalization rules:

In memos and briefs, the Bluebook and ALWD require capitalization of the word court in the following examples:

1. When naming any court in full:
   The U.S. Court of Appeals for the Fifth Circuit held ...

2. When referring to the U.S. Supreme Court
   The Supreme Court held ...

3. When referring to the court reading the document:
   This Court should find ...

ALWD includes a fourth rule for capitalizing the word court in memos and briefs:

4. When referring to the highest court in any jurisdiction after it has been fully identified.
   The Oklahoma Supreme Court held...
   In its ruling, the Court outlined...

Capitalize the amendments of the U.S. Constitution in text:

The First Amendment protects...

In memos and briefs, when referring to the actual parties involved in the matter being discussed, capitalize party designations:

Plaintiff, Defendant, Appellant, Appellee

See Bluebook Rule B10.6.2 and ALWD Rule 3.3.

Capitalize civil, professional, military, and religious titles only when they directly precede a personal name:

Judge Alexander, the judge   Secretary of State Rogers, the secretary of state

Two exceptions to the preceding rule apply. Both the Bluebook and ALWD capitalize the titles of U.S. Supreme Court Justices, even when used without proper names:

Chief Justice Roberts, the Chief Justice
Justice Ginsburg, the Justice

ALWD also capitalizes titles of honor when they substitute for a person's name:

Secretary of State Rogers addressed the UN...
In his speech, the Secretary of State...

&? ↪Quiz: Capitalization

Editing — Clearly or Obviously (Avoid Using)

Usually, when a legal writer uses the word *clearly* or *obviously*, the argument is neither clear nor obvious. Avoid using these words because they usually substitute for the logical reasoning that will make the argument clear and obvious. Similar terms to avoid are *plainly* and *certainly*.

Editing — Colons and Semicolons

The following are the most popular uses of a **semicolon**:

1. To separate items in a list when the items themselves have commas
2. To join two independent (but related) clauses without a coordinating conjunction
3. To separate items in a series when the items are separate, as in a statute

The following are the most popular uses of a **colon**:

1. To join two related independent clauses
2. To introduce a block quotation, a numbered list, or a list that further explains the object of the sentence

If the phrase following the colon is not a complete sentence, do not capitalize the first word following the colon (unless it is a proper noun).

&? ➥**Quiz: Semicolons and Colons**

Editing — Commas

Use a comma for the following purposes:

1. To separate items in a list:
   The prosecution introduced the murder weapon, the victim's diary, and photographs of the scene of the crime.

2. To offset an introductory phrase (optional for short introductory phrases):
   Because the police did not comply with the Fifth Amendment, the confession is inadmissible. In December 2002, the plaintiff moved for summary judgment.

3. To join two independent clauses with and, or, nor, for, so, but, or yet (coordinating conjunctions). Independent clauses are complete thoughts; they can stand alone as complete sentences.
   The defendant confessed to the crime, but the confession was not voluntary.

4. To offset a phrase that could be omitted without changing the meaning of the sentence:
   The defendant, who had been a close friend of the victim, had a key to the apartment.

5. To offset a dependent clause preceding an independent clause:
   Because she was tired, Lisa took a nap.

However, if the dependent clause follows the independent clause, no comma is necessary:

Lisa took a nap because she was tired.

&? ➥**Quiz: Commas**

Editing — Comparisons

In comparisons, the items compared should be of the same type.

Cases can be like other cases, defendants can be like other defendants, and evidence can be like other evidence. Cases cannot be like evidence.

Like the baton in *Goya*, the car in the present case was used as a weapon. OR
As in *Goya*, the evidence here was used as a weapon.

BUT NOT:

Like *Goya*, the car in the present case was used as a weapon.

⚇? ➥**Quiz: Comparisons**

Editing — Conciseness

Legal readers prefer documents that are concise, not wordy. Therefore, omit redundancy and irrelevancy. In addition, avoid phrases that can be replaced with a single word:

By way of, By means of ➥ By
For the purpose of ➥ To (unless purpose is a term of art)
In the event that ➥ If
Begin to develop ➥ Develop
Void and unenforceable ➥ Unenforceable
Period of five years ➥ Five years
Distance of 100 miles ➥ 100 miles
Due to the fact that ➥ Because
In the event that ➥ If
At this point in time ➥ Now
Be able to ➥ Can
Was aware of the fact ➥ Knew
Despite the fact ➥ Although
As a consequence of ➥ Because
In order to ➥ To

➥**See Conciseness**

Editing — Contractions

Because legal writing is generally formal writing, you should avoid using contractions such as *he's, we're*, or *didn't* unless you are quoting passages in which contractions are used.

Editing — Dangling Modifiers (see Misplaced and Dangling Modifiers)

Editing — Due to

The phrase *due to* should be used only in rare circumstances. It must follow a linking verb (for example, *is* or *seems*) and precede the phrase modifying the subject.

> The contract's termination was due to rescission.

⚇? ↪ **Quiz: Due to**

Editing — Effect vs. Affect (see Affect vs. Effect)

Editing — Farther vs. Further

Farther refers to spacial distances:

> He ran farther than he had ever run.

Further refers to nonspatial distances:

> He went further in proving Fermat's theorem than any mathematician before him.

⚇? ↪ **Quiz: Farther vs. Further**

Editing — Hyphens

You can use a hyphen to join together related modifiers:

> The tax-deductible expense was not included on the return.
> The two-year-old child did not take the witness stand.

However, do not use a hyphen to join proper names or if the modifiers follow a linking verb:

> The expense is tax deductible.
> The child is two years old.

⚇? ↪ **Quiz: Hyphens**

Editing — Italics

Italics may be used in the following situations:

1. To add emphasis to quotations
2. To mark foreign language words
3. For certain Bluebook and ALWD citations

Do not use italics to emphasize your own points. Instead, rewrite the sentence so the emphasis is clear without italics.

Editing — Legalese (Avoid Using)

Language like herein, aforementioned, and heretoformentioned often make legal documents difficult to read. Instead, consider substituting these terms with simple ones: here or above.

You might need to use legal language and terms of art because the analysis calls for them, but do not insert legal-sounding terms simply because they sound more lawyerly.

⚇? ⮕**Quiz: Avoid Legalese**

Editing — Misplaced and Dangling Modifiers (Avoid Using)

A modifier is misplaced when it modifies a term that the author does not intend. Moving the modifier cures a misplaced modifier.

Misplaced Modifier: Sitting on a flagpole, I saw three birds.
(According to this sentence, "I" refers to the one sitting on the flagpole.
Instead: I saw three birds sitting on a flagpole.)

A modifier is dangling if it does not modify anything in the sentence. Rewriting the sentence to insert the modified object cures a dangling modifier.

Dangling Modifier: To collect damages, three elements must be met.
(Instead: To collect damages, a plaintiff must meet three elements.)

⚇? ⮕**Quiz: Misplaced and Dangling Modifiers**

Editing — Nominalizations (Avoid Using)

A nominalization occurs when the writer makes a verb or an adjective into a noun. Although grammatically correct, nominalizations decrease sentence clarity and persuasiveness. Consider omitting nominalizations in your legal writing whenever possible.

Nominalization: enforcement - this is a noun
Instead: enforce = verb

Nominalization: justification - this is a noun
Instead: justify = verb

Nominalization: specificity - this is a noun
Instead: specify = verb or specific = adjective

⚇? ⮕**Quiz: Nominalizations**

Editing — Numbers and Quantities

According to Bluebook Rule 6.2 and ALWD Rule 4.2, spell out the numbers zero through ninety-nine. Use numerals for any numbers higher than ninety-nine.

They were locked up for fourteen days.
They were locked up for 144 days.

There are a number of exceptions to the above rule, including (but not limited to) the following:

1. Spell out numbers that begin a sentence.
2. Do not spell out numbers in a series where at least one number is 100 or greater.
3. Do not spell out numbers if used repeatedly for percentages or dollar amounts.
4. Use numerals for section numbers.

> Two defendants entered the courtroom.
> Three hundred people were called in for jury duty.
> The people killed in Iraq in three subsequent days were 25, 122, and 6.
> He received a score of 96% on one test and 84% on another.
> The fee was $223.

Use the words *number*, *fewer*, and *many* to discuss multiple things that can be counted.

Use the words *amount*, *less*, and *much* to discuss singular things that cannot be counted.

> The defense listed a number of objections to the prosecution's line of questioning.
> The plaintiff received a large amount of mail. OR
> The plaintiff received a large number of letters.

Use between to refer to two items; use among to refer to more than two.

> He had to choose between juror #212 and juror #21.
> He had to choose among juror #45, juror #567, and juror #14.

☹? ➥**Quiz: Numbers and Quantities**

Editing — Obviously or Clearly (see Clearly or Obviously)

Editing — Parallel Structure

Strive to use parallel structure when writing lists or rules with multiple elements.

> The judge ruled based on the following: the attorneys' briefs, oral arguments, and the sentencing guidelines.

NOT:

> The judge based her ruling on the following: the attorneys' briefs, the way in which they conducted oral argument, and her need to follow the sentencing guidelines.

☹? ➥**Quiz: Parallel Structure**

Editing — Passive vs. Active Voice (see Active vs. Passive Voice)

Editing — Pronouns

When using a pronoun, make sure that the word the pronoun refers to is clear. If it isn't, avoid using the pronoun and spell out the full term instead.

The following indefinite pronouns are singular:
another, each, either, every, neither, nobody, no one, nothing, one, other

> Neither of the parties is willing to settle.

The following pronouns can be singular or plural, depending on what follows:
all, any, more, most, none, some

All of the money is in my wallet. [*Money* is a singular, noncountable noun.]
All of the dollar bills are in my wallet. [*Bills* is a plural, countable noun.]

⚇? ➥**Quiz: Indefinite Pronouns**

Editing—Quantities and Numbers (see Numbers and Quantities)

Editing—Quotation Marks—Placement

Periods and commas go inside the quotation marks:

> Defendant said, "I will be there."

Semicolons and colons go outside the quotation marks:

> Defendant said, "I will be there"; Plaintiff said, "I will not."

Question marks go inside the quotation marks only if the question mark was part of the original quoted material:

> Defendant asked Plaintiffs, "Will you be there at noon?" Smith responded, "Maybe," and Jones responded, "Doubtful": Defendant decided not to attend.

Quotations of fifty or more words should be indented on the left and right, without quotation marks. See Bluebook Rule 5.1 and ALWD Rule 47.5.

⚇? ➥**Quiz: Quotation Marks**

Editing—Redundancy (Avoid Using)

Watch out for words that do not add any meaning but are redundant:

> any and all
> first and foremost
> null and void

➥**See Conciseness**

Editing—Semicolons and Colons (see Colons and Semicolons)

Editing — Sentence Fragments (Avoid Using)

Sentence fragments are phrases that are not complete sentences. They are grammatically incorrect because they lack a subject or verb or begin with a subordinating conjunction. One way to check for sentence fragments is to read each sentence out loud.

Sentence fragment: Whether she should come or go.

❓ ⇢ **Quiz: Sentence Fragments**

Editing — Sexist Language

Avoid language that can be construed as sexist:

> Firefighter,
> Not: Fireman

Avoid using awkward constructions such as *he* or *she* or *s/he*. Instead, choose the gender that applies to your client or specific situation.

An employee can feel uncomfortable if she is asked to perform menial tasks; Ms. Jones felt uncomfortable when asked to get Mr. Smith's shirts from the cleaners.

Editing — Short Sentences

Writing short sentences helps with clarity and conciseness.

Shorter sentences can also make your writing more persuasive; usually a short sentence has more "bang for the buck."

Editing — Since vs. Because (see Because vs. Since)

Editing — Split Infinitives (Avoid Using)

A split infinitive is when a word appears between "to" and the verb. Usually, writing teachers suggest avoiding the split infinitive because it distracts from the action. However, if splitting an infinite leads to clarity in legal usage, you may split it.

Editing — Strong Subject-Verb Combinations

English readers expect a subject and a verb and then an object, in that order.

When your writing interjects many words between the subject and the verb, the reader tends to become distracted and confused.

Although not all of your sentences need to follow a formulaic subject – verb – object pattern, be wary of the sentences that interject too many words in between the subject and the verb.

Editing — Subject-Verb Agreement

Keep the subject and verb of a sentence in agreement. Here are some tips:

When the subject of the sentence is plural (uses *and*), use a plural verb:

> The attorney and her client were in agreement.
> NOT: The attorney and her client was in agreement.

When the subject of the sentence is singular (uses *or* or *nor*), use a singular verb:

> Neither the attorney nor the client was ready for the verdict.
> NOT: Neither the attorney nor the client were ready for the verdict.

When the subject uses *each* or *every*, use a singular verb:

> Each of the defendants was ready for the verdict.
> NOT: Each of the defendants were ready for the verdict.

When the subject and verb of a sentence are not close together, it is sometimes difficult to ensure that they agree. To avoid this problem, ➥**see Strong Subject-Verb Combinations** and ➥**Short Sentences.** Also problematic are ➥**indefinite pronouns.**

Editing — That vs. Which

That and *which* are not interchangeable in legal writing.

That incorporates a limiting phrase, meaning it narrows the field of objects to the one being discussed:

> The case that the defense cited on page 27 of its brief has been overruled.

Which incorporates a descriptive phrase or a phrase that could be eliminated without changing the meaning of the object:

> The *Smith* case, which has been overruled, would have been helpful to the defense.

Use a comma before *which*, but not before *that*.

&? ➥**Quiz: That vs. Which**

Editing — Terms of Art (Avoid Varying)

In legal writing, terms of art are important; they are defined, analyzed, and argued. Therefore, when writing, you should keep the terms of art consistent. Do not vary them as you might have been taught in undergraduate studies.

Editing — Verb Tense

Use present tense in legal writing to refer to legal rules still in effect.

> *Miranda* requires officers to read suspects their rights before an arrest.

Use past tense to describe facts, reasoning, and holdings of prior case law. Also use past tense to describe any facts in your case that are complete as of the time of the writing.

> Plaintiff is a seventy-five-year-old woman who brought this action after she was terminated.

Whenever possible, maintain consistent tenses throughout a text.

&? → **Quiz: Verb Tense**

Editing — Which vs. That (see That vs. Which)

Editing — While vs. Although (see Although vs. While)

Editing — Who, Whom, and Whose

Who is a subject. **Whom** is an object.

> That is the man who was in the lineup.
> That is the man whom the witness identified.

Whose is the possessive of *who*, not to be confused with *who's* (a contraction for "who is").

&? → **Quiz: Who, Whom, and Whose**

Citation — ALWD and the Bluebook

Finding the authority referenced in a legal document is so important to the legal reader that rules have developed to standardize citation. Although most law students and practicing attorneys dislike citation rules, they are necessary to allow the reader to access the materials referenced. If a legal authority is improperly cited, the reader will have a difficult time finding the law. In addition, the legal reader might not trust the substance of the document; if the writer's citation is inadequate, then perhaps the research and writing are similarly inadequate or improper. Thus, citations for the legal reader are not only helpful for finding law, but they also have become a tool to measure the writer's credibility. Currently, there are two widely accepted citation reference manuals: the more recent ALWD (Association of Legal Writing Directors) and the more traditional Bluebook (which this site uses for legal citation).

ALWD

In 1997, the board of directors of the Association of Legal Writing Directors decided to create a citation manual to fulfill three primary goals: to simplify legal citation rules, to create one set of rules for all forms of legal writing, and to present these rules in a format that judges, lawyers, instructors, and students would find easy to use. The result was the ALWD Citation Manual: A Professional System of Citation, authored primarily by Dean Darby Dickerson of Stetson University College of Law. ALWD is now in its third edition, which was published in 2006 by Aspen Publishers.

THE BLUEBOOK

The first and most widely recognized citation standardization manual, titled The Bluebook: A Uniform System of Citation, was developed in the 1920s by a Harvard law student and is still published by the

Harvard Law Review. The Bluebook is the traditional citation manual used by courts, lawyers, and law schools, despite complaints by some that the book is difficult to use and inconsistent in places. The Bluebook is currently in its eighteenth edition, which was published in 2005.

Citation — Strategies for Legal Citation: ALWD

The trick for using ALWD is to learn these three things:

1. The purpose of citation
2. The design, layout, and basic rules of ALWD
3. Some of the often-used rules

1. **The Purpose of Citation:** Lawyers use citation to provide authority in legal documents and to find the law referenced in legal documents. The ALWD Citation Manual: A Professional System of Citation (or ALWD for short) is designed to provide a uniform system of citation rules so that lawyers can easily find and reference legal sources. Eventually, when electronic filings are required with links to each cited source, citation might become obsolete. But until that time, lawyers are required to use citation that permits other lawyers easy access to their references. ALWD and the Bluebook are the most commonly used citation systems. Using correct citation adds credibility to your writing; if a judge can trust your citations, she can also trust your analysis.

Citation — The Design, Layout, and Basic Rules of the ALWD Citation Manual

1. **Design:** Unlike the Bluebook, the ALWD Citation Manual does not have separate citation formats for scholarly writing and legal documents. Thus, a citation based on ALWD style appears the same, regardless of the type of document you are writing.
2. **Layout:** ALWD is divided into seven parts:

    Part 1: Introductory Material. This section summarizes the organization of the manual, discusses common citation problems that word processors may cause, and provides information regarding local citation formats.

    Part 2: Citation Basics. This section contains the basic rules for citing a source, including typeface, abbreviations, spelling, capitalization, numbers, page numbers, citing particular sections or divisions of a source, internal cross-references, and short citation formats. A careful review of these fundamental rules is necessary before using ALWD to cite a source.

    Part 3: Citing Specific Print Sources. This section focuses on print sources, both primary and secondary, and is divided into subsections by source type. At the beginning of each subsection, a "Fast Formats" table provides quick examples of correct citations for several commonly used sources.

    Part 4: Electronic Sources. This section discusses the proper citation for electronic resources from LexisNexis, Westlaw, e-mail, and the Internet. It also provides information regarding the citation of sources available both in print and electronic formats.

    Part 5: Incorporating Citations into Documents. This section explains how to place and use citations, how to use signals, how to order cited authorities, and when and how to include explanatory parentheticals.

Part 6: Quotations. This section discusses use of quotations, alteration of quoted material, and omission within quoted material.

Part 7: Appendices. The appendices contain more information about primary sources by jurisdiction, local court citation rules, abbreviations, federal taxation materials, federal administrative publications, and a sample legal memorandum showing proper citation placement.

ALWD also has a detailed table of contents and an index.

Throughout the manual, green triangles (▲) are used to designate spaces in citation formats, and green circles (•) are used to separate components of citations. On the inside front cover is a "Fast Format Locator" that gives the page numbers for the Fast Formats tables throughout the manual. On the inside back cover is a "Short-Citation Locator for Commonly Used Sources" that lists rule numbers for many short citation formats.

3. **Basic Citation**

➥**CASES (Rule 12):**

Citation of a U.S. Supreme Court Case:

> ➥**Lakeside v. Oregon,** 435 U.S. 333, 345 (1978).

Be sure to include both the first page of the cited case and a specific page if one is referenced.

Citation of a case decided by the U.S. Court of Appeals for the Eleventh Circuit:

> ➥**Campbell v. Sikes,** 169 F.3d 1353, 1366-67 (11th Cir. 1999).

Short form for cases:

> ➥**Campbell,** 169 F.3d at 1369.

➥**CONSTITUTIONS (Rule 13):**

Citation of Section 2 of the Eighteenth Amendment to the U.S. Constitution:

> ➥**U.S. Const. amend. XVIII, § 2.**

Citation of a state constitution:

> ➥**N.C. Const. art. III, §1.**

➥**STATUTES (Rule 14):**

Citation of an entire statute, as codified in the United States Code:

> ➥**Federal Trademark Dilution Act, 15 U.S.C. § 1125 (2000).**

Citation of an individual provision of the United States Code:

> ➥**15 U.S.C. § 1125 (2000).**

Short citation of provision of the United States Code:

> ➥**Id. at §1125 (where appropriate) or 15 U.S.C. §1125.**

➥**FEDERAL ADMINISTRATIVE AND EXECUTIVE MATERIALS (Rule 19):**

Citation of a particular provision of a regulation in the Code of Federal Regulations:

➥**49 C.F.R. §172.101 (2005).**

Cite all final federal administrative rules and regulations to the C.F.R.

Short citation of particular provision of a regulation in the C.F.R.:

➥**Id. at §172.101 (where appropriate) or 49 C.F.R. at § 172.101.**

➥**BOOKS, TREATISES, AND OTHER NONPERIODIC MATERIALS (Rule 22):**

Citation of a treatise:

➥**William L. Prosser & W. Page Keeton, Prosser and Keeton on the Law of Torts § 3.65 (5th ed., West 1984).**

Short citation of a treatise:

➥**Prosser & Keeton, Prosser and Keeton on the Law of Torts at § 3.65**

or, if using footnotes,

➥**Prosser & Keeton, supra n. 7, at § 3.65.**

Citation of a particular page in a novel:

➥**J. K. Rowling, Harry Potter and the Sorcerer's Stone 125 (Scholastic 1997).**

➥**LEGAL AND OTHER PERIODICALS (Rule 23):**

Citation of particular pages within a law review article:

➥**Mustave Hurt, Unimaginable Pain, 742 Geo. L.J. 801, 831-32 (2003).**

Citation of a magazine article:

➥**J. Madeleine Nash, Fertile Minds, Time 18 (Feb. 3, 1997).**

Citation of a newspaper article:

➥**Adam Gourna, Celiac Disease: A Killer, N.Y. Times F3 (Dec. 12, 1994).**

Citation — Often-Used ALWD Rules

The following are some of the most often-used rules in citation from the ALWD Citation Manual:

➥**Typefaces**
➥**Spelling and Capitalization**
➥**Basic Structure and Signals**
➥**Subdivisions and Pinpoint Cites**
➥**Short Citations**
➥**Abbreviations**
➥**Numbers**

➥ **Quotations**
➥ **Cases**
➥ **Constitutions**
➥ **Statutes**
➥ **Administrative and Executive Materials**
➥ **Books, Reports, and Other Nonperiodic Materials**
➥ **Periodicals**
➥ **Electronic Media**

Citation — Typefaces (Rule 1)

ALWD RULE	KEY POINTS
Rule 1.1: Typeface Choices	Most material should be presented in ordinary type. Italics may be presented either with *slanted type* or <u>underlining</u>. Periods are typically part of the citation component that they follow and should be underlined. Commas are not typically part of the citation component and so should not be underlined.

Rule 1.3: When to Use Italics in Citations	Italicize only the following:
	    Introductory signals
	    Internal cross-references
	    Case names, both in full and short citation formats
	    Phrases indicating subsequent or prior history
	    Titles of most documents
	    Topics or titles in legal encyclopedia entries
	    Names of Internet sites
	    The short forms id. and supra.

Rule 1.8: Italicizing Foreign Words	Generally italicize foreign words that have not been incorporated into normal English. Do not italicize words, such as ad hoc, amicus curiae, and habeas corpus, that have been incorporated into normal English. Consult Rule 1.8 or <u>Black's Law Dictionary</u> if you are unsure about a particular word.

Citation — Spelling and Capitalization (Rule 3)

ALWD RULE	KEY POINTS

Rule 3.1: Words in Titles	Retain the spelling of the title of a source, such as a book or law review article, from the original source.
	
	Change capitalization to conform to the following rules:
	    Capitalize the first word in the title
	    Capitalize the first word in any subtitle
	    Capitalize the first word after a colon or dash
	    Capitalize all other words except articles, prepositions, the word "to" when used as part of an infinitive, and coordinating conjunctions.
	
	Rule 3.1(c) contains special rules for capitalizing hyphenated words.

| Rule 3.2; General Rules | Generally capitalize the following:
     Professional titles and titles of honor or respect
     Organization names
     Proper nouns
     Adjectives formed from proper nouns
     Holidays, events, and epochs
     Defined terms in a document |
| Rule 3.3: Capitalizing Specific Words | Certain words, such as "Act," "Board," and "Circuit," have special capitalization rules. Consult Rule 3.3 for the full list and accompanying rules. |

Citation — Basic Structure and Signals (Rules 10, 43, and 44)

ALWD RULE	KEY POINTS
Rule 10: Internal Cross-References	Internal cross-references may be used to reference text, footnotes, appendices, or any other internal material to avoid repeating text or to help readers. They may not be used to reference outside sources that have been cited elsewhere in the document. For those, use the appropriate short citation forms (see Rule 11). To refer to material that appears earlier in the document, use <u>supra</u>. To refer to material that will appear later in the document, use <u>infra</u>.
Rule 43: Citation Placement and Use Rule 43.1: Placement Options	When a source relates to the whole sentence in the text, include the citation to that source in a separate citation sentence, beginning with a capital letter and ending with a period. When a source relates to only part of a sentence in the text, include the citation as a clause within the sentence, immediately after the text it concerns, and set the clause off with commas. Rule 43.1(e) discusses the use of footnotes in legal documents.
Rule 43.2: Frequency of Citation	Include a citation immediately after any sentence or portion thereof that contains a legal principle, legal authority, or thoughts borrowed from other sources.

Rule 44: Signals	Signals are words or terms that inform readers about the type and degree of support (or contradiction) that the cited authority provides.
	Use no signal if the cited authority directly supports the statement, identifies the source of a quotation, or merely identifies authority referred to in the text.

	Signals that indicate support include:
	   See
	   Accord
	   See also
	   Cf.

	Signals that indicate contradiction include:
	   Contra
	   But see
	   But cf.

	Other signals indicate background material, indicate an example, or draw a comparison.
	Signals should be capitalized if they begin a citation sentence, but not otherwise. Signals should be separated from the rest of the citation with one space, but no punctuation. Italicize or underline each introductory signal, unless it is used as a verb within the citation sentence.
	Consult Rules 44.7 through 44.8 for specifics regarding the use of multiple signals or the same signal for multiple citations.

Citation — Subdivisions and Pinpoint Cites (Rules 5, 6, and 7)

ALWD RULE	KEY POINTS
Rule 5.1: Initial Pages	When citing a source with page numbers that is contained within a larger source (for example, a law review article), always include the initial page number of the source being cited.
Rule 5.2: Pinpoint Pages	When citing specific material from a source, include a pinpoint page reference that provides the exact page on which the cited material is located. This rule applies both to material that is directly quoted and to specific information, such as a case holding, from a source. Consult Rules 5.3 and 5.4 for details on how to cite consecutive pages or multiple pages within a source.
Rule 6: Citing Sections and Paragraphs	If a source is divided into sections or paragraphs, cite the relevant subdivision using the section (§) and paragraph (¶) symbols, with a space between the symbol and the following number.

Rule 6.4: Subsections and Subparagraphs	Cite to the smallest subdivision possible when citing a section or paragraph. Use the original source punctuation to denote subsections. If the original source does not use punctuation to denote subsections, place subdivisions in parentheses, without inserting a space between the main section and subdivision.
	Example: Fed. R. Civ. P. 26(a)(1)(D).
	Rules 6.6 through 6.10 address citation of multiple sections, subsections, paragraphs, and subparagraphs.
Rule 7: Citing Footnotes and Endnotes	When citing a footnote or endnote, include the page on which the note begins and give the note number.
	One note is abbreviated as "n."; multiple notes are abbreviated as "nn." Place one space between the abbreviation and the note number(s).

Citation — Short Citations (Rule 11)

ALWD RULE	KEY POINTS
Rule 11.2: Short Citation Format	Only use short citation format after an authority has been cited once in full citation format and when the reader will not be confused as to which source is being referenced.
	Rules for each specific type of source should be consulted to find the short citation format for that source.
Rule 11.3: Id. as a Short Citation	Id. generally replaces whatever portion of the immediately preceding citation is identical with the current citation. For example, if a full citation is provided for a law review article with pinpoint citation after one textual sentence, the citation for the next textual sentence may substitute "id." for all the details regarding the article name, source name, and so on, and include only the new pinpoint page number:
	Example: "And so it goes in Bankruptcy Court these days." Susan Dinero, The Three Bs: Bankruptcy and Baby Boomers, 105 Harv. L. Rev. 233, 245 (2002). Dinero adds, "And so it should." Id. at 246.
	Id. may be used only to refer to the immediately preceding authority. In a paper with footnotes, if the preceding footnote has more than one citation, id. may not be used to refer because it would be unclear to the reader which citation is being referred to.
	Italicize id. (if you use underlining to represent italics, underline the period in id. also).
	Capitalize id. only if it begins a sentence.

Rule 11.4: <u>Supra</u> as a Short Citation	<u>Supra</u> can be used to cross-reference a full citation provided previously in the document.
	<u>Supra</u> is typically used for sources that are cited by author name, such as books and law review articles. Do not use <u>supra</u> as a short citation for cases, statutes, session laws, ordinances, legislative materials (other than hearings), constitutions, and administrative regulations.
	Example: Baker, <u>supra</u> n. 3, at 55.
	This citation provides the author name, the location of the original citation in the document, and a pinpoint citation to the page number in the original source.
	Rule 11.4(d) discusses the use of "hereinafter" to shorten <u>supra</u> citations or other short citations where a source has a particularly long title.

Citation — Abbreviations (Rule 2)

ALWD RULE	KEY POINTS
Rule 2: Abbreviations	Abbreviations are often used in legal citation for common sources, such as legal periodicals and case names, and also for other less common words and phrases.
	Consult Appendices 3, 4, and 5 for tables of standard abbreviations. Appendix 3 lists words, such as "commonwealth" or "insurance," that should be abbreviated in citations. Appendix 4 lists court abbreviations for both state and federal courts. Appendix 5 lists abbreviations for legal periodicals, such as law reviews.

Citation — Numbers (Rule 4)

ALWD RULE	KEY POINTS
Rule 4: Numbers	Numbers within citations should be presented as numerals unless the number appears in a title. If a number does appear in a title, present it as it is presented in the original.
	Numbers within textual material may be presented as either numerals or words, but whichever you use, remain consistent. The convention in law is to present numbers zero to ninety-nine as words, and numbers above 100 as numerals. Rule 4.3 addresses special rules for ordinal numbers (such as "first").

Citation—Quotations (Rules 47, 48, and 49)

ALWD RULE	KEY POINTS
Rule 47.4: Short Quotations	If a quotation is fewer than fifty words, or runs fewer than four lines of typed text, simply enclose it in double quotation marks (" "). Place the citation for the quoted material after the sentence containing the quoted material. In a footnoted document, place the note reference number immediately after the closing quotation mark, even if it is in the middle of the sentence. However, if a single textual sentence includes multiple quoted phrases from the same source and pinpoint reference, place the note reference number at the end of the sentence to reference all the quoted phrases.
Rule 47.4(d): Punctuation	Periods and commas should generally be placed inside quotation marks, regardless of whether they are part of the original quotation. Other punctuation, such as semicolons and question marks, should generally be placed outside the quotation marks unless they are part of the original quoted material.
Rule 47.5: Longer Quotations	If a quotation is fifty words or more, or exceeds four lines of typed text, present it as a block of type by single-spacing it and indenting it by one tab on both the right and left. Do not use quotation marks at the beginning or end of the block quotation. Separate the block quotation from the surrounding text by one blank line above and below.
Rule 47.7: Quotations within Quotations	Within a short quotation, set off quotations with single quotation marks (' '). Within a block quotation, set off quotations with double quotation marks (" ").
Rule 48: Altering Quoted Material Rule 48.1: Altering the Case of a Letter	When changing a letter from uppercase to lowercase, or vice versa, within a quotation, enclose the altered letter in brackets (for example, "[B]asketball" or "[f]ootball").
Rule 48.2: Adding, Changing, or Deleting One or More Letters	When adding, changing, or deleting letters from a quoted word, enclose the added, changed, or deleted material in brackets (indicate omitted or deleted material with empty brackets—[ ]).
Rule 48.4: Substituting or Adding Words	When substituting or adding words to a quotation, such as to clarify a detail for the reader, enclose those words in brackets.
Rule 48.5: Altering Typeface	When altering the typeface of quoted material, such as by adding or deleting italics for emphasis, describe the alteration in a parenthetical following the citation.
Rule 48.6: Mistakes within Original Quoted Material	When quoting material that contains mistakes, either correct the mistake and enclose changes in brackets as discussed above, or denote the mistake with "[sic]." Do not italicize or underline "[sic]."
Rule 49: Omissions within Quoted Material	Use ellipsis to indicate omission of one or more words. An ellipsis consists of three periods with one space between each (. . .). Insert one space before and after the ellipsis as well. Rule 49 contains many additional, more specific rules regarding the use of ellipses, particularly specifying spacing and punctuation.

Citation — Cases (Rule 12)

ALWD RULE	KEY POINTS
Rule 12.1: Full Citation Format	Example: <u>N.Y. Times Co. v. Sullivan</u>, 144 So. 2d 25, 40-41 (Ala. 1962), <u>rev'd</u>, 376 U.S. 254 (1964).
Rule 12.2: Case Name	Italicize or underline the case name, but not the comma following it. If a caption on a case lists more than one case, cite only the first case listed. If a single case has two different names, use the one listed first. Cite only the first-listed party on each side of the case, and do not use "<u>et al.</u>" or other terms to denote any omitted parties. If the party is an individual, use only the last name. If the party is an organization, include the organization's full name, but omit abbreviations such as "d/b/a" and any material following. Usually omit "The" when it appears as the first word in a party's name. Use the abbreviations listed in Appendix 3 to abbreviate listed words in case names pursuant to Rule 12.2(e)(3), unless doing so would create confusion for the reader. Other more specific rules regarding the presentation of a case name in a citation sentence are provided in Rule 12.2.
Rule 12.4: Reporter Abbreviation	After the volume number, include the abbreviation for the reporter in which the case appears. Abbreviations for reporters are found in Appendix 1. When submitting a document to a state court, check the local rules for that court (see Appendix 2) to determine which reporter to cite to. Remember that some states require parallel citation (citation of both official and unofficial reporters). When submitting a document to federal court, check the local rules for that court (see Appendix 2). For U.S. Supreme Court cases, typically cite to only one reporter, preferably the United States Reports (abbreviated "U.S."), or to other reporters listed in Rule 12.4(c) if a "U.S." cite is not yet available.
Rule 12.6: Court Abbreviation	Include the appropriate abbreviation for the court that decided the case in the parentheses following the page number, just before the year the case was decided. Check Appendices 1 and 4 for abbreviations of courts. No court abbreviation is required for U.S. Supreme Court cases because the name of the reporter indicates that the case is a U.S. Supreme Court case. Simply include the year the case was decided in the parentheses.
Rule 12.8: Subsequent History	Subsequent history should be included in a citation if the action is listed in Rule 12.8(a). Also indicate when a judgment in a cited case has been overruled. Consult the rules in Rule 12.8 directly for formatting and other details.

Rule 12.9: Prior History	Prior history may be included, but is never mandatory and should be used sparingly.
	Prior history should be presented in the same manner as subsequent history.
Rule 12.21: Short Citation Format	If <u>id.</u> is appropriate, use it as the preferred short citation for cases.
	If all or part of a case name is not included in the textual sentence, include some portion of the case name in the short citation to identify it for the reader.
	Example: The judge thought otherwise and ruled against the defendant. <u>Seel</u>, 971 P.2d at 924.
	If the case name, or part of it, is included in the textual sentence, simply include in the short citation the volume number, reporter abbreviation, the word "at," and then the pinpoint reference.
	Example: The judge in <u>Seel</u> thought otherwise and ruled against the defendant. 971 P.2d at 924.

Citation — Constitutions (Rule 13)

ALWD RULE	KEY POINTS
Rule 13.2: Full Citation Format for Constitutions Currently in Force	A citation to a constitution currently in force should include the name of the constitution and a pinpoint reference.
	Example: U.S. Const. amend. XIV, § 2.
	Check Appendix 3 for appropriate abbreviations for the jurisdiction, and then use the abbreviation "Const." for the word "constitution."
	Be as specific as possible with pinpoint references.
Rule 13.3: Full Citation Format for Constitutions No Longer in Force	For constitutions no longer in force, use the same citation format given in Rule 13.2, but use a parenthetical to explain why it is no longer in force and include the year in which it lost effect.
	Example: U.S. Const. amend. XVIII (repealed 1933 by U.S. Const. amend. XXI).
Rule 13.4: Short Citation Format	If appropriate, use <u>id.</u> as the short-form citation for constitutional provisions.

Citation — Statutes (Rule 14)

ALWD RULE	KEY POINTS
Rule 14.2: Full Citation, Print Format for Federal Statutes Currently in Force	Example: 18 U.S.C. § 1965 (2000). The official code for federal statutes is the United States Code, abbreviated "U.S.C." Do not include a publisher for U.S.C.
Rule 14.3: Full Citation, Print Format for Federal Statutes No Longer in Force	Cite as described in Rule 14.2, but include a statement that the statute was repealed or superseded, with the year in which the statute ceased to be in force. Example: 26 U.S.C. § 1071(a) (repealed 1995).
Rule 14.4: Full Citation, Print Format for State Statutes	Abbreviations and formats for state codes are included in Appendix 1.
Rule 14.6: Short Citation, Print Format for Federal and State Statutes	Use id., if appropriate. Otherwise, use all required components of the full citation, but omit the date. Example: The full citation "42 U.S.C. § 12101 (2000)" may be cited in short form as "42 U.S.C. § 12101."

Citation — Administrative and Executive Materials (Rule 19, Appendix 7(C))

ALWD RULE	KEY POINTS
Rule 19.1: Full Citation Format for Code of Federal Regulations	Whenever possible, cite all federal rules and regulations to the Code of Federal Regulations (C.F.R.) by title, section or part, and year. Examples: 28 C.F.R. § 540.71 (2003). 31 C.F.R. pt. 730 (2005).
Rule 19.2: Short Citation Format for Code of Federal Regulations	If id. is appropriate, use it as the preferred short citation for rules and regulations cited in the C.F.R. If id. is not appropriate, repeat all elements in the full citation except the date. Example: 28 C.F.R. at § 540.90.
Rule 19.3: Full Citation Format for Federal Register	Cite final rules and regulations not yet entered in the C.F.R., proposed federal rules and regulations, and notices to the Federal Register. Include a pinpoint cite if appropriate, and use a full date. Example: 70 Fed. Reg. 10868, 10870 (Mar. 5, 2005).
Rule 19.4: Short Citation Format for Federal Register	If id. is appropriate, use it as the preferred short citation for rules and regulations cited in the Federal Register. If id. is not appropriate, repeat all elements in the full citation except the date. Example: 70 Fed. Reg. at 10875.
Appendix 7(C): Administrative Materials	See Appendix 7(C) for help in citing Treasury regulations and other federal taxation materials.

Citation—Books, Reports, and Other Nonperiodic Materials (Rule 22)

ALWD RULE	KEY POINTS
Rule 22.1: Full Citation Format	Cite books, treatises, reports, or other nonperiodic materials by author, title (italicized or underlined), pinpoint reference (if appropriate), edition (if any), publisher, and year. Example: Joshua Dressler, <u>Understanding Criminal Law</u> § 10.04 (3d ed., Lexis 2001).
Rule 22.2: Short Citation Format for Works Other Than Those in a Collection	If <u>id.</u> is appropriate, use it as the preferred short citation for books. If <u>id.</u> is not appropriate, the format of the short citation varies. Example (document without footnotes): Dressler, <u>Understanding Criminal Law</u>, at § 12.08. Example (document with footnotes): Dressler, <u>supra</u> n. [note number], at § 12.08.

Citation—Periodicals (Rule 23)

ALWD RULE	KEY POINTS
Rule 23.1: Full Citation Format	Cite to articles in law reviews, journals, newspapers, magazines, and other periodicals by author, title (italicized or underlined), volume number (if any), periodical abbreviation, first page, pinpoint reference (if appropriate), and date. Use Appendix 5 to abbreviate periodical names and to determine whether the journal you are citing is consecutively or nonconsecutively paginated. Example (consecutively paginated periodical): Howard F. Chang, <u>Risk Regulation, Endogenous Public Concerns, and the Hormones Dispute: Nothing to Fear but Fear Itself?</u> 77 S. Cal. L. Rev. 743, 751 (2004). Example (nonconsecutively paginated periodical): Linda Buckley, <u>A Hole in the Safety Net</u>, Newsweek 40 (May 13, 2002).
Rule 23.2: Short Citation Format	If <u>id.</u> is appropriate, use it as the preferred short citation for periodicals. If <u>id.</u> is not appropriate, the format of the short citation varies. Example (document without footnotes): Chang, 77 S. Cal. L. Rev. at 752. Example (document with footnotes): Chang, <u>supra</u> n. [note number], at 752.

Citation—Electronic Media (Rules 12, 14, and Part 4)

Rule 12.12: Cases Published Only on LexisNexis or Westlaw	Include the case name (italicized or underlined), the database identifier, the name of the database (either LEXIS or WL) plus a unique document number, and a parenthetical containing the court abbreviation and a full date. Example: <u>Goodyear Tire & Rubber Co. v. Moore</u>, 2005 WL 1611323 (Va. App. July 12, 2005).
Rule 14.5: Statutes Available on Electronic Databases	Cite statutes according to Rules 14.2 and 14.4. In addition, include in the date parenthetical the name of the database provider and information about the currency of the database. Example: Ga. Code Ann. § 7-1-841 (Westlaw current through 2004 1st Spec. Sess.).
Part 4: Electronic Sources Rule 38: General Information About Online and Electronic Citation Formats	Cite only to print sources unless the material would be difficult for most readers to find or the source is more widely available in electronic form. In that case, include the electronic source information in a parenthetical. Example: U.S. Census Bureau, <u>Statistical Abstract of the United States</u> 119 (121st ed. 2001) (available at http://www.census.gov/prod/2002pubs/01statab/stat-ab01.html). For more about citing electronic sources, see Rules 38 through 42.

Citation—Strategies for Legal Citation: Bluebook

The Bluebook is not as intimidating as it appears at first glance. The trick for using it is to learn these three things:

1. The purpose of citation
2. The design, layout, and basic rules of the Bluebook
3. Some of the often-used rules

1. **The Purpose of Citation:** Lawyers use citation to provide authority in legal documents and to find the law referenced in legal documents. The Bluebook, officially titled, The Bluebook: A Uniform System of Citation, is designed to provide a uniform system of citation rules so that lawyers can easily find and reference legal sources. Eventually, when electronic filings are required with links to each cited source, citation might become obsolete. But until that time, lawyers are required to use citation that permits other lawyers easy access to their references. The Bluebook and ⇥ALWD are the most commonly used citation systems. Using correct citation adds credibility to your writing; if a judge can trust your citations, she can also trust your analysis.

Citation—The Design, Layout, and Basic Rules of the Bluebook

1. **Design:** The introduction in the Bluebook explains the purpose and function of the book. The Bluebook, in general, provides citation formats for scholarly documents, such as law review articles. The "quick reference" on the front inside cover is a cheat sheet for most-often used citations for law reviews.

Most practicing lawyers, however, cite to the law in legal documents, not scholarly articles. The Bluebook section called the Bluepages provides citation rules for court documents and legal memoranda. The Bluepages are organized by legal source (cases, statutes, constitutions, and so on) and provide easy-to-understand formatting and examples. A law student in a first-year class can use the Bluepages for simple citation format; for more complicated citations, use the rules and tables referenced in the Bluepages. In addition, the "quick reference" on the inside back cover of the Bluebook provides a cheat sheet for most-often used citations for legal documents. (The following rules and examples follow the Bluepages' citation rules for court documents unless otherwise noted.)

2. **Layout:** The main highlights of the Bluebook contain the following:
   1. **Citation rules**, which are organized by category:
      1. ➥**Cases (Rule 10)**
      2. ➥**Constitutions (Rule 11)**
      3. ➥**Statutes (Rule 12)**
      4. ➥**Administrative and Executive Materials, including Rules and Regulations (Rule 14)**
      5. ➥**Books, Reports, and Other Nonperiodic Materials (Rule 15)**
      6. ➥**Periodical Materials (Rule 16)**
   2. **Tables** (on white pages with a blue edge), which lay out specific requirements of:
      1. Federal and State Jurisdictions (T.1)
      2. Foreign Jurisdictions (T.2)
      3. Intergovernmental Organizations and Treaty Sources (T.3 - T.4)
      4. Abbreviations for Arbitral Reporter Sources (T.5)
      5. Abbreviations for Case Names and Court Names (T.6 - T.7)
      6. Abbreviations for Explanatory Phrases and Legislative Documents (T.8 - T.9)
      7. Abbreviations for Geographical Terms (T.10)
      8. Abbreviations for Judges and Officials and Months (T.11 - T.12)
      9. Abbreviations for Periodicals (T.13)
      10. Abbreviations for Publishing Terms and Services (T.14 - T.15)
      11. Abbreviations for Document Subdivisions (T.16)

In addition, the Bluebook contains a table of contents, which is helpful for finding rules on broad topics such as law reviews, and an index, which is helpful for finding rules on specific subjects such as pinpoint cites.

3. **Basic Citation**

➥**CASES (Rule 10):**

Citation of a U.S. Supreme Court Case:

➥**Lakeside v. Oregon, 435 U.S. 333, 345 (1978).**

Be sure to include both the first page of the cited case and a specific page if one is referenced.

Citation of a case decided by the U.S. Court of Appeals for the Eleventh Circuit:

➥**Campbell v. Sikes, 169 F.3d 1353, 1366-68 (11th Cir. 1999).**

Short form for cases:

> ➥<u>Campbell</u>, 169 F.3d at 1369.

➥**CONSTITUTIONS (Rule 11):**

Citation of Section 2 of the Eighteenth Amendment to the U.S. Constitution:

> ➥**U.S. Const. amend. XVIII, § 2.**

➥**STATUTES (Rule 12):**

Citation of an entire statute, the Federal Trademark Dilution Act of 1995, as codified in the United States Code:

> ➥**Federal Trademark Dilution Act, 15 U.S.C. § 1125 (2000).**

Citation of an individual provision of the United States Code:

> ➥**15 U.S.C. § 1125 (2000).**

Short citation of a provision of the United States Code:

> ➥**15 U.S.C. § 1125 or § 1125.**

➥**RULES AND REGULATIONS (Rule 14):**

Citation of a particular provision of a regulation in the Code of Federal Regulations:

> ➥**49 C.F.R. § 172.101 (2005).**

> Whenever possible, cite all federal rules and regulations to the Code of Federal Regulations (C.F.R.) by title, section, and year.

Short citation of a particular provision of a regulation in the C.F.R.:

> ➥**49 C.F.R. § 172.101 or § 172.101.**

➥**BOOKS (Rule 15):**

Citation of treatise:

> ➥**William L. Prosser & W. Page Keeton, <u>Prosser and Keeton on the Law of Torts</u> § 3.65 (5th ed. 1984).**

Citation of a particular page in a novel:

> ➥**J. K. Rowling, <u>Harry Potter and the Sorcerer's Stone</u> 125 (1997).**

➥**PERIODICAL MATERIALS (Rule 16):**

Citation of particular pages within a law review article:

> ➥**Mustave Hurt, <u>Unimaginable Pain</u>, 742 Geo. L.J. 801, 831-32 (2003) (discussing the requirements to show deliberate indifference).**

Citation of an entire magazine article:

> ➥**J. Madeleine Nash, <u>Fertile Minds</u>, Time, Feb. 3, 1997, at 18.**

Citation of a newspaper article:

➥**Adam Gourna, <u>Celiac Disease: A Killer</u>, N.Y. Times, Dec. 12, 1994, at F3.**

Citation — Often-Used Bluebook Rules

The following are some of the most-often used rules in citation. They are provided for practitioners' use in court documents and legal memoranda.

➥**Typefaces**
➥**Basic Structure and Signals**
➥**Subdivisions and Pinpoint Cites**
➥**Short Citations**
➥**Abbreviations**
➥**Cases**
➥**Constitutions**
➥**Statutes**
➥**Administrative and Executive Materials**
➥**Books, Reports, and Other Nonperiodic Materials**
➥**Periodicals**
➥**Electronic Media**

Citation — Typefaces (Bluepages 2, 8, 9, 10, 13 and Rule 2)

BLUEBOOK RULE	KEY POINTS
B2: Citation Sentences and Clauses: Blue-pages Tip Underscoring or italics may be appropriate in court documents or legal memoranda. However, check your local rules for the court's preference (Table BT.2). Example: <u>Pope v. Hightower</u> Rule 2: Typefaces for Law Reviews	Practitioners underscore or italicize all case names, including the "v." Where the Bluepages indicates to use underscoring, italics may be substituted. Be consistent with underscoring or italics throughout the document. In law reviews, three typefaces are commonly used: 1. Ordinary Roman (plain text) 2. Italics 3. Large and small capitals See Rule 2 for specifics.
B8: Books and Other Nonperiodic Materials B9: Journal and Newspaper Articles Example: <u>Killer Tornado</u>, Newsweek, Mar. 3, 1991, at 39.	Underscore or italicize the title of a book or the title of an article appearing in a periodical.

B13: Typeface Conventions This rule tries to clarify the distinction between the Bluepages typeface and law review typeface. It provides an exclusive list of underscored (or italicized) sources for practitioners. Words and Phrases Introducing Related Authority Example: <u>Red Sox Say Manager's Contract Won't Be Renewed</u>, N.Y. Times, Oct. 27, 2003, <u>available at</u> http://www.nytimes.com/aponline/ sports/AP-BBA-Red-Sox-Little.html.	Underscore or italicize subsequent case history. Underscore or italicize "<u>available at</u>" and other similar words and phrases referring to related authority. Underscore or italicize <u>id.</u> and <u>supra</u>.
If not specified as underscored or italicized, practitioners print everything else in ordinary Roman type. Example: U.S. Const. amend. XVIII, § 2	Print reporters, services, constitutions, statutes, Restatements, model codes, rules, executive orders, administrative materials, unpublished sources, and treaties in ordinary Roman type.
B10.6: Capitalization in Textual Sentences Examples: The Court of Appeals for the First Circuit held ... The Supreme Court held ... This Court should hold ... Examples: Here, Plaintiff claims Defendant ... In another case, the plaintiff made a similar claim against the defendant.	Capitalize "Court" in the following circumstances: 1. When naming any court in full 2. When referring to the U.S. Supreme Court 3. When referring to the court that will be receiving that document Capitalize party designations: Plaintiff, Defendant, Appellant, etc., when referring to those actual parties in your case only.

Citation — Basic Structure and Signals (Bluepages 2, 4, 11 and Rule 1)

BLUEBOOK RULE	KEY POINTS
B2: Citation Sentences and Clauses Example: See Jones v. Smith, 345 U.S. 322 (1985). Jones v. Smith, 345 U.S. 322 (1985); see also Cambridge v. Boston, 235 U.S. 412 (1977).	Citations in court documents and legal memoranda traditionally appear within the text rather than in footnotes or endnotes. A citation within the text can appear in a stand-alone sentence or in a citation clause. A citation sentence begins with a capital and ends with a period. If it contains multiple citations, it will include semicolons to separate each citation. A citation clause is set off from the text with commas.
Rule 1.1: Citation Sentences and Clauses in Law Reviews Example: [Footnote]2. Other authors have made similar assertions. Cf. Mustave Hurt, Unimaginable Pain, 742 Geo. L.J. 801, 831-32 (2003).	In law reviews, citations appear in footnotes. At times, an author might make an assertion within a footnote; here, a citation should appear in the footnote after the assertion.
B4: Introductory Signals Rule 1.2: Introductory Signals Example: See generally Killer Tornado, Newsweek, Mar. 3, 1991, at 39.	A signal is a sign to the reader indicating the type of authority about to be cited. Signals that indicate support are no signal, e.g., accord, see, see also, cf. A signal that suggests a useful comparison is compare ... with. Signals that indicate contradiction are contra, but see, but cf. A signal that indicates background material is see generally.
B4.5: Order of Signals Rule 1.3: Order of Signals Example: See Mustave Hurt, Unimaginable Pain, 742 Geo. L.J. 801, 831-32 (2003); see also Killer Tornado, Newsweek, Mar. 3, 1991, at 39. But see Adam Gourna, Celiac Disease: A Killer, N.Y. Times, Dec. 12, 1994, at F3.	Signals of different types must be grouped in different citation sentences. When more than one signal is used in a citation, the signals should appear in the order listed in Rule 1.2. Signals of the same type must be strung together with a single citation sentence and separated by semicolons.

B4.5: Order of Signals Rule 1.4: Order of Authorities Within Each Signal Example: See <u>Turner</u>, 482 U.S. at 89; <u>see also</u> 28 C.F.R. § 540.71 (2002) (establishing security as legitimate government interest).	Authorities within each signal are separated by semicolons. General Order: Constitutions, Statutes, Treaties, Cases, Legislative Materials, Administrative and Executive Materials, Resolutions of Intergovernmental Organizations, Records, Briefs, Petitions, Secondary Materials. In addition, the Bluebook has rules regarding the order within each one of these categories. However, if one authority is more helpful, it should precede the others.
B11: Explanatory Parentheticals Rule 1.5: Parenthetical Information Example: 28 C.F.R. § 540.71 (2002) (establishing legitimate government interest).	Additional information about a citation is added in a parenthetical at the end of the citation sentence or clause. The text in a parenthetical need not be a full sentence; omit extraneous words such as "the." Often, parentheticals begin with a present participle; however, a quotation or short phrase is also appropriate. Parenthetical information is recommended when the relevance of the cited authority might not otherwise be clear to the reader.

Citation — Subdivisions and Pinpoint Cites (Bluepages 5.1.2 and Rule 3)

BLUEBOOK RULE	KEY POINTS
B5.1.2: Reporter and Pinpoint Citation Rule 3.2(a): Pages, Footnotes, Endnotes, and Graphical Materials Example: <u>Campbell v. Sikes</u>, 169 F.3d 53, 66 (1999). Example: <u>McElligot v. Foley</u>, 182 F.3d 1248, 1256-58 (11th Cir. 1999). Example: <u>Rhodes v. Chapman</u>, 452 U.S. 337, 346, 349 (1981).	When referring to specific material within a source, include both the page on which the source begins and the page on which the specific materials appear, separated by a comma. When citing material that spans more than one page, give the inclusive page numbers, separated by a hyphen or dash. Always retain the last two digits, but drop other repetitious digits. Cite nonconsecutive pages by giving the individual page numbers separated by commas.

Citation — Short Citations (Rule 4)

BLUEBOOK RULE	KEY POINTS
In Bluepages, see specific sections for each appropriate short form (e.g., cases, statutes, and so on). Rule 4.1: "Id." Example: 1. Helling, 509 U.S. 25, 29 (1993). 2. Id. at 35-36. 3. See id.	Use id. when citing the immediately preceding authority. Capitalize id. when it appears at the beginning of a citation sentence; do not capitalize id. when it is not the beginning of a sentence. Id. may not be used to refer to one authority in a preceding footnote if the preceding footnote cites more than one source.
Rule 4.2: "Supra" and "Hereinafter" Example: Hurt, supra note 3, at 8.	Used to refer to legislative hearings, books, pamphlets, unpublished materials, nonprint resources, periodicals, services, treaties, international agreements, regulations, directives, and decisions of intergovernmental organizations. Do not use to refer to cases, statutes, constitutions, legislative materials, Restatements, model codes, or regulations. Supra form consists of the last name of the author, followed by a comma and the word "supra," then the footnote in which the full citation can be found, and the specific volume, paragraph, section, or page numbers cited.

Citation — Abbreviations (Rule 6)

BLUEBOOK RULE	KEY POINTS
Rule 6.1: Abbreviations	Abbreviations not found within the Bluebook should be avoided unless they are unambiguous and save substantial space.
Rule 6.2(c): Section (§) and Paragraph (¶) Symbols	Spell out the words "section" and "paragraph" in the text. In citations, the symbols should be used with a space between § or ¶ and the numeral.

Citation — Cases (Bluepages 5 and Rule 10)

BLUEBOOK RULE	KEY POINTS
B5.1: Full Citation Rule 10.1: Basic Citation Forms	U.S. Supreme Court case: Example: <u>Thornburgh v. Abbott</u>, 490 U.S. 401, 407-08 (1989). U.S. Court of Appeals case: Example: <u>Pope v. Hightower</u>, 101 F.3d 1382, 1383 (11th Cir. 1996). Do not use superscripts when abbreviating words like "11th."
B5.1.1: Case Name Rule 10.2: Case Names	Include only the necessary information in a case name and underline the entire case name up until the comma (do not underline the comma). Use only the surname. Omit words indicating multiple parties. Look up the abbreviations required in B5.1.1 and 10.2. Note that 10.2.2 provides extra rules for case names in citation sentences and clauses (as opposed to references to case names in text). 1. When a case name is used in a textual sentence (in text or footnotes), you should follow 10.2.1 (see below). 2. When a case name is used in a citation sentence or clause, you should refer to rules 10.2.1 and 10.2.2 (see below).

Rule 10.2.1: Case Names in Textual Sentences	Omit words indicating multiple parties, such as "et al.," and all parties other than the first listed on each side.
Example: <u>Harris v. Thigpen</u> NOT: <u>Harris et al. v. Thigpen, Kramer & Levin.</u> Example: <u>Alabama v. Carter</u>, 507 U.S. 411, 418 (1992).	Abbreviate only widely known acronyms and the following eight words unless the word begins a party's name: 1. & 2. Ass'n 3. Bros. 4. Co. 5. Corp. 6. Inc. 7. Ltd. 8. No.
Example: <u>Commonwealth v. Robertson</u> Not: <u>Commonwealth of Virginia v. Robertson</u> Example: <u>Montana Moving Co. v. Rhode Island Storage, Inc.</u> Not: <u>Montana Moving Co., Inc. v. Rhode Island Storage, Inc.</u>	Usually omit "The" as the first word of a party's name. Geographical terms: Omit "State of," "Commonwealth of," and "People of," except when citing decisions of the courts of that state. When citing decisions of the courts of that state, use "State," "Commonwealth," or "People." Business firms: Omit "Inc.," "Ltd.," "L.L.C.," "N.A.," "F.S.B.," and similar terms if the name also contains a word such as "Ass'n," "Bros.," "Co.," and "R.R."
Rule 10.2.2: Case Names in Citations Example: <u>Turner R.R. v. Safley</u>, NOT <u>Turner Railroad v. Safley</u>. NOT: <u>U.S. v. White</u>	Always abbreviate any word listed in Table 6 (T.6) and any geographic term in Table 10 (T.10), unless the geographical unit is a named party. Abbreviate other words of eight letters or more if the result is unambiguous and substantial space is saved. Do not abbreviate "United States" in the case name when the United States is the actual party. (However, abbreviate United States when it is part of the party's name - e.g., U.S. Steel.)
B5.1.2: Reporter and Pinpoint Citation Example: <u>Jones v. Smith</u>, 230 U.S. 432, 434 (1986).	When providing reporter information, you should provide the volume and abbreviation for the reporter as well as the page on which the opinion begins. A pinpoint cite or jump cite is a reference to the specific page(s) for your proposition.

B5.1.3: Court and Year of Decision Rule 10.4: Court and Jurisdiction Example: <u>United States v. White</u>, 490 U.S. 84, 87 (1990).	Give the name of the court and its geographical jurisdiction, abbreviating using Table 1 (T.1) or Table 2 (T.2), in the parenthetical immediately following the citation. Do not include the name of the deciding court in the parenthetical when citing the U.S. Supreme Court or the highest court of a state. Include the year of the decision in the parenthetical. Cite to the Supreme Court using U.S., not S. Ct., when the U.S. citation is available.
B5.2: Short Form Citation Rule 10.9: Short Forms for Cases Acceptable examples: <u>Jones</u> at 240. <u>Jones</u>, 250 S.E.2d at 240. <u>Id.</u> at 35-36. <u>See id.</u> at 35-36.	A short form is a shortened reference to a citation. You may use a short form if it clearly provides the correct reference, the full citation is provided in the same general discussion, and the full citation can be easily found if the reader wishes to do so. There are a number of acceptable short forms; most of them include "at" with a pinpoint cite. When using a name for a short form, use the first party's name unless it is a geographical term or government name. "<u>Id.</u>" may be used in court documents and legal memoranda to refer to a case cited in the previous citation. When used at the beginning of a citation sentence, capitalize the "i." However, when used in the middle of a citation sentence, do not capitalize the "i." Do not use "<u>supra</u>" to refer to previously cited cases in a court document or legal memorandum.

Citation — Constitutions (Bluepages 7 and Rule 11)

BLUEBOOK RULE	KEY POINTS
B7: Constitutions Rule 11: Constitutions Example: U.S. Const. amend. XVIII, § 2.	Abbreviate United States (U.S.). Use Const., not CONST. Short form: Do not use short citation form (other than id.) for constitutions. Cite state constitutions by the abbreviated name of the state and the word "Const." Abbreviate subdivisions of constitutions according to Table 16 (T.16). Example: Ala. Const. art. V, § 9.

Citation—Statutes (Bluepages 6 and Rule 12)

BLUEBOOK RULE	KEY POINTS
B6: Statutes, Rules, and Regulations Rule 12.1: Basic Citation Forms for Statutes Example: 42 U.S.C. § 1983 (1994). Example: 42 U.S.C. §§ 8401-8405 (2000).	Cite current statutes to the official code. (Cite U.S.C., not U.S.C.A. or U.S.C.S.) Place periods in between "U.S.C." Do not underline statute citations. Leave a space between "§" and the cited section numbers. When citing multiple sections, use "§§". Include the year the code was published in a parenthetical. Include the official name of the act when available.
B6.1.3: Rules of Evidence and Procedure: Restatements; Uniform Acts Rule 12.8.3: Rules of Evidence and Procedure Rule 12.8.5: Model Codes, Restatements, Standards, and Sentencing Guidelines Examples: Fed. R. Evid. 213 Fed. R. Crim. P. 11. Restatement (Second) of Torts § 84 (1989). Example: U.S. Sentencing Guidelines Manual § 5D2.1(f) (2001).	Do not include dates.
B6.2: Short Forms (for Statutes) Rule 12.9: Short Forms for Statutes Example: 42 U.S.C. § 1221 or § 1221.	Id. may be used in court documents and legal memoranda to refer to the previously cited statute or to a statute within the same title previously cited. Use chart from 12.9(c) to determine proper format for named statutes, U.S. Code provisions, state code provisions, and session laws.

Citation—Administrative and Executive Materials (Bluepages 6.1.4 and Rule 14)

BLUEBOOK RULE	KEY POINTS
B6.1.4: Administrative Rules and Regulations Rule 14.2: Rules, Regulations, and Other Publications Example: 28 C.F.R. § 540.71 (2003).	Whenever possible, cite all federal rules and regulations to the Code of Federal Regulations (C.F.R.) by title, section or part, and year.
B6.2: Short Form Citation Rule 14.10: Short Forms for Regulations Example: 28 C.F.R. § 540.71 or § 540.71.	Use chart in Rule 14.10(c) to determine proper format for regulations. Id. may be used in court documents and legal memoranda to refer to the previously cited regulation or to a regulation within the same title previously cited.

Citation—Books, Reports, and Other Nonperiodic Materials (Bluepages 8 and Rule 15)

BLUEBOOK RULE	KEY POINTS
B8: Books and Other Nonperiodic Materials Rule 15: Books, Reports, and Other Nonperiodic Materials Example: Noah Lee, <u>Deliberate Indifference: What's It All About?</u> 31 (3d ed. 2001).	Cite books, reports, and other nonperiodic materials by author, title (underlined), pinpoint page, section or paragraph, edition (if more than one), and date (in parenthetical).
B8.2: Short Form Citation Rule 15.9: Short Citation Forms Example: Stevens, <u>supra</u>, at 45.	If the work was cited as the immediately preceding authority, use <u>id.</u> If the work has been cited in full, but not as the immediately preceding authority, use <u>supra.</u>

Citation—Periodicals (Bluepages 9 and Rule 16)

BLUEBOOK RULE	KEY POINTS
B9.1.1: Consecutively Paginated Journals Rule 16.3: Consecutively Paginated Journals Example: Mustave Hurt, <u>Unimaginable Pain</u>, 742 Geo. L.J. 801, 831-32 (2003).	Include author, title of work, volume number, periodical name, first page of work, pages on which cited material appears, and year. Use Table 13 (T.13) to abbreviate the names of periodicals.

B9.1.2: Nonconsecutively Paginated Journals **Rule 16.4: Nonconsecutively Paginated Journals and Magazines** Example: <u>Killer Tornado</u>, Newsweek, Mar. 3, 1991, at 39, 40.	Cite works appearing within periodicals that are separately paginated within each issue by author, title, periodical name, date of issue, and first page of work and/or pages on which material appears. Use Table 13 (T.13) to abbreviate names of periodicals.
B9.1.4: Newspaper Articles **Rule 16.5: Newspapers** Example: Adam Gourna, <u>Celiac Disease: A Killer</u>, N.Y. Times, Dec. 12, 1994, at F3.	Use Table 13 (T.13) to abbreviate names of newspapers. Cite the same as for nonconsecutively paginated periodicals (Rule 16.4), but only the first page of the work need be cited.

Citation — Electronic Media (Rule 18)

BLUEBOOK RULE	**KEY POINTS**
Rule 18.1.1: Cases Example: <u>Ossining v. Brubaker</u>, No. CIV. A.02-2332, 2003 U.S. Dist. LEXIS 5130, at *1 (S.D. Ala. Jan. 6, 2003).	Provide the case name, docket number, database identifier, court name, and full date of most recent major disposition. Westlaw: WL Lexis: LEXIS Use when case is unreported, but available on widely used electronic database.
Rule 18.1.2: Constitutions and Statutes Example: Mich. Comp. Laws § 22.33 (West, Westlaw through 2003 Sess.). Mich. Comp. Laws Ann. § 22.33 (Michie, LEXIS through 2003 Legislation).	Cite statutes according to Rules 12.3 and 12.4. In addition, when citing statutes from an electronic database such as Lexis or Westlaw, give within a parenthetical the name of the database and information about the currency of the database instead of the year of the code according to Rule 12.3.2.
Rule 18.2.1: General Internet Principles Example: Judith Expert, <u>Allergy on the Net</u>, 5 New Eng. J. Med. 9, ¶ 10 (2002), <u>available at</u> ➥**http://www.nejm.org/expert/v5/allergy.html.**	If Internet material can be found elsewhere, use "<u>available at</u>"; however, where possible, the traditional source should be used.
Rule 18.2.2(c): Order of Authorities and Parentheticals Example: <u>See</u> H.R. 81, 108th Cong. (2003), <u>available at</u> ➥**http://thomas.loc.gov/bss/d108/d108laws.html**	

Editing and Citation — Quick Reference — Citation Signals

	Signals In Text	Proposition		Cited Authority and Meaning
Support	[No signal]			Directly states proposition.
	See See also			Clearly supports; obviously follows from proposition.
	Cf.			Analogous proposition.
	E.g., See, e.g.,			Multiple authorities clearly state the proposition.
Contradiction	Contra			Directly states contrary proposition.
Background	See generally			Helpful, related background material.
Comparison	Compare ... with ...			Comparison of cited authorities supports proposition.

Editing and Citation — Quick Reference — ALWD

- To use ALWD effectively, you should understand the following:
  o The purpose of citation
  o The design, layout, and basic rules of ALWD
  o Some often-used rules of ALWD

- The purpose of citation is to allow lawyers to easily find and reference legal sources.

- The design of ALWD:
  o Citation formats are the same for scholarly writing and legal documents.

- The layout of ALWD:
  o Part 1—Introductory Material
  o Part 2—Citation Basics
  o Part 3—Citing Specific Print Sources
      o "Fast Formats"—examples of citations for commonly used sources
  o Part 4—Electronic Sources
  o Part 5—Incorporating Citations into Documents
  o Part 6—Quotations
  o Part 7—Appendices
  o Detailed table of contents and an index
  o Green triangles (▲) designate spaces in citation formats.
  o Green circles (●) separate components of citations.
  o "Fast Format Locator" on inside front cover gives page numbers for Fast Format tables.
  o "Short-Citation Locator for Commonly Used Sources" on inside back cover lists rule numbers for short citation formats.

- Basic Citation in ALWD
  o Cases: Rule 12
  o Constitutions: Rule 13
  o Statutes: Rule 14
  o Federal Administrative and Executive Materials: Rule 19
  o Books, Treaties, and Other Nonperiodic Materials: Rule 22
  o Legal and Other Periodicals: Rule 23

- Often-Used Rules in ALWD
  o Typefaces: Rule 1
  o Spelling and Capitalization: Rule 3
  o Basic Structure and Signals: Rules 10, 43, and 44
  o Subdivisions and Pinpoint Cites: Rules 5, 6, 7
  o Short Citations: Rule 11
  o Abbreviations: Rule 2
  o Numbers: Rule 4
  o Quotations: Rules 47, 48, 49
  o Cases: Rule 12
  o Constitutions: Rule 13

o   Statutes: Rule 14
o   Administrative and Executive Materials: Rule 19, Appendix 7C
o   Books, Treaties, and Other Nonperiodic Materials: Rule 22
o   Legal and Other Periodicals: Rule 23
o   Electronic Media: Rules 12, 14, and Part 4

Editing and Citation — Quick Reference — Bluebook

–   To use the Bluebook effectively, you should understand the following:
  o   The purpose of citation
  o   The design, layout, and basic rules of the Bluebook
  o   Some often-used rules of the Bluebook

–   The purpose of citation is to allow lawyers to easily find and reference legal sources.

–   The design of the Bluebook:
  o   In general, provides citation formats for scholarly documents.
  o   "Quick Reference" on front inside cover provides most-often used citations for law reviews.
  o   Bluepages provide citation rules for court documents and legal memoranda.
  o   "Quick Reference" on back inside cover provides most-often used citations for court documents and legal memoranda.

–   The layout of the Bluebook:
  Citations:
  o   Cases: Rule 10
  o   Constitutions: Rule 11
  o   Statutes: Rule 12
  o   Administrative and Executive Materials, including Rules and Regulations: Rule 14
  o   Books, Reports, and Other Nonperiodic Materials: Rule 15
  o   Periodical Materials: Rule 16
  Tables:
  o   United States Jurisdictions: T.1
  o   Foreign Jurisdictions: T.2
  o   Intergovernmental Organizations and Treaty Sources: T.3 - T.4
  o   Abbreviations for Arbitral Reporter Sources: T.5
  o   Abbreviations for Case Names and Court Names: T.6 - T.7
  o   Abbreviations for Explanatory Phrases and Legislative Documents: T.8 - T.9
  o   Abbreviations for Geographical Terms: T.10
  o   Abbreviations for Judges and Officials and Months: T.11 - T.12
  o   Abbreviations for Periodicals: T.13
  o   Abbreviations for Publishing Terms and Services: T.14 - T.15
  o   Abbreviations for Document Subdivisions: T.16
  o   Table of Contents
  o   Index

- Basic Citation in the Bluebook
    - o   Cases: Rule 10
    - o   Constitutions: Rule 11
    - o   Statutes: Rule 12
    - o   Rules and Regulations: Rule 14
    - o   Books: Rule 15
    - o   Periodical Materials: Rule 16

- Often-Used Rules in the Bluebook
    - o   Typefaces: Bluepages 2, 8, 9, 10, 13 and Rule 2
    - o   Basic Structure and Signals: Bluepages 2, 4, 11 and Rule 1
    - o   Subdivisions and Pinpoint Cites: Bluepages 5.1.2 and Rule 3
    - o   Short Citations: Rule 4
    - o   Abbreviations: Rule 6
    - o   Cases: Bluepages 5 and Rule 10
    - o   Constitutions: Bluepages 7 and Rule 11
    - o   Statutes: Bluepages 6 and Rule 12
    - o   Administrative and Executive Materials: Bluepages 6.1.4 and Rule 14
    - o   Books, Reports, and Other Nonperiodic Materials: Bluepages 8 and Rule 15
    - o   Periodicals: Bluepages 9 and Rule 16
    - o   Electronic Media: Rule 18

Editing and Citation — Quick Reference — Grammar and Legal Usage

Strategies for Editing Grammar and Legal Usage:

- Focusing on sentence *structure, syntax,* and *word choice,* try the following strategies:
    - o   Read your document out loud.
        - If you are breathless, your sentences are too long.
        - If your reading sounds choppy, your sentences are too short.
    - o   Identify your grammar and usage weaknesses, and look for them in your document. (*See below for common weaknesses.*)
    - o   Edit one paragraph at a time, and take breaks so you stay focused.
    - o   Read your document backwards word by word to find typos.

Grammar and Legal Usage Rules:

- Active vs. Passive Voice
    - o   With active voice, the subject is doing the work.
        - Preferred in legal writing
        - Makes for concise writing
    - o   With passive voice, the subject is being acted on.
        - Can be helpful in persuasive writing
        - Helps the writer downplay an actor

- *Affect* vs. *Effect*
  - o Generally, *effect* is a noun.
    - ▪ Exception: when used to mean "to bring into being"
  - o *Affect* is a verb.
- *Although* vs. *While*
  - o *Although* is used to introduce a counterargument or for a causal relationship.
  - o *While* is used for temporal circumstances.
- Apostrophes
  - o Avoid using contractions.
  - o Use apostrophes to show possession.
    - ▪ Exceptions: possessive pronouns such as *hers, its, theirs, ours, yours,* and *whose. Its* is the possessive form.
- *Because* vs. *Since*
  - o *Because* is used to show causation.
  - o *Since* is used for temporal circumstances.
- Capitalization (*Bluebook and ALWD follow the same rules.*)
  - o Capitalize the word *court* in memos and briefs when
    - ▪ referring to a court by its full name.
    - ▪ referring to the U.S. Supreme Court.
    - ▪ referring to the court reading the document.
    - ▪ referring to the highest court in any jurisdiction after it has been fully identified. (*ALWD only*)
  - o Capitalize party designations in a legal memo or brief when
    - ▪ referring to the actual parties involved in the matter.
  - o Capitalize civil, professional, military, and religious titles only when they directly precede a personal name. BUT:
    - ▪ Capitalize titles of U.S. Supreme Court Justices, even when used without proper names. (*Bluebook and ALWD*)
    - ▪ Capitalize titles of honor when they substitute for a person's name. (*ALWD only*)
- *Clearly* or *Obviously*
  - o Avoid using.
- Colons and Semicolons
  - o Use a semicolon to
    - ▪ separate items in a list when the items themselves have commas.
    - ▪ join independent clauses without a coordinating conjunction.
    - ▪ separate items in a series when the items are separate.
  - o Use a colon to
    - ▪ join related independent clauses.
    - ▪ introduce a block quotation, numbered list, or list that further explains the subject of the sentence.
  - o If the phrase following a colon is not a complete sentence, do not capitalize the first word following the colon.
    - ▪ Exception: proper nouns

- Commas
  - Use a comma to
    - separate items in a list.
    - offset an introductory phrase (optional for short introductory phrases).
    - join two independent clauses with *and, or, nor, for, so, but,* or *yet.*
      - Independent clauses can stand alone as complete sentences.
    - offset a phrase that could be omitted without changing the meaning of the sentence.
    - offset a dependent clause *preceding* an independent clause.
- Comparisons
  - The items compared should be of the same type.
- Conciseness
  - Omit redundancy and irrelevancy.
  - Avoid phrases replaceable with a single word.
    - *By way of, By means of* — Use *by*
    - *For the purpose of* — Use *to* (unless *purpose* is a term of art)
    - *In the event that* — Use *if*
    - *Begin to develop* — Use *develop*
    - *Void and unenforceable* — Use *unenforceable*
    - *Period of five years* — Use *five years*
    - *Distance of 100 miles* — Use *100 miles*
    - *Due to the fact that* — Use *because*
    - *In the event that* — Use *if*
    - *At this point in time* — Use *now*
    - *Be able to* — Use *can*
    - *Was aware of the fact* — Use *knew*
    - *Despite the fact* — Use *although*
    - *As a consequence of* — Use *because*
    - *In order to* — Use *to*
- Contractions
  - Avoid contractions.
  - Exception: quoting passages in which contractions are used.
- *Due to*
  - Should be used in rare circumstances.
  - Must follow a linking verb and precede the phrase modifying the subject.
- *Farther* vs. *Further*
  - *Farther* refers to measurable distances.
  - *Further* refers to nonmeasurable distances.
- Hyphens
  - Use to join together related modifiers.
    - Exception: do not use a hyphen to join proper names.
    - Exception: do not use a hyphen if the modifiers follow a linking verb.

- Italics
    - o   Use to add emphasis to quotations.
    - o   Use to mark foreign language words.
    - o   Use for certain Bluebook and ALWD citations.
    - o   Do not use italics to emphasize your own points.
- Legalese
    - o   Avoid using legalese.
- Misplaced and Dangling Modifiers
    - o   A modifier is misplaced if it modifies a term you did not intend.
        - ▪   Move the modifier.
    - o   A modifier is dangling if it does not modify anything in the sentence.
        - ▪   Rewrite the sentence and insert the modified subject.
- Nominalizations
    - o   Avoid making a verb or an adjective into a noun.
- Numbers and Quantities
    - o   Spell out the numbers zero through ninety-nine.
    - o   Use numerals for any numbers higher than ninety-nine.
    - o   Exceptions include but are not limited to the following:
        - ▪   Spell out numbers that begin a sentence.
        - ▪   Do not spell out numbers in a series where at least one number is 100 or greater.
        - ▪   Do not spell out numbers if used repeatedly for percentages or dollar amounts.
        - ▪   Use numerals for section numbers.
    - o   Use the words *number, fewer,* and *many* to discuss multiple things that can be counted.
    - o   Use the words *amount, less,* and *much* to discuss singular things that cannot be counted.
    - o   Use *between* to refer to two items; use *among* to refer to more than two items.
- Parallel Structure
    - o   Use parallel structure when writing lists or rules with multiple elements.
- Pronouns
    - o   Use a pronoun only when the word the pronoun refers to is clear.
    - o   Singular indefinite pronouns include
        - ▪   *another, each, either, every, neither, nobody, no one, nothing, one, other.*
    - o   Some pronouns may be singular or plural, depending on what follows:
        - ▪   *all, any, more, most, none, some*
- Quotations
    - o   Periods and commas go inside quotation marks.
    - o   Semicolons and colons go outside quotation marks.
    - o   Question marks go inside quotation marks only if the question mark was part of the original quoted material.
    - o   Quotations of fifty or more words should be indented on the left and right, without quotation marks.
- Redundancy
    - o   Avoid words that do not add any meaning.

- Sentence Fragments
  o Avoid sentence fragments.
  o Check for sentence fragments by reading each sentence out loud.
- Sexist Language
  o Avoid language that can be construed as sexist.
  o Avoid awkward constructions; instead choose the gender that applies to your specific situation.
- Short Sentences
  o Use short sentences to help with clarity and conciseness.
  o In persuasive writing use short sentences for big impact.
- Split Infinitives
  o Generally, avoid split infinitives.
  o But if splitting an infinitive leads to clarity in legal usage, you may split it.
- Strong Subject-Verb Combinations
  o Avoid placing too many words between the subject and the verb.
- Subject-Verb Agreement
  o When the subject of the sentence is plural (uses *and*), use a plural verb.
  o When the subject of the sentence is singular (uses *or* or *nor*), use a singular verb.
  o When the subject uses *each* or *every,* use a singular verb.
- Terms of Art
  o Keep terms of art consistent.
- *That* vs. *Which*
  o *That* narrows the field of objects to the one being discussed.
  o *Which* incorporates a descriptive phrase or a phrase that could be eliminated without changing the meaning of the object.
    ▪ Use a comma before *which.*
- Verb Tense
  o Use *present tense* to refer to legal rules still in effect.
  o Use *past tense* to describe facts, reasoning, and holdings of prior case law.
  o Use *past tense* to describe any facts in your case that are complete as of the time of the writing.
  o If possible, maintain consistent tenses throughout a text.
- Who, Whom, Whose
  o *Who* is a subject.
  o *Whom* is an object.
  o *Whose* is the possessive of who.

More Ebook Interactivity

$\left[\text{edit}/_{\text{cite}}\right]$ *Editing and Citation — Quick References and Checklists*

QUICK REFERENCES

- 🖥 Citation Signals
- 🖥 ALWD
- 🖥 Bluebook
- 🖥 Grammar and Legal Usage

$\left[\text{edit}/_{\text{cite}}\right]$ *Editing and Citation — Class Exercises*

- ↦ Citation Exercise - Signals
- ↦ Citation Exercises (ICWs)
- ↦ ALWD
- ↦ Bluebook

$\left[\text{edit}/_{\text{cite}}\right]$ *Editing and Citation — Quizzes*

GRAMMAR

- ⚇? Active vs. Passive Voice
- ⚇? Affect vs. Effect
- ⚇? Although vs. While
- ⚇? Apostrophes
- ⚇? Because vs. Since
- ⚇? Binding vs. Persuasive
- ⚇? Capitalization
- ⚇? Commas
- ⚇? Due to
- ⚇? Farther vs. Further
- ⚇? Fragments
- ⚇? Hyphens
- ⚇? Indefinite
- ⚇? Legalese
- ⚇? Modifiers
- ⚇? Nominalizations
- ⚇? Numbers and Quantities
- ⚇? Parallel Structure
- ⚇? Quotation Marks

&? Semicolons and Colons
&? Signals
&? That vs. Which
&? Verb Tense
&? Who, Whom, and Whose

GRAMMAR IN GENERAL

&? Editing and Self-Assessment

CITATION

&? Signals
&? Citation Exercises (ICWs)
&? ALWD Citation Self-Assessment
&? Bluebook Citation Self-Assessment